The Long Quest for Identity

LISBON PHILOSOPHICAL STUDIES

uses of language in interdisciplinary fields

A Publication from the Institute of Philosophy of Language at the New University of Lisbon

PETER LANG
Bern · Berlin · Bruxelles · Frankfurt am Main · New York · Oxford · Wien

Gabriele De Angelis & Paulo Barcelos (eds)

The Long Quest for Identity

Political Identity and Fundamental Rights Protection in the European Union

PETER LANG
Bern · Berlin · Bruxelles · Frankfurt am Main · New York · Oxford · Wien

Bibliographic information published by die Deutsche Nationalbibliothek
Die Deutsche Nationalbibliothek lists this publication in the Deutsche Nationalbibliografie; detailed bibliographic data is available on the Internet at ‹http://dnb.d-nb.de›.

British Library Cataloguing-in-Publication Data: A catalogue record for this book is available from The British Library, Great Britain

Library of Congress Cataloging-in-Publication Data

The long quest for identity : political identity and fundamental rights protection in the European Union / Gabriele De Angelis & Paulo Barcelos (eds.).
pages cm. – (Lisbon philosophical studies uses of language in interdisciplinary fields ; vol. 3)
ISBN 978-3-0343-1083-3
1. Constitutional law–European Union countries. 2. Civil rights–European Union countries.
I. Barcelos, Paulo, 1984- II. De Angelis, Gabriele
KJE4445.L63 2013
342.2408'5–dc23

2013005756

ISSN 1663-7674 pb.
ISBN 978-3-0343-1083-3 pb.
ISSN 2235-641X eBook
ISBN 978-3-0351-0593-3 eBook

Hochfeldstrasse 32, CH-3012 Bern, Switzerland
info@peterlang.com, www.peterlang.com

Table of Content

Introduction

Gabriele De Angelis
Constitutionalising the EU. A Story of the Past? 7

Section I
Fundamental Rights and Political Identity in the EU

Paulo Barcelos
Vitangelo Moscarda's Syndrome.
The Charter of Fundamental Rights
and European Constitutionalization 27

Emma De Angelis
The European Identity in the Proceedings
of the European Parliament. Cultural Frames
and Political Processes 63

Section II
The Role of Fundamental Rights
in the Inter-institutional Struggle

Gabriele De Angelis
Enhancing Fundamental Rights Control in Europe.
The European Parliament's Scrutiny of Member States . . . 87

Justus Schönlau
Multi-Level Rights Protection in the European Union.
The Sub-national Dimension 135

Section III
Consequences of Constitutionalisation:
Legal Dilemmas, Legal Conflicts

GIOVANNI DAMELE
Legal Certainty in Europe. Legal Pluralism and Argumentative Practices of the European Court of Justice 157

TERESA BRAVO
The Unbearable Lightness of Fundamental Rights in the European Area of Freedom, Security, and Justice 173

TERESA VIOLANTE
Judicial Function in Context: Contextualising *judicial activism* in the US Supreme Court and the European Court of Justice 199

Section IV
Expectations and Reality

The Charter of Fundamental Rights After Its First Decade: Legal Impact and Political Consequences
A Conversation with MIGUEL POIARES MADURO 221

Constitutionalising the EU. A Story of the Past?

GABRIELE DE ANGELIS

The never ending ambiguity of the European project

Since its inception, the European Community, now European Union, has been caught in a political and institutional dilemma: to move further towards a supranational-communitarian structure of governance or to go on featuring substantial marks of intergovernmentalism. Thus far the EU political system displays mixed features of both a supranational entity and a (con-)federation of states.

Both the communitarian-supranational and the intergovernmental view correspond to different conceptions of a united Europe and its objectives. Both views have their normative, pragmatic, and political justifications (Shahin and Wintle 2000: 4). Those who advocate a more strongly communitarian structure of governance take seriously the aim of expanding the political integration towards an "ever closer Union" beyond national sovereignty in the name of common political principles, shared responsibilities, and post-national democracy (Habermas 1998). Those who wish to maintain a more inter-governmentally co-ordinated, rather than institutionally integrated, Union see in the EU a means to further national goals, instead of taking up supranational responsibilities and duties of solidarity. To the latter, the EU is still a mainly intergovernmental enterprise that avails itself of the, ideally, "technical" support of the Commission as well as of control and debate entities such as the European Court of Justice (ECJ) and the European Parliament.

In the 1990s and early 2000s a decisive step towards strengthening the communitarian level of governance seemed on the verge of being made. The subsequent setbacks on the process of Treaty ratifications as well as consistent resistances both on the side of governments and on the side of several countries' public opinions have led to the current mode of governance, in which the intergovernmental level has a far stronger say in several policy areas than the communitarian. The financial aspect, and in particular the Euro, belong to these policy areas.

At the end of the twentieth century European integration seemed indeed to have come to a watershed. Having been until then the result of piecemeal engineering, the single market and the single currency (the latter appeared, and had been presented as, the obvious consequence of the first) pointed to the necessity to move to the European level of governance much of the national competences in terms of fiscal, budget, and economic co-ordination. Integration-friendly politicians from different countries, not least Germany as a traditional key player in matters of integration, thought that such an encompassing shift of competences ought to be paired with a new, decisively more "federalist", stage of European integration (Fischer 2000; Shahin and Wintle 2000: 1). Two further elements contributed to pressure European policy makers: the increasing need to legitimise the EC/EU before its citizens and the prospective Eastern enlargement. The latter made necessary a restructuring of European governance, especially as far as Council's decision-making process was concerned. The former called for a stronger identification of citizens with Europe. Thus, a new institutional arrangement had to be coupled with a stronger European identity.

The Federalist Project

Federalist elements such as a increasingly powerful parliament (Corbett 1998: 263–266), a federal (constitutional) court, an independent policy co-ordinator such as the Commission, and EU law's direct effect and supremacy over national legislation, have enriched the EC/EU's political and legal system along the years. Indeed, the EU has evidently gone beyond the mere confederacy through the priority of the "acquis communautaire" over national legislations, the chief competence of EU institutions in several policy areas, and the supranational jurisprudence of the European Court of Justice. And yet, hardly anyone seems to have ever been deluded into believing that this path towards a post-national polity has ever been completed or have come near completion. The most keen supporters of deeper political integration have repeatedly underscored how the EU has being lacking a "constitutional moment", which some idealised as the fundamental stipulation by means of which European citizens would forge a fully fledged political unity (Wallace 1993; Weiler et al. 1995).

The dynamic towards a federal polity came to a head in the 1990s, as the institutional advances that set off as a consequence of the Single European Act (1986) seemed to propel the EU towards the goal of a tighter political union (though not yet of the federal kind dreamed of by the most keen supporters of the federal project). Indeed, during the 1990s and early 2000s, EU Member States seemed to have progressively made peace with the ideal of a more substantial political union, and steered therefore towards the acquisition of symbols apt to conjure up a stronger identification with the European polity: a flag, an anthem, and a set of constitutive rights and values. A European legal space of fundamental rights and values had also to be presented to the world as the marking characteristic of European politics (Wintle 2000; see also Smith 1992/1997, and Pocock 1991/1997). In part, such a codification of fundamental rights was the belated recognition that a European legal system was in fact already in place due to the ECJ's piecemeal engineering, and acted as a central catalyst of integration. More enthusiastic supporters of the federalist project envisioned, however, that the EU could finally reach the status of a fully fledged federal polity and go therefore beyond the shifting political wills and interests of member states (Garton Ash 1997). Due to the developments that characterised the decade and a half after the SEA, the EU has been depicted by and large as the supreme example of a construction of a post-national polity that transcends the sovereignty prerogatives of each individual member state and its national interests.

With the rejection of the "European Constitution" by French and Dutch citizens in 2005 the federalist strategy came, however, to a halt. The Lisbon Treaty includes some of the elements that characterised this project, such as the Charter of Fundamental Rights (CFR), but keeps a large part of European decision-making within the folds of intergovernmental bargaining. The federalist narrative is after all only half of the story, national belonging and national interest being the other half.

National interests and European integration

It has always been doubtful whether the federalist project gained the unrestrained allegiance of the political elite even of the founding member states. It is sometimes utterly difficult to tell where political will ends and rhetoric begins. As the former Irish minister of Posts and Telegraph Cruise O'Brien (1997: 79) once put it, it is questionable whether "the principal politicians who have been making the running, rhetorically, in the direction of the federalist goal, really mean that they want to get there". It is a truism that negotiations within Council and at Intergovermental Conferences have always been led in the name and with an eye on national interests. Its very institutional structure, which, as Richard Bellamy has remarked (1999: 202), satisfies Lijphart's criteria of "consociational confederalism",[1] has subjected the integration process to national interests.

For instance, the pillar structure of the Maastricht Treaty was motivated by the unwillingness of several governments to deliver foreign and security policy as well as justice and home affairs to supranational decision-making, especially because of the Commission's monopoly of legislative initiative, the EP's powers of co-decision, and the ECJ's powers of supervision and self-assigned judicial review (Baun 1996). The use of national opt-outs from treaty provisions is a telling sign of the difficulty of squaring the circle of intergovernmental bargaining versus political union within the framework of a single legal order that be the same for all.[2]

As a matter of fact, the increasing "Europeanisation" of ever more policy areas has led to quasi-federal arrangements, as for instance to the upgrading of the European Parliament to a proper legislative organ and the "downgrading" of the Council to a second chamber in which the votes are weighted on the basis of a compromise between the equal dignity of the member states and their different demographic weight (CDU-CSU Bundestagsfraktion 1994; Lamers 1994/1997: 108).[3] Thus, the EU political system results from the necessity of political efficiency, the balance of power among member states, and the quest for legitimacy and democratic representation, and is therefore the outcome of continuous bargaining among governments. Mutual economic solidarity and fiscal or otherwise financial redistribution are thereby an open wound, as we are experiencing in the current economic

1 These are the presence of a discernible political guidance through a "grand coalition" of countries, the segmental autonomy of decision-making organs, the proportionality of votes, and the option of a minority veto (Lijphart 1968; Cryssochoou 1994).

2 For an overview of the resistances to the process of legal constitutionalisation at the time of the Maastricht Treaty see Weiler (1999a: 230–231).

3 Bittberger (2007) sees the reason for the growing share of the EP in the legislative process in the perceived lack of democratic legitimacy in the eyes of the self-same national politicians and government leaders.

and financial crises.[4] What is commonly known as the process of EU constitutionalisation fully mirrors this fundamental ambiguity as to scope and ultimate aim of the integration process.

Constitutionalisation and political ambiguity

The so-called constitutionalisation of the European Union appears to have been a major goal of European politics from the late 1980s until recently. "Constitutionalisation" has a legal and a political aspect.

In its *legal* dimension, it consists of the instatement of a vertically integrated legal system within which all legal persons and entities within the territories of the member states are subject to the same rights and obligations that emanate from a common, supranational source.[5] As such, constitutionalisation results from the enactment of three classic doctrines of federalism by the ECJ, i. e. direct effect, supremacy of EU law, as well as of "pre-emption" (Mancini 2000: 1–2; Hix 2005: 121; Castiglione 2007a: 16–8).[6]

"Supremacy" means, in short, that EC/EU law enjoys higher law status than the national legislations of the member states, and is therefore pre-eminent in relation to previous and subsequent member states' law. "Direct effect" means, in general, that norms apply directly to a polity's citizens. The treaties restricted such a direct effect to regulations. Through a number of rulings,

4 It is remarkable how far the leading German political parties, namely CDU, CSU and SPD, are equally lukewarm on this point (Busch 2000).

5 Constitutionalisation is thus "the process by which the EC treaties evolved from a set of legal arrangements binding upon sovereign states into a vertically integrated legal regime conferring judicially enforceable rights and obligations on all legal persons and entities, public and private" (Stone 1995: 38), at least with regards to those areas covered by EC/EU law.

6 In a ruling of 1986 the ECJ explicitly refers to the "constitutional character" of the Treaties. See Ruling 294/83, Parti Ecologiste "Les Verts" v. European Parliament, 1986, ECR 1339.

the Court has progressively extended the direct effect well beyond the Treaties' provisions so as to cover directives that member states had failed to transpose into national law within the given time frame (Mancini 2000: 5). The doctrine of "pre-emption" affirms that policy areas covered by EC/EU law limit the right of member states to legislate for those areas even though such a coverage may be partial or potential (Mancini 2000: 7). Finally, the ECJ has given birth to an indirect judicial review on member state legislation through the practice of the preliminary rulings it gives on national courts' request (for further details and discussion see Damele's and Barcelos' contributions to this volume as well as the interview with Miguel Poiares Maduro).

The constitutionalisation and the vertical legal integration of the EC/EU is thus mainly the result of the ECJ's self-empowerment in the name of the coherence and hold of the EC/EU legal system. On the grounds that the Community is based on the rule of law, the Court has progressively advocated to itself the right to exert judicial review on the legislative acts of EU organs and their implementation, it has secured the horizontal and vertical effect of EC/EU legislation, and has accorded supremacy to the Treaties' provisions, to EU's secondary law as well as to the "general principles" of EU law, including fundamental rights as they result from the constitutional traditions common to the member states.

In its *political* dimension, the project to constitutionalise the EU reflects the federal ideal that was present in European intellectual and elite's discourse even before the integration process actually set in. As an institutional process, however, it has a date (whether it also has an expiry date is something to be assessed in the future). The late 1990s and early 2000s were definitely the heyday of its development.[7] In the wishes of several actors and observers, the project should fulfil the wish to systematise the EU's institutional structure. Its vanishing point would have consisted in a (ideally "ultimate") decision as to the competences of

7 For a more contrasted vision of the federalist and constitutional project in the early 1990s see Weiler (1999b).

EU organs and member states and the source of EU political legitimacy (i.e. democratic control and participation) (Castiglione 2007a: 22; 2007b: 27–30).[8] In sum, it should have brought the "constitutional moment" of the tradition of the social contract from the realm of shadows over into political reality (see Eriksen and Fossum 2007, and Longman 2007).[9]

In practice, the project consisted however of a set of political, symbolic, and legal elements that were intended to make the EU to a supranational community endowed with a political identity of its own as well as with a political legitimacy in the eyes of its citizens. How such a legitimacy had to be granted was in fact still unclear. From a symbolic point of view, it would result from forms of identification that consisted in endowing the Union with political symbols that European citizens know from their own (national) states (such as the flag, the anthem, etc.). From an institutional point of view, however, the Constitutional Treaty was far from achieving substantial results as regards popular participation and democratic control or from making a decisive step towards a federal Europe, if we espouse the doctrine according to which such a step would be made once the mechanisms to amend the Treaties would cease to be intergovernmental, i.e. international, and reside, instead, in the European citizens and their direct representatives, as is the case for national democracies.[10]

Nonetheless, the constitutionalisation of the EC/EU was an important part of the project of further integration that found such strong support in the 1990s. The codification of fundamental rights was been a milestone in this process. After the rejection of the so-called Constitutional Treaty at the hand of French and

8 On the relationship between constitutionalisation and "finality" or "finalité" see Paulo Barcelo's contribution to this volume.

9 Political theorists framed the situation in terms of the foundation of a post-national, rights-based community (Eriksen, Joerges and Roedl 2008) or discussed which kind of values a united Europe ought to represent internally and worldwide (Rumford 2007: 3–5).

10 What such a step would actually consist of is, however, controversial. For different criteria see for instance Weiler (2003: 19–20).

Dutch voters in 2005, the Charter of Fundamental Rights, as integrated in the Treaty of Lisbon, is the only survivor of this political project of constitutionalisation.

The Charter as part of the constitutional project

At its adoption, the Charter raised a number of recurring doubts, most of which boiled down to the question as to what its expected institutional impact would be. Contrary to the expectations it had initially raised (Reich 2001; Craig 2001; La Torre 2002; Fossum 2003), several observers registered an increased willingness on agreeing upon a language of constitutionalisation without making any decisive step towards a precise model of constitutionalism (Poiares Maduro 2003). On the one hand, the Charter included an autonomous list of fundamental rights that reached far beyond Community's competences as though it were the equivalent of a constitutional bill of rights. On the other hand, its wording reflected at times the will to state a list of political values in order to gain citizens' sympathies and allegiance, and had therefore a political value. At the same time, the Charter intended to appease those who feared that Union's competences would extend to the thus far national domain of the protection and promotion of fundamental rights with the guarantee than nothing substantial would be added or altered to the national protection of fundamental rights. The Charter also aimed to bind the Community's legislative acts to a then still fragmentary legal control of fundamental rights' conformity, and was therefore meant to put a certain restraint on Community decision-making.

In the light of these ambiguities, it is difficult to say whether the Charter was supposed to be part of the political or the legal process of EU constitutionalisation (see Barcelos's and De Angelis's contributions to this volume for a further discussion of the topic). Certainly, a chief motivation in promoting the CFR was to scrutinise Community acts for compatibility with fundamental rights, and therefore to enhance their protection at Union level; preserving the unity of the EC/EU legal order was another.[11] The prospective Eastern enlargement, political identity, and the protection of individual rights against abusive actions on the part of EU bodies were, however, as many important reasons to adopt a CFR. To this effect, the Charter had to be a legally binding instrument of law. The legally binding nature of the Charter gave rise to a yearlong controversy. The struggle for the Charter's implementation and incorporation into the Treaties is thus a prism through which the ambiguities of the process of constitutionalisation can be optimally observed.

This volume: after (political) constitutionalisation

Against the background of the current Euro-crisis, the pursuit of an "ever closer" and constitutionalised Union looks like a far echo of the past. National interests and intergovernmental bargaining are now at the centre of European business. Nevertheless, the process of constitutionalisation has had a profound impact on the European polity. While we wonder what will become of the European constitutional project, it is therefore still worthwhile to cast additional light onto what it was supposed to be until a very recent time and what is left of it.

Paulo Barcelos and Emma De Angelis open the volume by reminding us of the historical and political background that has accompanied both the entrenchment of fundamental rights and,

11 Thus, in an Opinion issued on behalf of the Committee on Constitutional Affairs, the EP's Committee on Legal Affairs and Internal Market, in the person of Charlotte Cederschiöld, affirms that "a high profile set of EU fundamental rights which would allow EU acts to be reviewed at European level" would maintain "the unity of the EU legal order" (PE 232.648/fin, 39) inasmuch as it would help bypass the scrutiny of national constitutional courts, which threatened to disapply parts of EU law for incompatibility with their own list or interpretation of fundamental rights.

more generally, the quest for political identity in relation to the drafting of the Charter of Fundamental Rights and the proceedings of the European Parliament, respectively.

Besides the ideal and ideological reasons that lay at the bottom of the entrenchment of fundamental rights as well as of the quest for political identity in Europe, both topics have also been a battlefield on which the institutions that are keen on increasing their share of influence in policy-making have fought their struggle for recognition. Gabriele De Angelis and Justus Schönlau highlight this in the cases of the European Parliament and the Committee of the Regions.

The ECJ's attempts to "constitutionalise" the EC/EU from a legal point of view hinged upon the effort to connect the legal traditions of the member states both in order to act as surrogates for the insufficiency of the EC/EU's own legal sources and to gain support from national courts. The ensuing pluralism of sources and traditions is the consequence of such a "double contingency" in the legal birth of constitutionalisation. After a failed attempt to build a European polity with a stronger political identity and more purposeful legal integration, *pluralism* is thus the legal hallmark of present day Europe. Teresa Bravo, Teresa Violante, and Giovanni Damele deal with the implications of pluralism in relation to legal certainty and the national legal jurisdictions in the key field of fundamental rights protection in Europe.

Finally, an interview with Miguel Poiares Maduro traces the route from the de facto constitutionalisation of Europe at the hands of the ECJ to the present state of constitutional pluralism, and confronts the expectations raised by the decision to entrench fundamental rights with the current legal practice.

Fundamental Rights and Political Identity

In his opening contribution, PAULO BARCELOS reconstruct the complex route towards the Charter of Fundamental Rights. After sketching the evolution of fundamental rights protection at EC/EU level along the years, he reminds us of the debate that scholars and legal practitioners have devoted to the scope, content, and legal significance of the Charter, and scrutinises the reasons and motivations that have been adduced for endowing the Union with such a legal and political instrument. He focuses in particular with the issue of political identity and European "finalité", and analyses the Charter and fundamental rights protection as a means by which European elites attempted to clarify scope and ends of the European polity.

EMMA DE ANGELIS tackles this same topic from the point of view of the institution that has most contributed to raising democracy and fundamental rights to the European core business: the European Parliament. She reconstructs the growing role of fundamental rights in Parliament's identity discourse through the lenses of the successive enlargement rounds, which she identifies as the events that have brought Parliament to develop and progressively modify its overall conception of the European polity. Finally, she shows the increasing difficulties that Parliament's identity discourse has had to face in recent times.

Fundamental rights and inter-institutional struggles

While the former essays introduce the topic of fundamental rights and political identity from both a theoretical and a historical point of view, the second section of the volume deals with the contribution that European institutions have given to the development and promotion of fundamental rights in Europe. In particular, Gabriele De Angelis and Justus Schönlau highlight the extent to which fundamental rights play a role in the inter-institutional struggle for influence on the legislative process and political visibility.

GABRIELE DE ANGELIS shows the evolution of the fundamental rights discourse at the EP since discussion on the CFR started over ten years ago. In the tendency to Europeanise national political battles as well as to frame the groups' political platforms in fundamental rights terms he sees the factors that have led Parliament to exert a growing scrutiny over member states' respect for fundamental rights. Although as far as the respect of fundamental rights in member states is concerned the EP still issues recommendations only, in the face of the growing inclusion of fundamental rights issues in EU policies such a tendency on the part of the EP prefigures the subordination of any field of national legislation to EU scrutiny.

In his contribution, JUSTUS SCHÖNLAU highlights the growing attention that the Committee of the Regions has devoted to the CFR along the years, and depicts the main contribution of the Fundamental Rights Agency to the multilevel fundamental rights protection in the European space. In particular, the Committee of the Regions represents one of the instruments by means of which subnational authorities may receive assistance and counselling from EU authorities, and can in turn play a role in promoting a Union-wide culture and practice as regards fundamental rights protection. In a political self-restriction on the part of the Commission as well as in a still insufficient inter-connection among local authorities and between the latter and the central EU authorities Schönlau sees, however, the reason why the subnational level of governance still lags behind its potential as regards its contribution to the EU multilevel system of fundamental rights protection. Nevertheless, in such a contribution he sees a considerable factor of democratic enhancement.

Legal dilemmas and legal conflicts

Scholarly literature has remarked early on that the piecemeal constitutionalisation that the ECJ has brought forth represents a challenge for legal certainty. Although this can be said to be a general characteristic of judicial review altogether, the legal practice of the ECJ in particular has represented a surprise for member states inasmuch as it has decisively contributed to strengthening the supranational character of European law far beyond the expectations of the signatories of the Treaties.

In his contribution, GIOVANNI DAMELE analyses legal pluralism and the "constitutional dialogue" among different traditions and legal agencies in Europe from the point of view of the argumentative forms that have shaped the jurisprudence of the ECJ. He remarks how much the persistent uncertainty as to the scope of EU competences and the prominent role of judicial interpretation in their determination represents an ongoing source of perplexity for the legal cogency of EU law and the legal status of its subjects. This is the more so as the "polyphony" of legal sources and the ensuing complexity of the Court's ruling has become a persistent mark of the ECJ's interpretive practice, a practice that spreads on national courts and irradiates well into national law.

TERESA BRAVO tackles the same topic from the specific point of view of criminal law. She highlights the role of the ECJ in the shaping of the European Area of Freedom, Security and Justice, and brings us through the main rulings that have determined the current legal landscape. Her contribution points out some highly problematic effects that the European legal practice has in relation to the Portuguese legal tradition and institutional arrangement, thus addressing the topic of the conflicts between the practice of the ECJ and its results, and the national constitutional traditions. She finally brings to attention to the resulting risks for fundamental rights protection in the Area of Freedom, Security and Justice.

TERESA VIOLANTE introduces the topic of "judicial activism". By means of a comparison between the practices of the ECJ and the

US Supreme Court, she recalls the rulings that have brought upon the ECJ the unflattering accusation of judicial "creativity" (or at least "activism"), and reconstructs the international debate on its role in European legal integration. She casts light on the factors that have determined the de facto acceptance of the ECJ's self-advocated role and the elements that have earned it Europe-wide legitimacy. She offers an explanation of the ECJ's successful "activism" by means of a comparison between the European and the US institutional context. Finally, she points out the ambiguities, the limitations, and the risks connected with the ECJ's role in the European legal landscape, and depicts the challenges it currently faces.

Expectations and Reality

In a conversation with MIGUEL POIARES MADURO, the expectations addressed to the CFR and the process of constitutionalisation in general are confronted with the reality of legal pluralism and interpretive polyphony. Poiares Maduro highlights how over ten years after its adoption, the Charter has neither predominantly become a tool for further political integration, nor has it put a limit to it. Nor is it legally clear whether the Union has competence to intervene in the internal affairs of the member states when fundamental rights are affected. Although a political will to intervene can be observed in some cases, and the ECJ equates fundamental rights to the EU's basic principles of law, the entrenchment of fundamental rights has not yet answered the question of competences, for the attitude of the political actors in such a matter is as unclear as ever. Going through a number of cases, Poiares Maduro gives this ambiguous state of affairs as regards fundamental rights a rich illustration. Legal pluralism and "polyphony" are also a consequence of the unsteady social and political nature of fundamental rights in our societies. Against such a background, codification is not a guarantee of legal cogency.

Poiares Maduro finally claims that a theory of fundamental rights, i. e. a theory about the meaning and function of fundamental rights in the EU, is what is most needed from a legal – and a political – point of view.[12]

References

BAUN, Michael (1996), *An Imperfect Union: The Maastricht Treaty and the New Politics of European Integration.* Boulder: Westview.

BELLAMY, Richard (1999), *Liberalism and Pluralism.* London and New York: Routledge.

BITTBERGER, Berthold (2007), Constructing Parliamentary Democracy in the EU: How Did It Happen? In Beate Kohler-Koch and Berthold Bittberger, eds. *Debating the Democratic Legitimacy of the European Union.* Plymouth: Rowman and Littlefield, pp. 111–137.

BUSCH, Klaus (2000), The Corridor Model: Towards the Further Development of an EU Social Policy. In Jamal Shahin and Michael Wintle (eds.), *The Idea of a United Europe. Political, Economic and Cultural Integration since the Fall of the Berlin Wall.* Houndsmill and London: Macmillan, pp. 52–70.

CASTIGLIONE, Dario (2007a), Constitutional Politics in the EU. In Castiglione et al., Constitutional Politics in the EU. The Convention Moment and Its Aftermath. Houndsmill, Basingstoke: Palgrave Macmillan, pp. 11–25.

— (2007b), Constitutional Moment or Constitutional Process? In Castiglione et all., *Constitutional Politics in the EU. The Convention Moment and Its Aftermath.* Houndsmill, Basingstoke: Palgrave Macmillan, pp. 26–45.

CORBETT, Richard (1998), *The European Parliament's Role in Closer EU Integration.* Houndmills-London: MacMillan.

CDU-CSU Bundestagsfraktion (1994), *Reflections on European Policy*, 1st September (Bonn).

CRAIG, Paul (2001), Constitutions, Constitutionalism, and the European Union. *European Law Journal*, Vol. 7, N. 2, pp. 125–150

CRYSSOCHOOU, D. N. (1994), Democracy and Symbiosis in the European Union: Towards a Confederal Consotiation?, *West European Politics*, Vol. 17, N. 4, pp. 1–14.

---

12 The research, the meetings, and the workshops on which this volume rests have been made possible by a funding of the Portuguese Foundation for Science and Technology (PTDC/FIL-ETI/108287/2008).

CRUISE O'BRIEN, Conor (1997), Pursuing a Chimera. In Peter Gowan and Perry Anderson (eds.), *The Question of Europe*. London and New York: Verso, pp. 77–84.

ERIKSEN, Erik Oddvar, Christian JOERGES and Florian ROEDL (2008), Europe's unsettled political order. In Eadem, eds., *Law, Democracy and Solidarity in a Post-national Union*. London-NY: Routledge, pp. 1–19.

ERIKSEN, Erik Oddvar, and John Erik FOSSUM (2008), A done deal? The EU's legitimacy conundrum revisited. In Erik Oddvar Eriksen, Christian Joerges and Florian Roedl (eds.), Law, Democracy and Solidarity in a Post-national Union. London-NY: Routledge, pp. 230–252.

FISCHER, Joschka (2000), Vom Staatenverbund zur Föderation. In Christian Joerges, Yves Mény and Joseph Weiler (eds.), *What Kind of Constitution for What Kind of Polity? Responses to Joschka Fischer*. Florence and Cambridge/MA: European University Institute and Harvard Law School, pp. 19–30.

FOSSUM, John Erik (2003), The European Union in Search of an Identity. *European Journal of Political Theory*, Vol. 2, N. 3, pp. 319–340.

GARTON ASH, Timothy (1997), Catching the Wrong Bus? In Peter Gowan and Perry Anderson (eds.), *The Question of Europe*. London and New York: Verso, pp. 117–125.

HABERMAS, Jürgen (1998), *The Inclusion of the Other: Studies in Political Theory*. Cambridge, MIT Press.

HIX, Simon (2005), *The Pol. System of the EU*. 2nd ed. Palgrave MacMillan. Houndmills, Basingstoke.

LA TORRE, Massimo (2002), The Law Beneath Rights' Feet. Preliminary Investigation for a Study of the Charter of Fundamental Rights of the European Union. *European Law Journal*, Vol. 8, N. 4, pp. 515–535.

LAMERS, Karl (1994/1997), Strengthening the Hard Core. In Peter Gowan and Perry Anderson (eds.), *The Question of Europe*. London and New York: Verso, pp. 104–116.

LIJPHART, A. (1968), Typologies of Democratic Systems. *Comparative Political Studies*, Vol. 1, N. 1, pp. 3–44.

LONGMAN, Chris (2007), The Debate on European Values. In Castiglione et all., *Constitutional Politics in the EU. The Convention Moment and Its Aftermath*. Houndsmill, Basingstoke: Palgrave Macmillan, pp. 186–204.

MANCINI, Federico (2000), The Making of a Constitution for Europe. In Idem, *Democracy and Constitutionalism in the European Union*. Oxford-Portland/OR: Hart, pp. 1–16.

POCOCK, J. G. A. (1991/1997), Deconstructing Europe. In Peter Gowan and Perry Anderson (eds.), *The Question of Europe*. London and New York: Verso, pp. 297–317.

POIARES MADURO, Miguel (2003), Is there Europe for a Constitution? In *Integration in an Expanding European Union: Reassessing the Fundamentals*, ed. by J. H. H. Weiler, I. Begg, and J. Peterson. Houndsmill, Basingstoke: Blackwell, pp. 34–37.

REICH, Norbert (2001), Union Citizenship – Metaphor or Source of Rights? *European Law Journal*, Vol. 7, N. 1, pp. 4–23.

RUMFORD, Chris (2007), Cosmopolitanism and Europe. In Rumford, ed. *Cosmopolitanism and Europe*. Liverpool: Liverpool University Press, pp. 1–15.

SHAHIN, Jamal, and Michal WINTLE (2000), Introduction: the Idea of a United Europe. In Eadem (eds.), *The Idea of a United Europe. Political, Economic and Cultural Integratoin since the Fall of the Berlin Wall*. Houndsmill and London: Macmillan, pp. 1–10.

SCHÖNLAU, Justus (2005), *Drafting the EU Charter. Rights, Legitimacy, and Process*. Houndsmill Basingstoke: MacMillan Palgrave.

— (2007), The Convention Method. In Castiglione et al., *Constitutional Politics in the EU. The Convention Moment and Its Aftermath*. Houndsmill, Basingstoke: Palgrave Macmillan, pp. 90–111.

SMITH, Anthony D. (1992/1997), National Identity and the Idea of European Unity. In Peter Gowan and Perry Anderson (eds.), *The Question of Europe*. London and New York: Verso, pp. 318–342.

STONE, Alec (1995), Constitutional Dialogues in the European Community. *Working Papers of the European University Institute* RSC, N. 95/38.

WALLACE, H. (1993), Deepening and Widening: Problems of Legitimacy for the EC. In S. Garcia (ed.), *European Identity and the Search for Legitimacy*. London: Pinter, pp. 95–105.

WEILER, Joseph (1999a), The reformation of European constitutionalism. In Idem, *The Constitution of Europe*. Cambridge: Cambridge University Press, pp. 221–236.

— (1999b), Fin-de-siècle Europe: do the new clothes have an Emperor? In Idem, *The Constitution of Europe*. Cambridge: Cambridge University Press, pp. 238–264.

— (2001), Federalism and Constitutionalism. Europe's Sonderweg. Jean Monnet Working Paper, Harvard University.

— (2003), A constitution for Europe? Some hard choices. In *Integration in an Expanding European Union: Reassessing the Fundamentals*, ed. by J. H. H. Weiler, I. Begg, and J. Peterson. Houndsmill, Basingstoke: Blackwell, pp. 17–33.

WINTLE, Michael (2000), The Question of European Identity and the Impact of the Changes of 1989/90. In Jamal Shahin and Michael Wintle (eds.), *The Idea of a United Europe. Political, Economic and Cultural Integration since the Fall of the Berlin Wall*. Houndsmill and London: Macmillan, pp. 11–30.

Section I
Fundamental Rights and Political Identity in the EU

Vitangelo Moscarda's Syndrome. The Charter of Fundamental Rights and European Constitutionalization

PAULO BARCELOS[1]

> No name. No memory today of yesterday's name; of today's name, tomorrow. If the name is the thing; if a name in us is the concept of every thing placed outside of us; and without a name you don't have the concept, and the thing remains in us as if blind, indistinct and undefined: well then, let each carve this name that I bore among men, a funeral epigraph, on the brow of that image in which I appeared to him, and then leave it in peace, and let there be no more talk about it.
>
> Luigi Pirandello, *One, No One, and One Hundred Thousand*

> Polonius: What do you read, my lord?
> Hamlet: Words, words, words.
>
> Shakespeare, *Hamlet*

A history of the charter, ten years later

The purpose of this text is to explore the motivations that prompted the drafting of a Charter of Fundamental Rights of the European Union (CFR), the significance attached to it, and the obstacles that prevented it from accomplishing the main task that it was expected to fulfil. I shall, more specifically, sustain that the main

1 PhD candidate at the Faculty of Social and Human Sciences of the Universidade Nova, Lisbon, researcher at the Instituto de Filosofia da Linguagem.

reason behind the process of creating a code assembling the rights that the European citizens enjoy is not primarily connected to legal or constitutional imperatives. Its primary intention seems, on the contrary, related to the concept of a European identity, and to the strategy toof its institutionalisation.

In the first two sections of the text I will sketch the protection of fundamental rights in the Community before the creation of the CFR, and assess the arguments usually employed to advocate a Charter. In the third section I will maintain that the basic motive underpinning the wish for this document was, in fact, the belief that it would crucially contribute both to legitimise the present institutional arrangements and to set a foundation for its future developments. This would be achieved by raising a common awareness of a "we-feeling" among the five hundred million EU citizens. The interpretation advanced here needs, therefore, to be understood against the ethical and political background that has been haunting the EU for decades: the much repeated identification of the Union as suffering from a *democratic deficit*.

In section four I will identify the idiosyncrasies that render ineffective the strategy behind the Charter: the heavy reliance on the axiological discovery of a common language of rights in detriment of clear political steps to enhance the citizens' power and participation; the particular content given to the proposed European *lingua franca*, which seems constantly to slip into the proclamation of cosmopolitan values instead of advancing a specific European conception of fundamental rights; and the peculiar "documental" strategy, coalescing around the drafting of a bill of rights, that seems to have been chosen to give shape to the idea of a European identity.

The protection of fundamental rights in the Communities, B.C.

In the pre-Charter period, the sources and scope of the judicial protection of fundamental rights were established by the European Court of Justice (ECJ). This is often understood as another facet of the fashioning of a "constitutional framework for a federal-type structure in Europe" through the creative deliberation of the judges, away from the "traditional international law methodology" (Stein 1981: 1; Mancini 2000a, 2000b). This story begins roughly in the late Sixties. Until that point, the European Communities (due either to their technical, economic nature or to the failure of other overtly political initiatives, such as the European Political and Defence Communities) were not regarded, and did not regard themselves, as raising human rights issues (Dauses 1985: 399; Mancini 2000: 11–14). This is visible in the absence of any declaration of attachment to a catalogue or source of rights either in the treaties of Paris and Rome or in the ECJ's *Stork* ruling. In it the judges declined the possibility of examining the compatibility of an act of the European Coal and Steel Community's High Authority with the dispositions of the German Constitutional law on the grounds that the Court did not have a mandate for meddling in that kind of crossed assessment.

The turning point came one decade later, and from that time on the ECJ's self-assumption as the granter of the respect of fundamental rights in every action included on the scope of European law grew steadily.

The new disposition was set in 1969, when the Court first referred to fundamental rights as "enshrined in the general principles of Community law and protected by the Court".[2] It was, certainly, a very vague reference in operational terms. Its contours began to take shape a year later in the *Internationale Handels-*

2 Judgment of the Court of 12 November 1969. Erich Stauder v City of Ulm – Sozialamt, Paragraph 7. Reference for a preliminary ruling: Verwaltungsgericht Stuttgart – Germany. Case 29–69.

gesellschaft case, in which the Court defined the sharing of responsibilities between itself and the member states. It designated, in particular, the different constitutional traditions as sources of inspiration for the decisions, but at the same time ascertained its exclusive responsibility as decision-maker in matters concerning the scope of Community law.[3] With *Nold* there came a reinforcement of its reference to domestic constitutional principles, declared inexpugnable, and an enrichment of the set of references to be safeguarded, with the inclusion of those codes of international law subscribed to by the member states.[4] Nevertheless, as stated in *Hauer*, even if the fundamentals granted by each national constitution define the borders that cannot be crossed by Community institutions' actions, the assessment of the latter is done by the ECJ alone, taking in consideration the contents of Community law.[5]

After arrogating to itself the right of judicial review on acts of EC institutions, the ECJ turned its consideration to the conduct of member states when implementing European law. As *Wachauf* demonstrated, States also could, in certain circumstances, be subject to assessment in relation to fundamental rights.[6] The ques-

3 Judgment of the Court of 17 December 1970. Internationale Handelsgesellschaft mbH v Einfuhr- und Vorratsstelle für Getreide und Futtermittel, Paragraph 4 . Reference for a preliminary ruling: Verwaltungsgericht Frankfurt am Main – Germany. Case 11–70.

4 Judgment of the Court of 14 May 1974. – J. Nold, Kohlen- und Baustoffgroßhandlung v Commission of the European Communities. – Case 4–73. This idea was materialized the following year, with a remission to certain articles of the European Convention for the Protection of Human Rights and Fundamental Freedoms. Vide Paragraph 32 of Judgment of the Court of 28 October 1975. Roland Rutili v Ministre de l'intérieur. Reference for a preliminary ruling: Tribunal administratif de Paris – Case 36–75.

5 Judgment of the Court of 13 December 1979. – Liselotte Hauer v Land Rheinland-Pfalz, Paragraph 14 (vide also paragraphs 15 and 16). Reference for a preliminary ruling: Verwaltungsgericht Neustadt an der Weinstraße – Case 44/79.

6 Judgment of the Court (Third Chamber) of 13 July 1989. – Hubert Wachauf v Bundesamt für Ernährung und Forstwirtschaft, Paragraph 19. – Reference for a preliminary ruling: Verwaltungsgericht Frankfurt am Main – Case 5/88.

tion of knowing under which conditions the ECJ could supervise, via preliminary rulings, member states' respect for human rights standards in their domestic activities has witnessed some fluctuation. A few years before *Wachauf,* the Court had ruled out the possibility of examining any action of member states.[7] A few years later, however, *ERT* undertook an extension of the scope of judicial review to certain undertakings of states: those whose mandate derives directly from Community law.[8]

One could say that, in the absence of a formal document and in the impossibility of knitting a patchwork out of the very incomplete puzzle of fundamental rights protection clauses present in the founding treaties, the ECJ has devised, in a series of rulings spanning from the late sixties, an evolving framework of judicial protection of human rights. Through the doctrines of supremacy and direct effect the ECJ has composed its own immaterial and plastic bill of rights. This was done either "in anticipation of the elaboration of its own charter" (Dauses 1985: 418), or even, as is also claimed, obviating altogether to the need for such document.

The way how the ECJ has read "an unwritten bill of rights into Community law" (Mancini 2000: 13) was not without contestation. The most famous set of charges against the Court's stance are Coppel and O'Neill's (1992) concerns as to how serious were the rights being taken in the (supposed) rhetorical strategy of the Court. They employed a two stage reading of the Court's motivations to have developed such an activist position in rulings involving human rights.

---

7 Judgment of the Court of 11 July 1985. – Cinéthèque SA and others v Fédération nationale des cinémas français, Paragraph 26. – References for a preliminary ruling: Tribunal de grande instance de Paris – Joined cases 60 and 61/84. S. Judgment of the Court of 30 September 1987. – Meryem Demirel v Stadt Schwäbisch Gmünd, Paragraph 28. Reference for a preliminary ruling: Verwaltungsgericht Stuttgart – Case 12/86.

8 Judgment of the Court of 18 June 1991. Elliniki Radiophonia Tiléorassi AE and Panellinia Omospondia Syllogon Prossopikou v Dimotiki Etairia Pliroforissis and Sotirios Kouvelas and Nicolaos Avdellas and others, Paragraphs 42–43. Reference for a preliminary ruling: Monomeles Protodikeio Thessalonikis – Case C-260/89.

According to the authors, in a first stage, the ECJ instrumentally "discovered" and imported a vocabulary of fundamental rights and principles into its decisions, declaring them "general principles of European Community law" despite the absence of a unified codification in the Treaties. This constituted a "defensive" strategy to retain the prerogatives that the Court had ascribed to itself in the previous years, and that were challenged in the 1970s by the German and Italian Constitutional Courts (1992: 227–230).

After having reinforced in that way the status of the supremacy and direct effect as widely accepted properties of the supranational EU law, the Court has gradually worked for the strengthening and expansion of the Community's powers against the sovereignty of the member states. Fundamental rights rhetoric is, again, merely the means to achieve an end. In this way, Coppel and O'Neill assert that their protection was the perfect alibi to sustain the ECJ's struggle to extend its jurisdiction in areas previously reserved for the autonomous space of the states' domestic judiciaries. The defence and promotion of the fundamental rights lexicon for private purposes was done this time with an "offensive, even imperial, purpose".

The conclusions adduced by the authors as to the sense of this jurisprudential evolution have been, however, forcefully disputed by Joseph Weiler and Nicholas Lockhart (1995). Not contesting that the 'defensive' preoccupation with the maintenance of the foundations of the Community's legal order played an important role in the introduction of human rights' considerations in the ECJ's rulings, they provide a richer picture of the reasons that underlie it.

The complementary reasons are directly related to the theme of this text. Apart from a connection to a favourable historical moment (Menéndez 2001),[9] Weiler and Lockhart defend that a

9 Menéndez also sustains that the ECJ sensed that a change would have to occur, to make the Community respond adequately to the international panorama of the 60s and 70s, which involved the Community's first enlargement, the Cold war geopolitics, and the EC's own development aiming at an extension of its powers and policy scope. What is more, rights were one of the main goals, if not the main one, of European integration from its

major explanation for the human rights shift of the ECJ's jurisprudence, since the days of *Stork*, was the perception of the troubling nature of the Community's democratic deficit. The citizens' connection to the European polity could be enhanced by counterbalancing the structure of coercion through the ring-fencing of the citizens' basic rights. Likewise, such a commitment would also be a way to address the structural problem of the ECJ, that, unlike national courts, is not backed by the existence of a clearly constituted and demarcated demos, to whom the Court would symbolically relate as a *pouvoir constitué* (Weiler and Lockhart 1995: 625).

Why a Charter?

Regardless of how critical we are towards the ECJ's activism in what concerns this particular case law, we could hardly predict that the protection of the individuals' basic rights would be threatened if this informal system subsisted. The status quo could simply be maintained (Weiler 2000).

Another option was the access to an external system of protection that would assess the actions of Community institutions. The accession of the Community as a whole, following the individual accessions of all the member states, to the European Convention of Human Rights was object of several proposals and initiatives (Moura Ramos 2001: 181–187), but was indefinitely set

very first design by the *founding fathers*. This is not more often recognized, according to Menéndez, since the rights protection and promotion was done using an indirect strategy: not through visible declarations and treaties but by steps that would contribute to "establishing the *preconditions* for the protection of civic, political and social rights in Europe". This involved focusing on the preservation of values such as peace and economic stability, as well as on the judicial empowerment of the individual and the inclusion of human rights into judicial citizens' protection via the ECJ (Menéndez 2001).

aside after the ECJ's Opinion requested by the Council on that matter. The ECJ rejected the possibility of accession to the Convention simply by means of the conditions defined in the article 235 of the Treaty of Rome, which establishes that measures not defined in the treaties, but needed to attain one of the Community's objectives, could be taken by Council after due consultations with the Assembly. A change of such magnitude in the EC political system would have to imply heavier procedural requirements.[10] After that, the member states dropped the subject, choosing instead to make reference to the Convention and to the need to respect fundamental rights in the Maastricht Treaty (Article F). The former practice of judicial review was thus maintained as the only option until the Cologne Council of 1999.

There are surely many valid reasons that justified, and even rendered necessary, a strengthening of fundamental rights protection in the EU at that time. The incoming Eastern enlargement, which included countries that until recently were ruled by dictatorships, induced for instance the need to set a clear European standard for human rights protection. The same need was felt in relation to the approaching "functionalist" completion of the audacious plan for a monetary union. A growing emphasis on human rights could, furthermore, serve as a protective device against the rise of far-right parties in many European countries. It would also contribute to a harmonization of the different levels of protection in each of the Union's pillars, and strengthen the ECJ's legitimacy to work as a check mechanism in the Union (for further reasons s. McCrudden 2001; Bellamy and Schönlau 2004: 418–419).

And yet, all this did not have to inevitably lead to the drafting of a bill of rights. From the literature and the discussions concerning the Charter we can discern three main reasons adduced to support it. Dealing with each of them, I will also try to sustain that those improvements either did not require a Charter to be implemented, or that they would require much more than the Charter of Fundamental Rights as it was conceived.

10 Opinion 2/94 of the court of 28 March 1996 (96/C 180/01).

Increasing visibility and legal certainty

To some, even if the Charter achieves no more than a mere codification and consolidation of existing legislation, it serves already some important purposes (Menéndez 2001: 13–14; 2003: 27; Eriksen 2003: 49–58; Twomey 1994: 128).

First of all, the Charter enhances citizens' participation in the debate concerning the constitutional principles of the EU. The visibility granted to the official rights on the basis of European integration, through their publication in an aggregated document as opposed to the former dispersion in a myriad of legal sources, allows a more intense and democratic public scrutiny of the catalogue. By knowing exactly what rights are to be counted on, citizens may challenge them and press for further refinement.

Secondly, a code favours *legal certainty*, in that a single source may replace the variety of sources from which the ECJ derived the rights to be applied and their interpretation. The multi-layered structure of fundamental rights would not disappear, but individuals would have an unified pictures of what rights they have vis-à-vis the Community institutions. Moreover, if one is favourable to the taming of the ECJ's creative jurisprudence, it can be alleged that a Charter tilts the process of fundamental rights protection away from the monopoly of the courts, since they now have a clearly defined set of rights to refer to.

If the first argument seems to be valid, it is however hard not to relativise the possible deliberative empowerment of the European citizens. It is true that the charter-making process was much more open than the treaty-making one, with a multi-level and multi-institutional Convention, with the residual participation of some organizations stemming from civil society, and the body's meetings having a semi-public character. Nevertheless, we cannot say that there was a true popular participation in the conception of the document (Delouche Gauchez 2002; de Búrca 2001b). Also, no process of periodical revision of the Charter is on the horizon, not was it defined a way how to initiate one. It seems that the document was not thought to be revised, and not at the public's request or with its direct participation.[11]

Actually, the crystallization of rights in a formal document might even have counterproductive effects, since it may lead politicians and voters to "cease to think about rights and discuss them from themselves", placing such issues away from the legislature and returning the decision-making concerning interpretation and extension of rights to the judicial branch (Bellamy and Schönlau 2004: 432). Moreover, if it is not accompanied by the empowerment of citizens through institutional change, a bill of rights might contribute to divert emphasis from issues of distribution of power, and therefore to stagnate claims for a more effective popular participation in the public sphere of deliberation (Twomey 1994: 129). Such democratic enhancement, in the case of the EU, would probably imply some hard choices in the direction of a more markedly parliamentary logic in its institutional ordering. This would, in turn, have as a consequence a redesigning of the modes of functioning and electing Commission and Council. In fact, independently on what kind of changes are required to foster a European public sphere, its existence seems to be a sine qua non condition for the experience of a genuine *constitutional moment* in the EU.

As to the second argument, if it is true that individuals get a clearer picture of the rights they are entitled to in the European space, this fact is still not powerful enough to justify the creation of a Charter instead of, for instance, having taken profit of one of the recent processes of treaty amendment in order to materialize the much requested collective accession to the European Convention (Krüger 2004). The option followed does not seem to amount to an increase in fundamental rights protection by comparison to what already exists through judges. There are other, more direct and robust ways of promoting the protection of citizens' funda-

11 The only existing mechanism of direct democracy, the *European Citizens' Initiative*, was introduced with the Treaty of Lisbon (Article 11, Paragraph 4 TEU).

mental rights. As to sources of fundamental rights protection, a surfeit of them, rather than a deficit, seems to be the rule in the EU (Dauses 1985: 416; Weiler 2000: 95).

Inclusion of emerging rights

A further reason that seemed to render a Charter necessary can be said to be the filling of a certain void in terms of codification, in order to upgrade rights protection by "enshrining certain 'new' rights which already exist but have not yet been explicitly protected as fundamental rights" (European Commission 2000). The emergent rights are those connected to the protection of privacy in information technologies, issues of bioethics, or the right to good administration. The enlargement of the catalogue of rights to be protected derived, as stated in the Charter's Preamble, from the need to accompany the "scientific and technological developments" of the last decades.

This argument, however, does not seem convincing, since the problem it signals is inevitable in every legal code, and the solution is either only temporarily effective, or would require a constant flow of drafting Conventions. The fact that social developments and the changing cultural self-understanding of a community might give rise to the perception and legal codification of new emerging rights does not compel to entrench them by constant bill of rights' revisions, each one possibly already behindhand by the time it is proclaimed. Any 'constitutional' enunciation of rights needs not have the presumption of being exhaustive. That is what is enunciated, for instance, in the Ninth Amendment of the United States Constitution: "The enumeration in the Constitution of certain rights shall not be construed to deny or disparage others retained by the people". An example from the European panorama is the European Convention on Human Rights, where the ageing problem of any such document is dealt with in a dual way: on the one hand, by the inclusion on the legal text of successive Protocols; on the other hand, by the European Court of Human Rights' interpreting the meaning of the rights enshrined in the Convention as including the possible extension and actualization of its scope (Krüger 2004: xix).

Vehicle for constitutionalisation

The reasons alluded so far point to a 'technical' need to actualize and publicize the fundamental rights that apply cross-cuttingly to the citizens of the Union. In fact, such a task, due to its specialized and non-creative nature, would be fit for a small group of academics and practitioners, an expert group working, say, under one of the Commission's Directorates-General. If, however, the exercise of drafting the Charter was entrusted to an inter-institutional team composed of some heavy political figures, it is surely because the members of the Cologne European Council were expecting a more grandiose role for the document.

The purpose of a bill of rights, indeed, is not limited to the accomplishment of pragmatic functions (i.e. protecting the individuals). It also conveys the symbolic force of a political instrument of legitimation, working as the guarantor of the same personal autonomy to every signatory of the "social contract" and is, consequently, justificatory of the exercise of coercion from the political institutions towards the citizens to whom they are accountable. The borders of a political organization are defined by who is included in the rights framework established by the founding documents of a polity. That is why "human rights form the constitutional bedrock of a legal order, be it national or transnational" (Twomey 1994: 121; see also Dutheil de la Rochère 2001: 2; Duff 2000: 14).

According to this view, if the plan is to give a new foundation to the EU through the crystallization of a common ethos of constitutional principles, their jurisprudential protection from an amalgam of sources is clearly insufficient. Such a labyrinth, of which only the juridical specialists possess the Ariadne's thread, is unable to raise among the individuals a perception of belonging to the same body of citizens. Those fundamental principles require a formal document in which they are clearly enunciated (Dauses 1985: 413). The Charter would, therefore, have emerged as a "constitutional moment".

Even if the EU was already in some sense constitutionalised at the legal level, and in some measure in terms of institutional supranationalism; even if a narrative of integration has already been developing since the first stages of the Community's history, the Charter would not only provide it, at last, with a set of justificatory principles, as it would establish rights as the *lingua franca* to discuss the shape of the EU to come (Menéndez 2001: 15).

What would be at stake with the Charter, then, could not simply be an *a posteriori* legitimation for an already defined polity, but a true reorientation of the European ethic. This redefinition of the very narrative of integration would make it shift from the functionalist prevalence of the founding economic objectives towards an emphasis on the shared axiological core, that is, a "commitment to a range of fundamental values which transcend purely market goals" (de Búrca 2001: 7).

The roots of this putative reorientation are less a matter of extension of the supranational authority's remit in what concerns fundamental rights, than the diffusion of the fundamental rights purview into every step of the creation of secondary law (de Búrca 2001; von Bogdandy 2000: 1333–4; Dauses 1985, 416). This could, finally, raise the issue of the possible *incorporation* of those rights in the legal systems of the member states, in the same way as the American Supreme Court incorporated the first ten amendments of the American Constitution in the sphere of the federated states. It would mean that all of the member states' domestic activities would be monitored by the central supranational institutions in terms of their respect for the Charter's provisions.

These ideals, nevertheless, collide with one fundamental paradox in the way the EU works. This has been powerfully stated by Philip Alston and Joseph Weiler (1998), who signal a gap between the EU's official rhetoric and external profile, and its own internal institutional commitment in what concerns human rights protection. In fact, there is on the one hand a proliferation of declarations and treaty dispositions in which the EU pledges itself to the respect of fundamental rights. Likewise, its foreign and enlargement policies in terms of international commerce and humanitarian assistance, as well as in the setting of the criteria needed for new members to accede, is guided by clear human rights requirements. On the other hand, this stance is not accompanied by a "fully-fledged human rights policy" inside the Union's borders.

This is due to the heritage of facing the protection of human rights as something to be accomplished solely through the vigilance of the ECJ. The *praetorian* conception of human rights monitoring, unaccompanied by policy initiatives that would proactively promote and incite the respect of the defined rights standards, has sanctioned a "negative" conception of integration of human rights in the functioning of the Communities, that is, one that privileges the establishment of legal bans on the action of institutions over the "positive" enhancement of the protection of fundamental rights. The latter would require the creation of those institutional means that allow a departure from a focus solely on the principle of non-violation towards its backing by an "affirmative human rights policy". This touches upon the same idea exposed earlier on: the concept of "infusion" of every piece of community legislation with what Weiler and Alston title a "human rights clause", this time endowed with the 'teeth' to protect and empower the individuals to react against violations of their fundamental rights (1998: 20–21).

The creation of a Bill of rights seems to be connected, then, to the will to provide a thicker constitutional legitimacy to the EU, which would project itself through a coming into force of a lexicon of individual rights. Indeed, from the text of the Charter we can discern a will of the drafters to transcend the limited field of application of the document and to give it a truly constitutional significance as a sign of the mutual consensus on rights that would lay at the basis of the Union's political life.

Nevertheless, the strategy employed to put that intention into practice raises some perplexities. Surely, if it revolves solely around the drafting of a text not intended to lead to very significant practical changes in what concerns citizens' protection, then the incorporation of the fundamental rights lens in every Community sphere of action cannot have been the ultimate aim of such a document. It seems, all in all, that what is at stake is not just the establishment of fundamental rights as the paramount principles in the internal and external action of the Union's institutions, placing them as the nucleus of the EU's ethos. As I shall try to sustain in the next section, what was sought to be incited was another kind of process, to which this former one is a precondition – the one that arguably goes from the proclamation of an *ethos* to the creation of a *demos*.

The "demos half" of democracy

> [C]itizens often ask us what this Charter of Fundamental Rights is for. Fundamental rights are recognised in our constitutions. The member states of the European Union respect fundamental rights. There is a Rome Convention, upheld by the Court in Strasbourg, which is the ultimate guarantee in the event of a violation. So what is this Charter for?

This question of Iñigo Mendez de Vigo, Chairman of the European Parliament Delegation at the drafting Convention of the Charter, issued at one of the EP's sessions in which the Charter was discussed,[12] summarises a great deal of what I have been trying to sustain. None of the reasons more often referred to earlier on has enough substance to explain in itself the need for a Bill of rights, and more specifically why this old idea has emerged in the late 1990s. Surely, all those reasons play their part, but they seem subsidiary to a more central motive, to a keystone narrative that gives sense to the whole.

---

12 European Parliament, Plenary Session of 14 March 2000. Available at: www.europarl.europa.eu/sides/getDoc.do?pubRef=-//EP//TEXT+CRE+20000314+ITEM-008+DOC+XML+V0//EN.

We can perhaps start to discern what is mainly at stake with the Charter by looking at the mandate that was issued in the Cologne European Council of June 1999. In the first paragraph of the Presidency Conclusions, Annex IV, we can read the following:

> There appears to be a need, at the present stage of the Union's development, to establish a Charter of fundamental rights in order to make their overriding importance and relevance more visible to the Union's citizens.

From the first two segments of the sentence we can infer that the purpose of an EU bill of rights, as the representatives of the peoples perceive it, is not independent of a certain context. It is a reaction to a given state of affairs: the "present state of the Union's development". That status quo, it seems clear, is one of democratic malaise and lack of popular legitimation, which prevents the granting to the Union of the status of an effective constitutional polity (Tarschys 2003: 173).

We could perhaps state, following the etymological decomposition of the word into *demos* and *kratos*, that the concept of *democratic* deficit applied to the EU might be broken down as follows. It might convey an institutional deficiency in the system of governance (of *power* and *rule*) and representation of the citizenry that need to be fixed to compensate the growing extension of the Union's policy remit. It might as well, on the other hand, point to a more foundational issue of the constitutionalisation of a polity: the indefiniteness concerning the composition of the *pouvoir constituant*, the group of citizens who act as ultimate holders of sovereignty and that, by agreeing to be ruled under the existing institutions, provide legitimisation for the system of governance.

The first notion is a widely discussed issue, and the statements of insufficiencies in the institutional working of the Union are well-known and generally accepted.[13]

---

13 Here is a classical list (vide Weiler, Haltern and Mayer 1995 and Follesdal and Hix 2006):

1) The EU is dominated by the executive branch in detriment of the parliamentary one. Two of the main contributors for the decision-making process are composed of national representatives (the Council) and of Commis-

As to the second aspect of the democratic deficit, the diagnosis is also a common one. The EU has established itself as a quasi-federative regional arrangement, designating the provisions emanated from its legislative institutions as the *supreme law of the land*, directly applicable to the domestic legal systems. It has also acquired institutional powers through progressive transfers of sovereignty from the member states to the supranational institutions, and fulfils therefore the constitutional requirements of a polity in legal and institutional terms. However, if we are to search for the normative foundation of the European constitutionalism, we are inevitably led to conclude that it has not been detached from the sum of the individual agreements between member states, in the tradition of *pacta sund servanda* (Weiler 1995: 220). The states, through the chosen national representatives, can still be counted as paramount agents in what concerns decisions over the Union's primary legislation. Thus, even if one understands the EU, to a certain extent, as a postmodern, multi-level polity (Caporaso 1996), it is hard not to see that its normative foundations still derive to a large extent from the modern confederative tradition in international relations.

---

sioners appointed by national governments, which are not controlled on an equal footing by each of the national parliaments or the European Parliament.
2) Even after successive treaty reforms, the European Parliament is still far from being powerful enough to achieve a balance between the representation of EU citizens and that of national governments. Most of all, there is still no nexus between the European 'government' and the composition of the Parliament emanated from each election.
3) European elections are still *second order national contests*, with the national perspective contaminating each of the separate campaigns opposing different sets of national parties in terms of discussed issues, candidates and explanation of results. We are still very far away from the idealized transnational contest between supranational parties.
4) The EU structure of governance in too 'unidentified' in what concerns the typical standards of a domestic democracy to be adequately perceived by the non-specialist citizen. We do not find, at the European level, a clear demarcation between executive and legislative powers, corresponding to one government and one or two parliamentary chambers, nor a monolingual legislative deliberation, following well-known codes of political debate.

Is there, truly, a people of Europe, recognizing itself as the normative author of the Union's laws and institutions? One is forced to answer negatively in what concerns psychological and empirical respects. Concerning the first aspect, consider the usual turnout of European elections, the salience of the issues pertaining to the Union in the national public spheres, the attachment proclaimed by the peoples to the Union's institutions, the level of we-feeling among Europeans, and, in this past couple of years, the level of economic solidarity shown between countries. It is hard to detect a strong sense of collective identification between the different peoples and fidelity towards the political institutions. In empirical terms, the time where the Union's elites decided to provide it with its own *Philadelphia moment* by means of drafting and approving a Constitution, ended with a failure, rejected by the very *people* that would be symbolically instituted as such.

This second aspect of the European democratic deficit can be said to be a foundational one, since it puts in question the very redrawing of the political boundaries between national and supranational polities. It would jeopardise the legitimacy of the Union even if, hypothetically, all the 'instrumental' requirements of a democracy were in place. Even then we would not have more than a "constitution without constitutionalism" (Weiler 1995: 220).

'I name this people the Europeans', or How to do things with words

Drafting a Charter of Fundamental Rights seems to have been perceived as a solution to the above mentioned challenges. Such a document would underpin the international extension of the idea of social contract, anchoring it in a common axiological attachment and not on some ancestral connection. Its expected consequence was the revelation of a communitarian cement out of values and democratic procedures (not necessarily in a federalist sense).

Interestingly enough, these intentions replicate the components of a notion that has been the focus of a growing interest in political theory: *constitutional patriotism*. This concept, emerged in post-war Germany to be applied domestically, has been extended to the EU sphere in the work of philosophers such as Jürgen Habermas or Jean-Marc Ferry.

Constitutional patriotism is an ideal of civic bond in which the common ground that makes citizens recognize themselves as compatriots is not the traditional ethno-historical co-extensiveness, but a common commitment to abstract principles: to those norms, values and procedures embodied in a (written or consuetudinary) constitution.

This kind of attachment does not intend to replace the bonds of affection towards those who share the same ethnic origin, language, religion, etc. It needs to adapt to a world submitted to what John Rawls terms "the inescapable fact of pluralism", in which no cultural or religious affiliation may exclusively lay claim to the ultimate truth about things and therefore rise up as the official comprehensive doctrine of the State. As Rawls states, a society needs to find a set of rules that mediate the relationship between people of different origins and creeds, a group of procedures to which anyone can consent. Those rules cannot, therefore, impose a given all-encompassing vision of the world. They have to be political: a set of principles that allow citizens to engage in mutual contact through fair terms of co-operation, granting them at the same time the possibility to maintain their regimes of partiality. The principles are those present in each democratic constitution. What is established as the binding feature between different people is, in this way, a common political culture, even if its precepts might be interpreted from different cultural perspectives (Habermas 1996: 500). Furthermore, the attachment is not to the constitution text itself, but to the principles of justice it embodies.

The application of this domestic idea to the EU might seem intuitive, given the Union's obvious empirical constraints. Certainly, in a very heterogeneous group of States, fractured in terms of all the basic components of national identity, the enunciation of a common ground can hardly be made through an archeology of a putative *Volksgeist* or an ethno-cultural affinity.

Adapting the ideas of Rawls, thought to apply to the domestic sphere, to the international one, the social bond of a polity whose motto is *In varietate concordia*, and whose desideratum, as is famously enunciated in the Treaty of Rome, is to "establish the foundations of an ever closer union among the European peoples", would have to be strictly political, impermeable to any of the classic traits that form national identity. It would, in that way, have to develop from a civic ideal of fair terms of co-operation and of common participation in the (transnational) society's public sphere. The concept embodying this ideal is, in fact, already created: European citizenship. Not intending to replace the primary attachment of an individual to his domestic polity, but being "additional" to it, as stated in the Maastricht Treaty, that notion of citizenship at the supranational scale seeks to complementary create a double layer of affiliation in each member states' national. An affiliation, however, that does not overlap with any 'organic' understanding of nationality. It is, instead, solely derived from the values implicit in the liberal-democratic political culture (see also Weiler 1995: 243).

Aware or not of the precise existence of this concept and of the academic debates surrounding it, the European policy-makers that designed the mandate for the Charter, and those that have drafted it, seem to coincide in their purposes with the supranational adaptation of the ideal of constitutional patriotism as a strategy to tackle the democratic deficit and establish the foundations for a supranational attachment. As I have tried to show, the main reason behind the creation of such a document does not pertain to the enhancement of the citizens' protection and awareness of the rights they enjoy, or the inclusion of new ones. It is mostly connected to the exercise of providing the notion of European peoplehood with a substantive content. The purpose was, certainly, one of visibility, but what has been rendered visible was not the rights as instruments for the individuals' autonomy, but as contours of the community.[14]

Some incongruences can be remarked in the strategy of encouraging a demos-creating European constitutionalism through the drafting of a Charter, namely between the expectations placed on the Charter and what the document effectively delivers.

1) It is to place a fair amount of trust in the power of speech and rhetoric to expect that a declaration unaccompanied by substantive changes in the rights protection regime could incite the kind of desired civic attachment. It is as if the Charter worked as a performative utterance, by which an action, and not just a description of some aspect of the world, is brought about by the speech act itself. The Charter would be, then, expected to "do something rather than merely saying something" (vide Austin 1976). It is as if the Charter would be expected to set the condi-

14 Two more examples that could be presented are the assertions of Johannes Voggenhuber (Greens/European Free Alliance) and Elena Paciotti (Party of European Socialists), both of them members of the drafting Convention's delegation of the European Parliament, in the already quoted European Parliament plenary session (see endnote 12). Andrew Duff, also member of the Parliament delegation to the Convention, extends the views of his colleagues in terms of the expected institutional consequences of finding this aggregative narrative for a European identity. In a text about the significance of the Charter, Duff claims that its intended effect is not to alter the institutional balance of the EU, making it lean ever more towards supranationalism. That, to him, is already assumed as the telos of integration. What is needed, therefore, is the incorporation of flesh in the institutional skeleton under way. In other words, what is still lacking is a "European federal society" that accompanies and provides legitimisation through "popular loyalty" to the institutional system of authority (2000: 14). The purpose of the Charter would, thus, first of all be to define the underlying "collective patrimony of values and rights which bind Europeans together and underpin all the Union's policies" (2000: 26). It is, precisely, that diagnosis that leads many of the opinions expressed in the debates surrounding the Charter to claim for the constitution of the commonality that binds Europeans together in a common identity. More than a constitution we could call it a restitution, since what is at stake is the rendering visible of what was opaquely already there.

tions needed to effectively "establishing the citizenship of the Union" (as we can read in its Preamble), as the Priest in the church, by saying to a couple 'I now pronounce you man and wife' effectively performs the act of marrying those two people.

2) As Austin explains, however, for a speech act to be performant (or *felicitous*), certain contextual conditions must apply. Some are connected to the appropriate "particular persons and circumstances" in each of the given cases where a performative is issued.

We could say that the participants of a polity, in order to transfer a part of their affective allegiance to the set of principles and procedures that guide their state, must follow a certain 'appropriate' model of citizenship. That is, being a citizen-voter enjoying the negative rights that the state allocates is not enough. To be a constitutional patriot requires more in terms of engagement in the public sphere, it involves a *republican* ideal of public participation.

Indeed, the shifting of loyalty from nationhood (as an unilateral and exclusive way to create collective identity) to constitutional patriotism comes from the strict importation of a number of principles from an outside source as well as from the engagement of all the individuals in a process of common deliberation. What should be the object of such a *public reasoning*? Precisely what is sensed to separate peoples as relatively sealed cultural containers: each county's national history, the incongruences between the different national visions of the same events (many times depicting clashes between nowadays EU member states), the collective traumas, and the histories of oppression between nationalities.

This is a crucial process for achieving a sense of collective identification that is not exactly post-national as post-nationalist (Müller 2007: 63). It proceeds in two steps. The first implies an internal destabilization, through public and academic scrutiny and contestation, of national official narratives, narratives that are so many times mythically conveyed through amnesia and selective rewriting. The second requires the establishment of a European public forum in which the crossed histories of the member states might be collectively assessed and reframed by means of the clash of interpretations. This second step is, indeed, an extension of the movement initiated by the first, since the corollary of a self-critical stance towards one's own national memories is the recognition of the *other* through the wrongs our country might have committed, in the recent or more distant past, against him. In fact, to Jean-Marc Ferry, it is this "overcoming of the identitarian narcissism", the result produced when the relations between states are mediated through the principles of "historical justice", that can be the cement granting stability to a project such as the EU (Ferry 2000: 23–24, 145–147).

The agonism and controversy that will likely emerge are not, in this way, something to be avoided. They are strictly connected with one of the main purposes of a democratic regime: to settle disagreements among individuals through fair procedures. Indeed, if the EU is to be constituted as a supranational democracy, it should replicate at its scale the connection between "autonomy, accountability and memory" (Müller 2007: 35). It is, in fact, precisely this process of assessing the European common past and the narratives each country has created to project its place in history by means of commonly accepted moral standards and procedures of discussion that might serve as an engine for placing those same values and procedures as constituents of a European axiological consensus. Ultimately, according to Ferry, it is here that resides the key that might impel the contemporary actualization and extension of the Kantian project of perpetual peace through *cosmopolitan justice* (Ferry 2000: 136–142).

However difficult we might find it to render operational this commonality by way of anamnesis, it should be quite consensual that there is a need for the EU to provide the conditions for the existence of a meaningful public sphere of deliberation as way to give an empirical shape to the concept of citizenship (Habermas 1990: 506). As the literature concerning the democratic deficit keeps reminding us, despite Euronews, the Financial Times, and the Erasmus programme, the EU is still lagging behind in the realisation of that plan. As we have also seen, the Charter itself was not conceived via a process of true public deliberation, nor is it envisaged to be revised in that way. Finally, concerning the content of the Charter itself, if there is an extensive list of negative rights, that other kind of positive rights that ensure the citizens' public autonomy, the possibility and incentive to participate in the public sphere are inexistent besides the classic right to vote, to stand as a candidate to some elections, and to petition the European Parliament (Articles 39, 40 and 44). As John Erik Fossum states, "the Charter in its present form, and within the context of the present treaties, cannot credibly be said to produce the essential *mutually reinforcing* character of private and public autonomy, which constitutional patriotism presupposes" (Fossum 2003: 236).

3) Constitutional patriotism is anchored in the values espoused by liberal-democratic regimes, which are sensed to have a universal validity. The assessment of political practices and institutions and the rules of social deliberation that are contained in the ideal of critical citizenship is based on those values.

Yet, if constitutional patriotism is not only a strategy for such evaluative critical citizenship but also a way to cement the collective identity of a given community, those allegedly universal principles of justice must be embedded in, and interpreted according to, a particular social co-operation scheme. The attachment is not exactly to the abstract principles themselves, but to the specific ways how they are interpreted by a given society, to the ways in which the social ethos integrates and shapes those ideals. Indeed, as Müller affirms, constitutional patriotism "is not a free-standing theory of political boundary-formation", it "cannot by itself generate large degrees of social solidarity" (2007: 48).

Presupposing existing political communities, with some level of homogeneity among its dwellers, the kind of uniformity required is not, of course, in the nationalistic sense. It does not imply, in the same way, a bounded system of borders, impermeable to inclusions of outsiders. To the contrary. What must unite citizens is a common constitutional culture, a political ideal of social co-operation that organizes the public forum. On the other hand, however, this idea does not entail the absolute negation of the relevance of the concept of borders in the consideration of a a model of community creation. It does not lead to espousing a communitarian affiliation between humanity at large. Constitutional patriotism is not cosmopolitanism. It relies on existing political communities as significant entities, endowed with moral relevance, even if that significance is not attached to the concept of nationality but to the understanding of political units as schemes of social co-operation having each a certain axiological distinctiveness.

In this way, in order for the attachment to the constitutional fundamentals of a society to be effective, the social interpretation of those principles cannot be made in strictly rational, abstract, terms. It needs to be deployed on solid ground, through the specific ethos of a given community. It needs to rely, that is, on "supplements of particularity" (Müller 2007: 10–11, 47, 68–70). It might be the delineation of an other which allows, from its repudiation, to draw the boundaries of the common self (as, for instance, undemocratic regimes and movements). Or a particular way to orient the public sphere as an *Agora* that develops community awareness by means of common deliberation. This is the strategy proposed by the defendants of a constitution of a public European memory through the joint assessment and dispute of the crossed histories among the peoples that compose the EU. Another possible strategy is to delineate a particular way of interpreting the general principles of justice, or to define a set of core values and procedural practices that structure a particular polity in a particular way. That could be the role of a Bill of rights, if it defined a nucleus of rights specifically connected to the European experience, regulating the relations between citizens is a distinctive way.

Thus, the Charter could establish a great number of positive rights of direct citizens' participation in the Union's affairs, go along with adequate institutional changes, and establish an exceptional regime of citizens' protection in what concerns human rights. As we have seen, however, not only the Charter did not innovate in what concerns the traditional focus on negative rights in documents alike as it was not accompanied by the kind of institutional rearrangements that would spur a step further in the protection of rights in the Union space.

More significantly still, in the very text of the Charter, there appears to be some ambivalences in what concerns the scope and content of the catalogue of rights. The document has, indeed, assimilated an inner tension that pervades all of the European project, and in such a way that it can hardly be considered as a clear blueprint for the community to come. In fact, as Miguel Maduro has noted, the Charter mirrors an ambiguity as to the kind of constitutional model to adopt: a mainly intergovernmental EU, in which a catalogue of fundamental rights has the sole purpose of guaranteeing the conformity between the actions of supranational institutions and the domestic systems of rights protection, or an effective supranational regime. The latter would also imply the existence of a post-national community. Individuals would have an allegiance to both layers of governance that manage their lives.

The "ambiguous" constitutional status of the Charter is visible in some contradictions, noted by Maduro (2003a, 2004), between the official declaration of the role it is expected to play and some of its internal aspirations. On the one hand, the original mandate bestowed on the drafting body was very clear in its limited breadth. On the other hand, the "horizontal clauses" of the Charter's text, especially Article 51, are clear in curtailing any pretension for the Charter to lead to developments in terms of the powers and scope of activity of the community institutions. They also define strictly the conditions in which member states' activities can be monitored in terms of respect for the Charter's provisions.

Contrary to the two previous ideas, however, the range expressed by the rights included in the Charter is not consonant with a document mandated to express the sectoral rights exclusively applied to the actions of the EU's institutions towards its citizens, and to those of the member states when applying or derogating from European legal acts. Indeed, as Maduro points out, in some instances of the document one can perceive a drive to become a general bill of rights, endowed with global reach. That can be detected in the inclusion of clauses, such as the one concerning death penalty, that are clearly outside the breadth of the EU policy-making activities. The text seems, hence, to create its own impasse, placing itself between a document to be strictly applied to the European institutions in their relation to citizens and one *universal* declaration which, having a cosmopolitan scope, applies to areas outside of the Union's attributed tasks.

4) Even those segments of the Charter supposed to fulfil the desideratum of founding *ex post* a supranational polity through a constitutional patriotic attachment are affected, as well, by a structural ambiguity in their intention. They do not seem to point to any specific direction, to any particular European mode of conceiving rights and substantiating the basic principles of justice. There seems to be, on the contrary, an overall vagueness and indefiniteness as to the content that should embody the axiological substance sensed to become the ground to which the European peoples feel attached to.

The Preamble is particularly illustrative. If it signals a clear commitment to the "common values" (1st and 3rd paragraph), to the "spiritual and moral heritage" that provide the aegis under which the "ever closer union" among the peoples of Europe stands, there is no indication of what precisely those values are. Indeed, when we find direct references to what kind of values the EU is committed to, of what is the overall moral substance that can be discerned out of the group of rights amalgamated in the catalogue, there is a sliding towards monist cosmopolitanism. The values are those which are "indivisible" and "universal": human dignity, freedom, equality and solidarity (2nd paragraph). The reference to the European moral heritage is both truncated, for the EU does not take inspiration from, but is merely "conscious" of it (La Torre 2003: 89; Schönlau and Bellamy 2004), and inconclusive.

Only once can we find a reference to values that do not entail obligations towards the "human community" as a whole (6th paragraph), and that can therefore be recognized as specific to the EU. Such is a reference to those economic rights that were the genetic basis of the European Communities: "free movement of persons, goods, services and capital, and the freedom of establishment" (3rd paragraph).

This is not to say that we cannot, or should not, understand the process of Europeanization as a growing cosmopolitan awareness in what concerns individual and institutional stances towards otherness. It depends on the notion of cosmopolitanism. The EU fits perfectly in the cosmopolitan project if by the latter we understand openness to otherness, enmeshment between different (European and non-European) cultures, cultural hybridization, moral responsibility towards distant others. All of these performed away from the appanage of uniformity that has been the traditional approach to nation-building, and that sometimes still underpins the demands for a European federalism (Beck 2007: 41–49). Nevertheless, as Ulrich Beck admits, the understanding of a cosmopolitan Europe needs to be one where people have “roots and wings”. There needs to be a common, even if non-ethnic, denominator. That idea overlaps perfectly with the constitutional patriots claim for a nucleus of post-national attachment defined in strictly political terms. Common and specific values, interpretations of the universal principles of justice, or approaches to the protection and enjoyment of fundamental rights are therefore required if the plan is to bestow the peoples composing the EU with some substantial cohesiveness. What is not consistent with an intention of post-nationalist and supranational constitutionalisation and demos-formation is an understanding of these processes as leading to (and requiring) the suppression of the moral pertinence of the concept of borders, both in what concerns the cultural boundedness of the supranational polity as the cultural specificity of the different *demoi* that compose it.

Unless the drafters of the Charter envisage the EU as a preliminary state to the building of a world citizenship, a much clearer awareness of what can be the specific axiological European narrative would be required to engage those *supplements of particularity* needed to create collective attachment. The Charter’s text, on the contrary, seems to expose a lack of decision concerning the very content of an European patriotism. It reflects an indefiniteness as to what ethos might be coined as European, or at least what kind of interpretation or apprehension of universal rights might be mobilized to enhance the perception of a shared ethical and political identity among the European peoples (McCrudden 2001: 10).

A little less conversation, a little more action

I have tried to demonstrate in this text, firstly, that the drafting of a Charter was not necessary in order to ensure the protection of the fundamental rights of European citizens. Also, some of the usual reasons employed to justify the need for such a document do not, for themselves, demonstrate that there was any need of it. Another intention seemed to prevail. That reason, it appears, was a tentative solution to both the problem of the incomplete substantial constitutionalisation of the EU and that of the *demos* part of the democratic deficit. The solution would consist in defining a model of attachment to the Euro polity via constitutional patriotism (as it is termed in the academic literature, not in political practice).

I have maintained that the formulation of such an ideal of demos-creation by means of a Charter does not work as a model of collective identity unless it is accompanied by those institutional changes that effectively prompt the protection of rights and their incorporation in the supranational sphere, as well as contribute to the advancement of the citizens' deliberative power. It will not work, furthermore, if it does not provide any kind of specifically European narrative or interpretation of rights and social life. Facing them but facing them through the same kind of universalist generality as the usual declarations of that kind is not enough.

It does not, all in all, seem to build the conditions to constitute itself as an antechamber in the way for an European "emphatic constitution" (Müller 2007: 97), to be that document which would help to weave the patchwork and forge a sense of belonging to a *pouvoir constituant* by the part of the European peoples.

This intention behind the Charter seems to assume that an idea of European demos is something in latency, that needs to be properly activated, or summoned by calling it by its name. Nonetheless, perhaps what is truly distinctive about the EU, and what differentiates it from the previous federal experiences, is that it might not need any kind of narrative uniting the different peoples that compose it. It does not need to forge a sense of communitarian identity, a particular European constitutional patriotism. All the member states being already, in themselves, somewhat constitutional patriots (Müller 2007: 124), the EU need not to relapse in the automatism of constituting itself as a polity through the classic strategies of nation-building. It can, on the contrary, assume itself as a patchwork: an overarching entity composed of multiple *demoi* (Weiler 1995: 252; Nicolaïdis 2004).

In fact, it is the decoupling between citizenship and nationality, proposed by the constitutional patriots, that allows us to keep fidelity to the pluralized motto present in the preambles of the treaties. What the EU is about concerns not the creation of one unitary Leviathan but the possibility of an "ever closer union among the European *peoples*".

What would, then, in the absence of an identity politics, be the justification of European integration, and the propellant for further steps? The answer, according to Kalypso Nicolaïdis, does not differ from what, since its outset, has driven the states to such a common enterprise: mutual beneficial achievements. In her words, it is desirable to place the sense of belonging and commitment to the EU "on the doing more that the being, on shared projects and ambitions, both internal and external" (Nicolaïdis 2004: 85).

Faithful to the constitutional-patriotic ideal of critical citizenship, the sense of belonging to the second layer of political affiliation would emerge out of the sharing of the joint enterprise, out of the bonds of interdependence. The root of EU identification would thus be immunized against those classic and crystallizing concepts such as nationality, ethnicity, language, etc., and would happen in the sign of tolerance and inclusion vis-à-vis the alterity that imbues each co-citizen, each different nationality. The EU would, in that way, understand itself as a "community of others" (Nicolaïdis 2004: 84; see also Weiler 1995).

Notwithstanding the practical seductiveness of this claim for less ontology and more action, it does seem to maintain untouched two crucial and pretty much inescapable deficits of European integration as it is today.

First, if one may defend a type of affiliation to the principles and procedures of the EU which does not correspond to the thick ideal of a "community of destiny" (as Ernst Renan's would put it), it is manifestly insufficient to expect a common awareness of mutual benefit to be enough. It would work if the EU was still a confederative arrangement devoted to the consensual harmonization of the member states' positions in what concerns mainly technical issues. However, despite the fluctuations in the measurement of the intergovernmental-supranational balance, it is hard to see the EU of today merely as a "regulatory state" (Caporaso 1996). The Union's output concerning its members is not limited to common benefits and *Pareto efficient* results. It is also a system of coercion, putting constraints on the individuals' lives and developing some heavily political measures that are far from reaching consensus in the European electorates. Need one to remind itself of the current tortuous path towards financial integration?

It is this fact that, putting in question the legitimacy of the EU as a polity involving mutual coercion, incites the need of some sort of collective narrative to be established. That seems to be the condition for the dwellers of the Community's space, connected to each other by effective, not just formal, bounds of citizenship, to recognize the law-making system as the legitimate producer of rules.

Envisaging a process of polity consolidation without projecting an (axiological) common ground for the different *demoi*, we might end up by relapsing in what René Pollesch termed, in one of his plays, a "community of non-communitarians": one which, understanding itself as founded by an "act of communication", takes it as "that of communicating at all times an absent meaning".[15] As this paradox demonstrates, an absent meaning, or a purely instrumental one, is not sufficient to make five hundred million individuals regard themselves as peers.

15 René Pollesch, *Ich schau dir in die Augen, gesellschaftlicher Verblendungszusammenhang!* ("I'm looking into your eyes, social context of deception!"), a production of Volksbühne am Rosa-Luxemburg-Platz, Berlin.

Secondly, and finally, to put the emphasis on the doing, instead of the abstractness of being, does not erase the relevance of the way by which we do things. Likewise, the problem of the Union's legitimacy cannot evidently be solved by the sole finding of an appropriate civic narrative to give content to an ideal of European constitutional patriotism. Since that group of principles will undoubtedly be connected to the notion of individual autonomy and citizenship, the means to achieve it must be safeguarded and enhanced. The EU cannot, therefore, avoid considering the institutional roots of its democratic deficit. To do something, we need to do it right.

References

ALSTON, Philip, and J. H. H. WEILER (1998), An 'Ever Closer Union' in Need of a Human Rights Policy: The European Union and Human Rights. *European Journal of International Law*, Vol. 9, pp. 658–723.

AUSTIN, John (1975), *How to Do Things With Words*. Cambridge, MA: Harvard University Press, 2nd Edition.

BECK, Ulrich (2007), Reinventing Europe – a cosmopolitanism vision. In C. Rumford (ed.), Cosmopolitanism and Europe. Liverpool: Liverpool University Press, pp. 39–50.

BEITZ, Charles (1979), *Political Theory and International Relations*. Princeton: Princeton University Press.

BELLAMY, Richard (2006), The Challenge of European Union. In J. Dryzek, A. Phillips and B. Honig (eds.), *The Oxford Handbook of Political Theory*. Oxford: Oxford University Press, pp. 245–261.

BELLAMY, Richard, and Justus SCHÖNLAU (2004), The Normality of Constitutional Politics: An Analysis of the Drafting of the EU Charter of Fundamental Right. *Constellations*, Vol. 11, N. 3, pp. 412–433.

BOGDANDY, Armin von (2000), The European Union as a human rights organization? Human rights and the core of the European Union. *Common Market Law Review*, Vol. 37, pp. 1307–1338.

BOON, Vivienne, and Gerard DELANTY (2007), Cosmopolitanism and Europe: Historical Considerations and Contemporary Applications. In C. Rumford (ed.), *Cosmopolitanism and Europe*. Liverpool: Liverpool University Press, pp. 19–38.

BÚRCA, Gráinne de (2001a), Human Rights: The Charter and Beyond. *Jean Monnet Working Paper No. 10/01*. Available at: http://centers.law.nyu.edu/jeanmonnet/archive/papers/01/013601.rtf (last accessed October 11, 2012).

— (2001b), The Drafting of the European Union Charter of Fundamental Rights. *European Law Review*, Vol. 26, 2001, 126–138.

CAPORASO, James (1996), The European Union and Forms of State: Westphalian, Regulatory or Post-Modern?. *Journal of Common Market Studies*, Vol. 34, N. 1, pp. 29–49.

COMMON MARKET LAW REVIEW (1996), Editorial Comments. Fundamental Rights and Common European Values. *Common Market Law Review*, Vol. 33, pp. 215–222.

COPPEL, Jason, and Aidan O'NEILL (1992), The European Court of Justice: Taking Rights Seriously?. *Legal Studies*, Vol. 12, pp. 227–245.

DEHOUSSE, Renaud (1998), *The European Court of Justice: the Politics of Judicial Integration*. London: Palgrave Macmillan.

DELOCHE-GAUDEZ, Florence (2002), The Convention on a Charter of Fundamental Rights: A method for the future?, *Groupement d'Études et de Recherche 'Notre Europe' Research and Policy Paper No. 15*. Available at: http://www.notre-europe.eu/en/axes/european-democracy-in-action/works/publication/the-convention-on-a-charter-of-fundamental-rights-a-method-for-the-future/ (last accessed October 11, 2012).

DUFF, Andrew (2000), Towards a European Federal Society. In K. Feus (ed.), *The EU Charter of Fundamental Rights. Text and commentaries*. London: The Federal Trust for Education and Research, pp. 13–27.

ERIKSEN, Erik Oddvar (2003), Why a Constitutional Bill of Rights. In Erik Oddvar Eriksen, John Erik Fossum and Agustín Menéndez, *The Chartering of Europe: The Charter of Fundamental Rights and its Constitutional Implications*. Baden-Baden: Nomos Verlagsgesellschaft, pp. 48–70.

ERIKSEN, Erik Oddvar, and John Erik FOSSUM (2000), Post-national integration. In Eriksen and Fossum (eds.), *Democracy in the European Union: integration through deliberation?* New York: Routledge, pp. 1–28.

ERIKSEN, Erik Oddvar, John Erik Fossum and Agustín Menéndez (2003), The Charter in Context, in E. Eriksen, J. Fossum and A. Menéndez, *The Chartering of Europe: The Charter of Fundamental Rights and its Constitutional Implications*. Baden-Baden: Nomos Verlagsgesellschaft, pp. 17–29.

EUROPEAN COMMISSION (2000), *Communication on the Charter of Fundamental Rights of the European Union*. COM (2000) 559, Brussels, 13.9.2000.

FERRY, J.-M. (2000), *La question de l'État européen*. Paris: Gallimard.

FOLLESDAL, Andreas and Simon Hix (2006), Why There is a Democratic Decit in the EU: A Response to Majone and Moravcsik. *Journal of Common Market Studies*, Vol. 44, N. 3, pp. 533–562.

FOSSUM, John Erik (2003), The European Charter – Between deep Diversity and Constitutional Patriotism?. In E. Eriksen, J. Fossum and A. Menéndez, *The*

Chartering of Europe: The Charter of Fundamental Rights and its Constitutional Implications. Baden-Baden: Nomos Verlagsgesellschaft, pp. 228–255.

— (2003), The European Union – In Search of an Identity. *European Journal of Political Theory*, Vol. 2, N. 3, pp. 319–340.

HABERMAS, Jürgen (1996), Appendix II: Citizenship and National Identity. In *Between Facts and Norms: Contributions to a Discourse Theory of Law and Democracy*. Massachusetts: MIT Press, pp. 491–515.

— (2003), Why Europe needs a Constitution. In E. Eriksen, J. Fossum and A. Menéndez, *The Chartering of Europe: The Charter of Fundamental Rights and its Constitutional Implications*. Baden-Baden: Nomos Verlagsgesellschaft, pp. 256–274.

KRÜGER, Hans Christian (2004), The European Union Charter and the European Convention on Human Rights : An Overview. In A. Ward and S. Peers (eds.), *The European Union charter of fundamental rights*. Oxford: Hart publishing, pp. xvii–xxvii.

LA TORRE, Massimo (2003), The law beneath rights' feet: law, politics and the Charter of Fundamental Rights of the European Union. In E. Eriksen, J. Fossum and A. Menéndez, *The Chartering of Europe: The Charter of Fundamental Rights and its Constitutional Implications*. Baden-Baden: Nomos Verlagsgesellschaft, pp. 71–92.

LEBECK, Carl (2006), National Constitutionalism, Openness to International Law and the Pragmatic Limits of European Integration – European Law in the German Constitutional Court from EEC to the PJCC. *German Law Journal*, 7(11), pp. 907–945.

MADURO, Miguel (2003a), The Double Constitutional life of the Charter of Fundamental Rights. In E. Eriksen, J. Fossum and A. Menéndez, *The Chartering of Europe: The Charter of Fundamental Rights and its Constitutional Implications*. Baden-Baden: Nomos Verlagsgesellschaft, pp. 199–227.

— (2003b), Contrapunctual Law: Europe's Constitutional Pluralism in Action. In N. Walker (ed.), *Sovereignty in Transition*, Oxford: Hart Publishing, pp. 502–537.

— (2004), Carta dos Direitos Fundamentais: limite ou instrumento do processo de integração europeia. *Europa: Novas Fronteiras Espaço de liberdade, segurança e justiça*, 16/17, pp. 71–77.

MANCINI, Federico (2000a), The Making of a Constitution for Europe. In *Democracy and Constitutionalism in the European Union*: Collected Essays. Oxford: Hart Publishing, pp. 1–16.

— (2000b), Democracy and the European Court of Justice. In *Democracy and Constitutionalism in the European Union: Collected Essays*. Oxford: Hart Publishing, pp. 31–50.

— (2000c), Europe: The Case for Statehood. In *Democracy and Constitutionalism in the European Union: Collected Essays*. Oxford: Hart Publishing, pp. 51–66.

McCrudden, Christopher (2001), The Future of the EU Charter of Fundamental Rights. *Jean Monnet Working Paper No. 10/01*. Available at: centers.law.nyu.edu/jeanmonnet/archive/papers/01/013001.rtf (last accessed October 11, 2012).

Menéndez, Agustín (2002), Chartering Europe: The Charter of Fundamental Rightsof the European Union. *ARENA Working Papers, WP 01/13*. Available at: http://www.sv.uio.no/arena/english/research/publications/arena-publications/workingpapers/working-papers2001/01_13.xml (last accessed October 11, 2012).

Müller, Jan-Werner (2007), *Constitutional Patriotism*. New Jersey: Princeton University Press

Nicolaïdis, Kalypso (2004), The new constitution as european 'demoi-cracy'?. *Critical Review of International Social and Political Philosophy*, Vol. 7, N. 1, pp. 76–93.

Ramos, Rui Moura (2001), A Carta dos Direitos Fundamentais da União Europeia e a protecção dos direitos fundamentais. Available at: http://www.defensesociale.org/02/17.pdf (last accessed October 11, 2012).

Rawls, John (1993), *Political Liberalism*. New York: Columbia University Press.

Rochère, Jacqueline Dutheil de la (2001), Droits de l'homme La Charte des droits fondamentaux et au delà, *Jean Monnet Working Paper No. 10/01*. Available at: http://centers.law.nyu.edu/jeanmonnet/archive/papers/01/013501.html (last accessed October 11, 2012).

Rousseau, Jean-Jacques (1994 [1755; 1762]), *Discourse on Political Economy and The Social Contract*. Oxford: Oxford University Press.

Schmitter, Philippe (1996a), Examining the Present Euro-Polity with the Help of Past Theories. In G. Marks, F. Scharpf, P. Schmitter and W. Streeck, *Governance in the European Union*. London: Sage Publications, pp. 1–14.

— (1996b), Imagining the Future of the Euro-Polity with the Help of New Concepts. In G. Marks, F. Scharpf, P. Schmitter and W. Streeck, *Governance in the European Union*. London: Sage Publications, pp. 121–150.

Stein, Eric (1981), Lawyers, Judges and the Making of a Transnational Constitution. *American Journal of International Law*, Vol. 75, N. 1, pp. 1–27.

Tarschys, Daniel (2003), Goal congestion. Multi-Purpose Governance in the European Union. In E. Eriksen, J. Fossum and A. Menéndez, *The Chartering of Europe: The Charter of Fundamental Rights and its Constitutional Implications*. Baden-Baden: Nomos Verlagsgesellschaft, pp. 161–178.

Twomey, Patrick (1994), The European Union: Three Pillars without a Human Rights Foundation. In D. O'Keefe and P. Twomey (eds.), *Legal Issues of the Maastricht Treaty*. London: Chancery Law Publishing, pp. 121–131.

Weiler, Joseph H.H. (1995), Does Europe Need a Constitution? Demos, Telos and the German Maastricht Decision. *European Law Journal*, Vol. 1, N. 3, pp. 219–258.

— (1999), To be a European citizen: Eros and civilization. In J.H.H. Weiler, *The Constitution of Europe. 'Do the new clothes have an emperor' and other essays on European integration*. Cambridge: Cambridge University Press, pp. 324–357.

— (2000), Editorial: Does the European Union Truly Need a Charter of Rights?, *European Law Journal*, Vol. 6, N. 2, pp. 95–97.

— (2001), Federalism without Constitutionalism: Europe's *Sonderweg*. In K. Nicolaïdis and R. Howse (eds.), *The Federal Vision: Legitimacy and Levels of Governance in the US and the EU*. Oxford: Oxford University Press, pp. 54–70.

WEILER, Joseph H. H., and Nicolas Lockhart (1995), 'Taking Rights Seriously' Seriously: The European Court of Justice and its Fundamental Rights Jurisprudence, Parts I&II. *Common Market Law Review*, Vol. 32, pp. 51–95 and 579–627.

WEILER, Joseph H. H., Ulrich HALTERN and Franz MAYER (1995), European Democracy and its Critique. *West European Politics*, Vol. 18, N. 3, pp. 4–39.

The European Identity in the Proceedings of the European Parliament. Cultural Frames and Political Processes

Emma De Angelis[1]

The quest for European identity

The European Parliament's engagement in the construction of a common European identity is not often recognised, although this is in fact a task that MEPs have undertaken since the infancy of this institution. There is of course a wealth of literature exploring the idea of European identity in general and within the context of the EU in particular. Sociologists, historians of ideas and even generalist historians have for instance written about whether there is such a thing as a European identity, what it includes and how it evolved over time. Many scholars of the EU, on the other hand, have discussed the idea of European identity within the Union, and especially the idea of political identity, focusing on the developments of the 1990s/2000s and processes of constitutionalisation and institutionalisation. Not much exists, however, in the way of historical accounts of identity construction within the European Union's institutions. It is therefore very much worth exploring more thoroughly the way in which the idea of European identity has developed as part of the evolving political discourse within the EU's institutional arena, and in particular to highlight the way

1 Emma De Angelis completed her PhD in International History at the LSE with a thesis on the history of the European identity discourse in the European Parliament. She is currently Editor of the RUSI Journal (Royal United Services Institute).

in which the European Parliament and its members have, over time, elaborated and communicated a specific interpretation of European identity.

The European Parliament is often overlooked by historians as the lesser of the Community institutions, whose powers only started to grow in the 1980s and 1990s, periods that historical scholarship of European integration does not usually cover. This admittedly undeniable lack of power, however, did not mean that the EP did not from its very inception engage – purposefully and repeatedly – in the discursive construction of what MEPs thought were the defining values and characteristics of 'Europe', as embodied first by the European Community and then by the European Union.

A key opportunity for the construction and elaboration of this identity discourse presented itself every time the EC/EU considered enlargement to new member states. The decision whether to allow a new country to join the European club did, after all, impinge directly on the question of the overall purposes, fundamental values, and common characteristics that brought existing and potential member states together. The European Parliament was widely involved in enlargement debates from the 1970s, even though it did not actually have any formal role in the enlargement process. In fact, this institution started to use the possibility of enlargement as a way to debate the defining values of the Community as early as 1962, when the famous Birkelbach Report seized the opportunity provided by the alleged interest of Franco's Spain in applying for membership to unequivocally state that democracy (and the respect of human rights) was the quintessential prerequisite for Community membership. Ever since then, European Parliament discourse on enlargement continued to refine the political, but also historical and cultural elements that constituted the 'European identity' that tied together the Community and its member states. Over decades of integration, this discourse maintained and strengthened the political elements of the European identity first laid out in the 1960s, while also venturing into historical and cultural factors, which remained, however, rather more fluid and somewhat unrefined.

The European Parliament's identity discourse was first and foremost an exercise in legitimisation of the enlargement process: MEPs were concerned with the need to place enlargement within the wider goals of European integration, in order to bring European public opinion on board and explain the rationale of enlargement beyond the immediate economic aspects. Already evident in the 1970s, the concern with public opinion and the need to justify and legitimise enlargement in the eyes of the Union's citizens grew in the mid-1990s and 2000s.

This discourse, however, was also largely intertwined with the EP's development as an institution: MEPs claimed from the early 1950s that their parliament was the one body within the EC/EU's institutional make-up that truly represented the fundamental political value embodied (or that should be embodied) by the Community, namely democracy. This became especially important after the first direct elections in 1979.

Democracy and Europe's political identity

The most thoroughly developed, and arguably most successful, element of European identity developed over the long term was the political one. The gradual elaboration and institutionalisation of this political identity, which pivots around the twin principles of democracy and human rights, is a largely well-known story.

Democracy had not always been a dominant feature of the European Community's political discourse. It was not present in the Treaties of Rome and, whilst all six founding members of the EEC were democratic, democracy was not their primary concern: peace, stability and prosperity within the Western camp were of much greater immediate importance. The preamble of the Treaties of Rome makes general references to 'liberty' and article 237 states that any European nation 'may apply to become a member of the Community'. Nowhere in the Treaties did the Six make democracy a prerequisite for membership or even quote it as one of the fundamental values underpinning the movement towards 'closer union'. In fact, Daniel Thomas has claimed in a recent article on the constitutionalisation of Europe that the omission of democracy and human rights from the Treaties was a deliberate shift away from the 'constitutionalisation of democracy and human rights' found in previous treaties such as the 1948 Brussels Treaty or the 1949 Statute of the Council of Europe (Thomas 2006). Thomas also points out that the first Commission President, Walter Hallstein, clarified in 1958 that the Community would be open to any European state whose economies and regulatory structures were compatible with the establishment of a common market.

The European Parliament, however, focused on democratic principles ever since the very first sittings of the European Parliamentary Assembly: this was to a large extent due to the fact that, as a Parliament, this institution saw itself as the most democratic element of the Community's institutional set-up and aimed, through the introduction of direct elections (first discussed in detail by the Assembly as early as 1960) and the increased attempts to exercise a true parliamentary role vis-à-vis the Commission and the Council, to enhance the democratic nature of the EEC. The very decision to call itself 'European Parliament', taken in 1962, was part of the assembly's quest to embody the democratic nature of the EEC.

Tracing the introduction and development of the concept of democracy in European Parliament debates shows two intertwined threads: democracy as a defining feature of the national system of existing and potential member states, and hence as a criterion for membership, and democracy at the level of EC institutions and hence the question of institutional reform and of the role of Parliament as the "democratic" representative of the peoples of Europe. Moreover, there were other themes that emerged in conjunction with democracy, such as stability, human rights, and the rule of law. These were also important at different stages of the EP's definition of the political character of the Community. In fact, the human rights theme became so entangled with the idea of Europe as represented by the EC/EU that over time it came to represent, together with democracy, the key tenet of the European political identity.

The beginning of 1962 saw the Assembly debate the report drafted by socialist MEP Willy Birkelbach following the work of the Political Affairs Committee between November and December 1961 on the political and institutional aspects of accession ("adhésion") or association with the Community. This was the first time that the Assembly held a general debate on the principles of enlargement. The Birkelbach Report appeared against a dynamic background in terms of potential accession and association agreements: whilst the UK did not pose problems of principle in terms of political eligibility, Spain's increasing overtures towards the Community and open interest in associating itself with the EEC with a view to becoming a member were potentially much more problematic, as the country was still in the grips of the Francoist regime and was not even a member of the Council of Europe. Moreover, in June 1961 the EEC had concluded an association agreement with Greece, the first of such agreements with a European country and hence a step which marked out Greece as a potential future member of the Community.

In presenting the report to the Assembly, Birkelbach affirmed the desire to establish guidelines ("lignes directrices") for accession and association. He highlighted the fact that democracy, in the form of the respect of fundamental rights and freedoms, was to be considered an essential requirement for Community membership:

> Pour ce qui est des conditions politiques, nous sommes d'avis que seuls les états qui garantissent sur leur territoire des pratiques gouvernmentals vraiment démocratiques et le respect des droits fondamentaux et des libertés fondamentales peuvent devenir membres de notre Communauté.[2]

He went on to affirm that, even if the Community was at the time a customs union, he and the Political Affairs Committee that had drafted the report considered it to be an "élement politique" and

2 Birkelbach, Débats, 23 January 1962, Aspects politiques et institutionnels de l'adhésion ou de l'association à la Communauté.

that any country wishing to gain membership should be made aware of the true, political nature of the Community institutions so that “ils ne puissent plus avoir aucun doute quant à la signification de ces institutions”.[3] Even though the question of political principles and the democratic requirement remained only a small element of his presentation and subsequent debate, this was a very significant starting point that firmly put the idea of a fundamental political identity on the agenda.

Although most speakers did not focus on the democratic element as a membership requirement, almost all of them focused on the larger issue of political aspects by stressing the fact that the Community was intended as a political union and that this should be not only acknowledged but also shared by potential new member states: Guy Jarrosson spoke of a political entity (“une entité politique, une véritable Communauté”),[4] German Socialist Ludwig Metzger spoke of the possibility of enlarging the Community to include all European democracies,[5] Camille Béguè of the need for a political union, and the Italian Christian Democrat Emilio Battista supported the idea of the Community as a political enterprise based on shared values which should constitute the “philosophie” that should shape the Community’s approach to demands of membership and association. The report was unanimously approved for transmission to the Council on 25 January 1962, as a contribution to the elaboration of a doctrine of accession and association.[6] This was a new step towards a definition of Europe’s democratic political identity by the European Parliament. It was also a step that had no contemporary equivalent amongst the other Community institutions. Whilst the debate on the Birkelbach Report did not therefore provide an exact definition of what constituted the Community’s political identity beyond a

3 Ibid.

4 Jarrosson, Débats, 23 January 1962, Aspects politiques et institutionnels de l’adhésion ou de l’association à la Communauté.

5 Ludwing Metzger, Débats, 23 January 1962, Aspects politiques et institutionnels de l’adhésion ou de l’association à la Communauté.

6 Assemblée Parlementaire Européenne, Résolution du 25 Janvier 1962, Documents de Séance, 25 Jan 1962 p. 186.

general commitment to 'democracy', the debate's significance largely lay in introducing the idea of a political identity itself. The following decades would witness a continued focus on the political principles at the basis of the integration process, as MEPs from all political sides searched for the definition of what 'Europe' meant.

The hypothetical problem of being faced with an association or membership application quickly turned into reality when Spain made a formal request for talks in February 1962, showing the intention to seek association with a view to membership (Powell 2009). Clearly undeterred by the Assembly's discussion of the democratic criterion, the Spanish government put forward a request for talks with the EEC to negotiate association and eventual integration into the Community (Thomas 2006). Willy Birkelbach's response on behalf of the socialist group in the Parliamentary Assembly came in the form of the first oral question to the Council ever asked by a representative of the new parliament: after asking whether the Council and the Commission would find it appropriate to consider such an application, coming from a country whose "political philosophy" and "economic practice" were in complete opposition to the "conceptions and structures" of the EEC. Birkelbach continued by quoting the reference to "freedom" in the Preamble of the Rome Treaties and linking it directly (at a considerable stretch) with human rights and fundamental democratic liberties, giving an interpretation based on the values shared by the Six and that it would be hard for them to reject.

The European Parliament was not the only political actor pressing in this direction: trade unions and transnational political movements across Europe were also vocal in their opposition to the eventuality of a Spanish accession (Thomas 2006). The EP thus served as the main conduit into the European Community's institutional system of concerns that existed quite widely within European society, but may likely have been ignored by both the Council and the European Commission. Eventually, the potential impasse between the EP and its fellow institutions lost its immediate relevance once the first enlargement talks came to a premature halt in early 1963.

The debate on the role of democracy within the political identity of the Community came back to the fore in 1967 when the Colonels' coup in Greece gave rise to a new problem: how was the Community to react to such developments in the first European state to have signed an association agreement with the EEC? The European Parliament first debated the Greek developments on 8 May 1967, when Edoardo Martino, chairman of the Political Affairs Committee, addressed an oral question to the Council expressing the committee's anxiety about the suspension of civil and political rights in Greece and its incompatibility with the principles at the basis of the Community, which also formed the basis of the association agreement. He also affirmed that Parliament considered itself the 'democratic guarantor' of freedom in Europe, and that it would do everything in its power to facilitate the return of democratic legality in Greece.[7] In the ensuing debate, the president of the Committee of association with Greece, Dutch Christian Democrat Wilhelmus Schuijt, explicitly asked for the freezing of the association agreement with Greece until parliamentary democracy was restored.[8] His request was echoed by Socialist Walter Faller and Liberal Cornelis Berkhouwer, who also

7 'Dans ce Parlement, qui constitue le garant démocratique des libertés européennes, nous savons qu'aujourd'hui, notre tache, notre devoir, consiste à dénoncer l'extrème gravité de la situation née du coup d'état [...] à favoriser tous les moyens dont nous disposons le retour a la legalité démocratique de ce pays ami. La Grèce ne peut pas ne pas retourner à cette legalité si elle désire vraiment poursuivre avec nous le chemin qui mène a l'unité européenne, Martino, Débats, Question orale n. 4/67 avec débat relative a l'association CEE-Grèce, 8 May 1967.

8 He said: 'la Commission n'éstime-t-elle pas qu'on devrait interrompre toute activité des institutions prévues par l'accord d'association entre la Grèce et la Communauté? [...] N'estime-t-elle pas, en effet, que la simple participation autour d'une même table des représentants des Communautés avec des représentants du gouvernement hellenique actuelle comporterait une reconnaissance implicite de la legitimité de ce gouvernement?', Schuijt, Débats, Question orale n. 4/67 avec débat relative a l'association CEE-Gréce, 8 May 1967.

insisted upon the idea of the European Parliament as a guarantor of European democracy introduced by Schuijt.[9]

Parliament's position was strengthened by the fact that Greece was a clear candidate for future membership of the Community and the democratic criterion had already been established in the Birkelbach report. On 11 May 1967 all party groups unanimously approved a resolution asserting that the Association Agreement could only be applied once Greece re-established its "structures démocratiques et les libertés politiques et syndicales", effectively demanding that the Association be suspended until democracy were re-established.[10] The association agreement with Greece would remain frozen until the end of the Greek dictatorship in 1974.

The debates on the freezing of the association with Greece enhanced the idea of the European Community as a community of values with both the right and the duty to uphold democracy within the European continent. This idea of the European Community as a guarantor of democracy and of the European Parliament, in its turn, as the keeper of the democratic values of Europe above and beyond the borders of the Community was a novel one: it tied in with the democratic criterion established by the Assembly in 1962, but it was based on an interpretation of the Treaties of Rome that had to be constructed over time. The speakers continually referred to the idea of "liberté" in the Preamble to the Treaty, and interpreted this as parliamentary democracy, the rule of law and individual civil and political rights along the lines of the Council of Europe. It was, in fact, an interpretation that reflected very much the nature of the institution that was putting it forward. As an appointed assembly with a consultative role and no real powers over the Community executive bodies, the Assembly

9 'Nous, qui voulons être les représentants de nos peuples au niveau d'une démocratie parlementaire européenne, ne devons pas rester indifférents aux événements qui se deroulent dans les pays de l'Europe occidentale. Notre cause peut être en jeu', Berkhouwer, Question orale n. 4/67 avec débat relative à l'association CEE – Gréce, 8 May 1967.

10 Résolution sur l'association entre la C. E. E. et la Grèce, Débats, 11 May 1967, Association C. E. E. – Gréce.

deliberately interpreted its own existence as the embodiment of a commitment to the creation of a democratic supranational Europe and hence of democracy as a defining value of the Community's political identity. It was on the basis of this self-image that the European Parliament appointed itself as the champion of democracy within Europe and that it took the opportunity to advance this concept by publicly shifting the enlargement debate to the field of political values. In claiming democracy as a defining element of the political identity of the Community in its discussions of the Spanish and Greek cases, the European Parliament appealed to the one value that no member within its assembly could reasonably object to and that no Council member or Commission could refute.

While the question of identity did not feature prominently in the early-1970s enlargement debates over the accession of the UK, Ireland, Denmark and Norway (the latter eventually voted against membership), it played a major role in the mid-1970s to early-1980s discussions over the accession of Greece, Spain and Portugal.

The Discourse on Democracy and the Spanish, Portuguese, and Greek Accession

The idea of enlargement as a way of anchoring the new Mediterranean democracies to democratic Western Europe has already been analysed in the existing literature. Many studies of the applicant states show that they themselves interpreted accession to the European Community as a confirmation of their successful transition to democracy and an official acceptance back into the fold of the 'true' Europe. Tsoukalis shows how there was a widespread consensus among the Spanish political elites, and indeed its population at large, on EC membership as a way of stabilising the volatile political situation while in Greece the pro-membership elite saw membership as a way to consolidate democracy and referred to the freezing of the Association Agreement and the

EC's denunciation of Greece's military regime to support this argument (Tsoukalis 1981). Moreover, the Community's focus on democracy stood in marked contrast with the attitude of NATO and the United States, who had not denounced the dictatorship in the same way. This strengthened the claim that by joining the Community Greece would be joining a pole of democracy. De la Guardia (De la Guardia 2004) also identifies Spanish motivations for entry with the consensus amongst Spanish political and social forces on the necessity of European integration to engineer the socio-economic modernisation and full democratisation of the country after the collapse of Franco's dictatorship. This consensus was shared by Spanish public opinion, which was based on an idealistic, and rather vague, understanding of 'Europe' coupled with the desire for international recognition (De la Guardia 2004). Charles Powell also focused on the idea of democracy as an essential aspect of Spain's desire to join the EC (Powell 2009).

This perception of the EC as a champion of democracy is all the more intriguing when considering that, at the time, the democratic aspect of integration was still being greatly overlooked in the practical functioning of the EC: the European Parliament was not yet directly elected and talk of the democratic deficit was beginning to emerge, and the accessions of 1973 had had no impact on the idea of democracy. And yet the image of Europe as a champion of democracy not only persisted from the stances taken in the 1960s, but it grew to become the defining element of the EC's political identity as it was perceived by the outsiders who were seeking to join it. In fact, the Council recognised it in its 1973 declaration on European identity, in which the Nine declared that

> sharing as they do the same attitudes to life, based on a determination to build a society which measures up to the needs of the individual, they are determined to defend the principles of representative democracy, of the rule of law, of social justice – which is the ultimate goal of economic progress – and of respect for human rights. All of these are fundamental elements of the European Identity.[11]

---

11 Declaration on European Identity, in Bulletin of the European Communities, December 1973, No 12.

The European Parliament worked hard on the consolidation and expansion of this democratic image of the Community. Parliamentary rhetoric started more and more to equate the Community with Europe, intended as the sole legitimate representative of the value-based politics of democracy, the rule of law, and human rights. The image of a Community based on common values and supranational co-operation came to embody the very idea of Europe. In the 1970s and 1980s, belonging to the EC became, in the discourse of Parliament, belonging to Europe.

MEPS debated the political developments in Portugal, Spain and Greece throughout the 1970s. In 1975, Peter Corterier affirmed that the accession of Greece would 'make it possible to safeguard democracy in that country and to strengthen democracy in Europe generally' – an opinion that had already been voiced by his colleagues in earlier debates.[12] The idea of strengthening democracy through membership would become ever more dominant in Parliament's discourse.

In July 1977, in a debate on the situation in Spain, Parliament approved a resolution drafted by the Political Affairs Committee on the result of the first free democratic elections held in the Iberian country. Praising the orderly and free elections, the mover of the resolution also said that its real purpose was to show that, in the view of the assembly, the restoration of democratic life also restored Spain to its place in Europe and that Parliament was 'willing to acknowledge [Spain's] right to take its place in our Community at the earliest opportunity'. In passing this resolution, the European Parliament was strengthening the primacy of the democratic criterion over all others: it was a re-affirmation of the political character of enlargement, an expression of political support for Spain on the part of the EP, and an assertion that, despite all the technical, economic, and financial difficulties, the one and only reason that had so far precluded its entry had been

12 Peter Corterier, Socialist, Germany, EP Debates, Recommendations of the EEC-Greece Joint Parliamentary Committee adopted on 27 June 1975 – Additional Protocol to the EEC-Greece Association Agreement, 12 November 1975.

the rejection of the Community's political values. Democracy was again being given a primary defining role in the Community's identity.

The first fully-fledged parliamentary debate on enlargement was held on 1 October 1977, after the new democratic governments of all three countries had officially applied for accession (after Greece, Portugal and Spain applied in March 1977 and July 1977 respectively).This debate showed how the European Parliament was interpreting enlargement as a way of ensuring that democracy would take root in the Mediterranean applicants, and that there was a widespread consensus among parliamentarians on the idea that the European Community was the representative of democracy in Europe. This idea constituted a shift in the image that the EP was constructing: democracy was no longer just a requirement for Community membership, a feature of the national political systems of the member states to which applicant states needed to adjust in order to be able to accede. The European Community was now, in and of itself, a guarantee of democracy in its member states. The concept of the Community as a "guarantor of democracy" introduced in 1967 in relation to the authoritarian coup in Greece became the crucial element of the new discourse on enlargement. The European Parliament constructed an image of the EC, with its system of institutionalised supranational co-operation between parliamentary democracies, as a superior political system, upholding values of democracy and human rights. It also equated belonging to this system with belonging to Europe: for instance, in 1975 it was possible to say that Portugal "belonged only potentially to Europe", even if this country was a founding member of NATO, the OECD and EFTA, and that only its full democratisation and membership of the EC would realise this potential.[13]

The first directly elected European Parliament hailed the accession of Greece in 1981 as a symbolic moment in the affirmation of the Community's democratic identity. On welcoming the Greek delegation of euro-MPs, the EP President, Simone Veil, highlighted

13 Ernest Glinne, EP Debates, 11 April 1975, Situation in Portugal.

not merely Greece's return to democracy, but the fact that by accepting Greece, "the mother of democracy", the Community was affirming its identity as "Europe".[14] Furthermore, the European Parliament increasingly adopted a language in which joining the European Community was indicated as "joining Europe", so that only by becoming an EC member would a country be able to completely fulfil its European vocation. The European Parliament was equating the European Community with the one legitimate representative of the positive European political values. It was also establishing the equation between the European Community and Europe in a way that depicted those who remained outside the European Community and did not subscribe to its political values as, implicitly, less European. To join the Community was slowly becoming an affirmation of a country's European nature.

The democracy theme emerged clearly in the 1982 and 1985 enlargement debates on the entry of Spain and Portugal.[15] Again, there was consensus on the fact that the primary objective of enlargement was to 'safeguard democracy in Spain and Portugal'.[16] The only dissenting voices on this point were those of the French and Greek Communists, but even within the Communist group, the idea of the Community as a democratic force that would act as guarantor of democracy in Western Europe was accepted by the Italian representatives, who in developing an independent foreign policy path for their party during the 1970s had come to

14 EP President Simone Veil said: 'In welcoming Greece the mother of democracy, the Community becomes Europe in the fullest sense. For all of us your country remained the cradle of our civilisation, the land in which the term 'politics' in its noblest sense was first coined thousands of years ago', and again: 'we are very happy to be able to join you in the task of forging a European identity that will be enriched by that vision of mankind so dear to the Greece of antiquity, a vision of which we have the most acute need if we are to be in the fullest sense the democratic Community that our institution is called upon to represent'. EP Debates, 12 January 1981, Welcome to Greek members.

15 General debates on southern enlargement were held in November 1982, January, May and September 1985.

16 Otto von Habsburg, EP Debates, 17 January 1985, Accession of Spain and Portugal.

uphold the widespread understanding of the inherent link between democracy and the EC.[17]

In September 1985, for the first time in its institutional life, Parliament debated the Accession Treaty and approved a resolution that it considered the equivalent of a ratification, stating that is was not trying to usurp the rights of national parliaments, but endorsing them.[18]

The end of the Cold War and the ongoing quest for identity

In 1989, the unexpected and sudden collapse of the Communist dictatorships in Central and Eastern Europe and the prospect of German re-unification opened up a completely new series of problems for the definition of the Community's identity. On the one hand, the collapse of the only truly alternative system of organising political life in Europe was a confirmation of the success of the Western European model. The claim of Central and Eastern European countries that they wished to rejoin Europe confirmed the political image of the EC as the symbol of democratic Europe. However, the collapse of the Cold War order created significant problems for the definition of Europe's identity. The international political framework within which the European actors, and hence also the European Parliament, had constructed their discourse suddenly crumbled, together with the strategic structure that had allowed Western Europe to safely develop its Community. The ideological undercurrent of previous enlargement debates, when

17 Pancrazio De Pasquale (Communist and Allied Groups, Italy), EP Debates, 8 May 1985, Enlargement.

18 The Communist and Allied Group, with the exception of the Italian delegates, voted against. The Danish Social Democrats also voted against the resolution, but for different reasons: they believed that the European Parliament was usurping a prerogative of the national parliaments. See Christiansen, 11 September 1985, EP Debates, Explanations of Vote.

anchoring a country to the Community had also meant anchoring it to the Western camp in the Cold War, disappeared. While this could be conceived of as a victory of Western European political values embodied by the Community, the end of the Cold War division of Europe also presented the EP and the EC with a new situation in which the Community's identity forged in a suddenly outdated geopolitical and ideological context could not remain unchanged.

Throughout the 1990s, the challenges of German re-unification, strategic uncertainty, and the demands of Central and Eastern European countries created a need to finally articulate the details of European identity beyond general notions of 'democracy', explaining what this democratic nature actually entailed and how the EC would now act as a guarantor for democracy throughout the continent.

The European Parliament, paradoxically, found that the success of its construction of a political identity for the Community now created the need to re-introduce cultural and historical elements into its image of Europe in order to both integrate the Central and Eastern European countries into a comprehensive idea of Europe, and at the same time to place limits upon the extent of this new idea of Europe.

The political identity elaborated through the parliamentary discourse of the first three decades of European integration was formalised in 1993, when the European Council in Copenhagen institutionalised the principles of democracy and respect of human rights as the foremost political criteria to which states had to adhere in order to qualify for membership of the European Union.[19] This institutionalisation meant that the EP's elaboration of a European identity was no longer a question of introducing and reinforcing the democratic principle as the foundation of the process of European integration as it had been in the 1960s, or of turning the European Union into a guarantor of the democracy of

19 For more on the Copenhagen criteria, visit: http://europa.eu/legislation_summaries/glossary/accession_criteria_copenhague_en.htm (last accessed October 11, 2012).

its member states: both developments were now firmly ensconced at the heart of the European self-image. The enlargement discourse of the 1990s up to 2004 was the culmination of parliament's reinforcement of this political identity. Nonetheless, what should have been the triumph of political identity actually ushered in a new era of soul-searching and a search for new historical and cultural elements to complement the political ones within a wider European identity. While the concern for democracy and human rights remained paramount (as exemplified by the cases of Slovakia and the Benes decrees in the Czech Republic), the EP's emphasis in justifying enlargement shifted to broader historical and cultural themes.[20]

Throughout the enlargement debates of the late 1990s up to 2004, a historical narrative of Europe emerged as a crucial component of the identity discourse. The universality of the political values hailed thus far as the key identity of the EU could not be used as the sole element of European identity in the post-Cold War context. After all, before 1989 there were other, broader layers of geopolitical nature that determined the composition of what was essentially a Western European club. After 1989, on the other hand, the wave of new democracies in former Communist territories showed very clearly that anyone could in fact abide by principles of democracy and human rights, no matter how close or far in cultural, historical or geographical terms. These could thus no longer provide sufficient justification for the 'Europeanness' of the Union. There must hence be other identifiable features, cultural or historical, binding certain countries together and excluding others, regardless of their common adherence to a certain set of political values. Such characteristics ought to be something that could be used to discern between candidates that had a legitimate claim, and countries that would remain outside the Union.

20 On the need to provide the European public with a legitimate explanation and justification for enlargement, and engage with the public on this issue, see for instance the debate of 3 October 2000, especially contributions by Pat Cox and Miguélez Ramos (PES). MEPs also discussed polls on public attitudes to enlargement in September 2001.

The MEP's quest for such characteristics led them to the elaboration of a strong historical narrative of integration and enlargement as a key component of the justification of the 2004 enlargement.

The EP's historical narrative was based on a long-standing historical myth of European integration and its founding fathers: integration was presented as a peace process, the basic tenet of a new, positive, 'enlightened' phase of European history after decades of bloodshed and conflict. This was coupled with a long-standing narrative of European history as a 'negative other', with anything before 1950 presented as a negative legacy that must be eschewed in favour of integration as the only means to avoid the pitfalls of nationalist animosity that had twice resulted in such bloody and brutal confrontations in the twentieth century (den Boer, Bugge and Waever: 1995). This was, indeed, a narrative that had existed in European integration discourse ever since its beginning, fostered by politicians but also historians and other observers of European integration. It was also compounded by a long-standing conception of the EU as an enterprise projected into the future: with a past so dark, only the previous fifty years, with their positive experience of integration within the EC/EU, could be held as a positive, shared historical experience.

There was, of course, an inherent contradiction sitting at the heart of this narrative: it was a quintessentially Western European representation of recent history, which essentially excluded Eastern European countries. And yet, justifying their accession was a key purpose of the EP's re-elaboration of its identity discourse. How, then, could MEPs reconcile its historical narrative with the need to justify enlargement to these countries?

In response to this conundrum, MEPs weaved an intricate, yet superficial and ultimately quite inaccurate narrative of pre-world wars European unity, a time, before wars and then external powers (conveniently placing the blame on the USSR and, for those who may seek to find it there, the US) tore it and kept it apart. In this interpretation, enlargement would in fact be righting the wrongs of the past fifty years that had denied Eastern Europe its rightful place with the democratic and free countries of Western Europe. This was then tied with a discourse of 'moral obligation' towards those countries that, through no fault of their own, had ended up on the wrong side of the Iron Curtain (Sedelmeier: 2005; Gowan and Anderson: 1997). However, even in this re-elaboration, the EP's historical narrative remained based on the experiences and views of a select few countries on the Western side of the Iron Curtain, to which a slightly convoluted additional discourse of 'older' common history was tacked on in order to bring the CEECs into the fold. The contradictions and imprecision remained, and, more importantly, so did the specificity of this historical identity to the cases of the 2004 enlargement.

Throughout the 1990s and early 2000s, the one element that kept trying to break to the surface of the identity discourse, yet was never fully taken up or developed by MEPs, was the idea of a European cultural identity. Many MEPs mentioned a common culture as a clear indication of mutual 'belonging', yet none attempted to actually define or elaborate the elements of this alleged common culture. The cultural elements of the European identity discourse developed by MEPs during their enlargement debates were extremely varied and did not necessarily amount to a coherent or consistent narrative. They showed, in fact, how a cultural definition of Europe was consistently harder to achieve than a political or even a historical one – to the extent that EP President Nicole Fontaine could still declare in November 2000 that Europe's cultural identity sorely needed to be discussed and defined in order to set the limits of enlargement:

> Even if the issue still seems to be taboo, we simply cannot avoid discussion of the final frontiers of the Union, by which I mean the geographical and cultural criteria which will determine not only the extent of the Union, but above all, its long-term cohesion and workability.[21]

No cultural definition of Europe was achieved, however, with the partial exception of cultural references linked to the discourse on political identity, in which MEPs identified the European "political culture": the idea that the core political values of democracy

21 Speech by Nicole Fontaine, President of the European Parliament to the European Conference, Sochaux, Thursday, 23 November 2000.

and human rights are derived from the European cultural heritage. The cultural and 'civilisational' foundation of the Community's political identity was a constant sub-theme throughout parliamentary debates on enlargement: ancient Greece and Rome, and the enlightenment, were examples of the cultural references underpinning the political identity discourse. However, often even these cultural references remained no more than an unspoken undercurrent implicit within the use of the phrase 'European civilisation'. Yet other cultural references remained steeped in either the personal experiences or particular national cultures of the speakers, so that it would be difficult to identify a cultural definition of Europe beyond the generalised claims that there was indeed such as thing as "European culture".

The limits of the EP's identity discourse

A European cultural identity thus continued to escape a set definition, and the limits of 'European civilisation' were as difficult to delimit as the geographical borders of Europe, just as the differences between European and Western civilisation were shown at times to be quite blurred. Furthermore, MEPs were constantly striving to find a balance between the idea of a common European culture and the perceived need to valorise the national and regional traditions that formed the 'European mosaic' in order to maintain the image of a Europe based on the principle of 'unity in diversity'. Culture is in fact often considered national and has been linked with the idea of sovereignty and the nation state: the idea of a Community 'version' of European culture could thus also potentially create tension – something that the slogan of 'unity in diversity' is meant to soothe (Ellwood 2009). The many and varied cultural elements that interspersed the EP's enlargement discourse fell short of constructing a strong and coherent cultural identity for the European Union. This absence was further compounded by the fact that even when not engaging in a conscious attempt to construct such an identity, the cultural references that MEPs chose to employ in their speeches do not show any kind of convergence that could point to a set of commonalities amounting to a collective cultural identity.

The EU's identity discourse developed within the enlargement context between 1962 and 2004 was therefore based on a strong elaboration of the political elements before 1989, consolidated after the end of the Cold War during the process of "constitutionalisation" started in the 1990s, with attempts to elaborate historical and cultural elements in order to bolster a common identity beyond universalist principles of democracy and human rights in the 1990s and 2000s meeting only partial success.

References

DEN BOER, Pen, Peter BUGGE and Ole WAEVER (1995), The history of the idea of Europe, Vol. 1 in the series *What is Europe*. Milton Keynes: Open University/London: Routledge.

DE LA GUARDIA, Ricardo (2004), In search of lost Europe. In W. Kaiser and J. Elvert (eds.), *European Union Enlargement*. London: Routledge.

ELLWOOD, W. (2009), Is there a European culture? *Journal of Modern Italian Studies*, Vol. 14, N. 1, pp. 109–122.

POCOCK, J. G. A. (1997), Deconstructing Europe. In P. Gowan and P. Anderson (eds.), *The Question of Europe*. London-New York: Verso.

POWELL, Charles (2009), The long road to Europe: Spain and the European Community, 1957–1986. In J. B. Cruz and C. C. Montero (eds.), *European integration from Rome to Berlin, 1957–2007: history, law and politics*. Brussels: P. I. E. Peter Lang.

SEDELMEIER, Ulrich (2005), *Constructing the path to Eastern enlargement: the uneven policy impact of EU identity*. Manchester: Manchester University Press.

THOMAS, Daniel C. (2006), Constitutionalisation through Enlargement: the Contested Origins of the EU's Democratic Identity. *Journal of European Public Policy*, Vol. 13, N. 8, pp. 1190–1210.

TSOUKALIS, Loukas (1981), *The European Community and its Mediterranean enlargement*. London: Allen & Unwin.

Section II
The Role of Fundamental Rights in the Inter-institutional Struggle

Enhancing Fundamental Rights Control in Europe. The European Parliament's Scrutiny of Member States

Gabriele De Angelis[1]

The European Parliament and fundamental rights: an ambiguous relationship

Fundamental rights were bound to be an important component of European constitutionalisation since the beginning. Despite the fact that the inclusion of the Charter of Fundamental Rights (CFR) in the Treaties was subject to controversies, the will to wrap up the Union's political principles in a representative document to hold up to citizens and candidate countries alike as a sign of political identity and commitment has accompanied the very idea of constitutionalisation all along. The necessity to close ranks around a core set of political principles was not least motivated by the prospective Eastern enlargement and the necessity to clarify what kind of commitment was expected by newcomers and how high the bar would be set for accessing and remaining within the Union. Hence the introduction from the Treaty of Amsterdam onwards of Art. 6 and 7 TEU: an "atomic bomb" meant to secure a minimum standard of democratic life common to all member states. The idea of exerting a control upon the democratic guarantees of member states was implicit in such an institutional innovation. And yet, the monitoring on the part EU institutions was all but taken for granted by both member states and Parliament.

1 Gabriele De Angelis is "Ciência 2007" Researcher in Political Theory at the Instituto de Filosofia da Linguagem, Universidade Nova, Lisbon.

Despite the inclusion in the Amsterdam Treaty of a series of references to fundamental rights – an area in which EU primary and secondary law had been weak until then – it is only with the Charter that a systematic interest for fundamental rights sets in at EU level. A monitoring of the respect of fundamental rights in the domestic domain of member states was, however, not part of the plot. The debates on fundamental rights that have taken place at the European Parliament (EP) over the past ten years (i.e. from 2000, when the Charter was being discussed, until the present) show nevertheless a clear evolution towards an ever more extensive parliamentary control on the state of fundamental rights in the European space – also as regards the member states. At the same time, Parliament has been loudly requesting additions to be made to EU secondary law in order to include ever more fundamental rights policies in EU law. Both tendencies are entirely due to the EP's own initiative, and clash with the interpretation that prevailed at the beginning of the twenty-first century of how the Union was supposed to deal with fundamental rights.

Initially, the Charter was supposed to carry along little changes in the protection of fundamental rights in Europe. Neither was it supposed to extend EU competences in this domain. Subsequent developments show that, contrary to these early expectations, the inclusion of fundamental rights in the Treaties opened the door to increasing EU competences and institutional monitoring over member states in the realm of fundamental rights, i.e. virtually on nearly any national policy. Besides the Treaties' provisions, it is also the political dynamics inside the EP that exert a growing pressure to subject member states to a broad scrutiny. Surely, when the EP discusses fundamental rights issues, it only produces recommendations. And yet, the evolution of the way in which Parliament deals with fundamental rights illustrates once more how much the European polity evolves not in virtue of political will and institutional planning, but as a result of clashing institutional and political interests and their unintended consequences.

The beginning: role and status of the Charter of Fundamental Rights

From the Cologne European Council onwards, in which the drafting of a Charter was given the green light, the EP has being strongly supportive of the idea of endowing the Union with a bill of rights that may both hold up the Union's founding values vis-a-vis public opinion and fill some of the gaps in the European institutional architecture. In fact, Parliament detached to the Convention a team of indisputable competence,[2] and devoted to the Charter two plenary debates in the year 2000, the first while the drafting Convention was at work (14 March), the second after a draft Charter had been tabled (3 October). The latter is particularly interesting in that it takes place just before the Biarritz informal Intergovernmental Conference of 13–14 October 2000, and shows how much the Charter got caught in the whirl of the political struggle that inflamed EU institutions over the internal balance of power and the institutional reform of European governance, which the impending renovation of the Treaties made urgent.[3]

At the first plenary session of 14 March 2000, with the unsurprising exception of Euro-sceptic or far right groups alongside a member of the EPP-DE, members of the European Parliament (MEPs) expressed an overwhelming support for the Charter (Table 1). The most debated topic is the Charter's legal status, which receives as enthusiastic a support as the very idea of drafting a Charter (17 statements), while only a tiny minority (2, from an MEP of EPP-DE and one from UEN, respectively) maintains that the Charter should not pass of a simple political statement.

2 On the role and importance of MPs and MEPs' participation in the drafting Convention see Bellamy and Schönlau (2004: 419–420).

3 On the history of Parliament's struggle for power and influence in the concert of EU institutions see Corbett (1998: 263–266), Smith (1995: 72–83), Kreppel (2002: 76–87) and Rittberger (2003). On the contingent nature of Parliament's successes and the need to renew the battle now and again see a striking illustration in Judge and Earnshaw (2002).

Support	56	Representatives of EP Committees, Commission, Council, EPP-DE, PSE, GUE/NGL, Verts/ALE, ELDR
Strong Opposition	5	UEN, EDD, TDI
Moderate Opposition	1	EPP-DE

Table 1: Expressions of support or opposition to the adoption of a CFR, 14 March 2000.

In the MEPs' opinion, the Union needs a Charter for reasons both symbolic and substantial. The first are tied up with the process of legitimacy through constitutionalisation, i.e. with the attempt to endow the Union with the characteristics of a polity that citizens know from their nation states: a bill of rights, a constitutional entrenchment of its values and principles, an anthem, a flag, etc.[4] The latter reflect, instead, the widespread worry that increasing EU competences in the area of internal security and justice would require stronger and more reliable mechanisms of fundamental rights control than the fragmented and occasional ones available up to that point. Fundamental rights had been so far included in EU law either "indirectly" through the case law of the European Court of Justice, or occasionally through specific Directives, but had never been the object of a systematic legislative process, let alone a constitutional entrenchment.[5] Moreover, the Charter is supposed to fill some of the gaps that characterise the Union's institutional architecture, in particular as far as individual rights' protection is concerned. Hence the MEPs insistence upon the Charter's binding character, which is meant to go along with the justiciability of its provisions through the citizens' direct access to the European Court.[6]

Accordingly, MEPs adduce both substantive and "symbolic" reasons in favour of the Charter. The latter are those aimed at improving the "image" of the Union in the perception of its citi-

4 See the Introduction to this volume.

5 See the contributions of Miguel Poiares Maduro, Teresa Bravo, and Teresa Violante to this volume as well as Bravo (2011).

6 See the Introduction to this volume.

zens, i.e. to give it some constitutional traces that may make it resemble the kind of polity that citizens were accustomed to from member states. This has to include the Union's normative basis, of which fundamental rights protection is such an important component, as an identity mark.[7] Thus, the Charter would help strengthen the Union's constitutional character and give it a clearer identity a profile (Table 2). Citizenship is thereby often referred to not so much as a conjoint of legally enforceable rights, but as a sense of belonging. "Symbolic" reasons underscore the building of a European polity as a post-national community based on rights, instead of cultural, national, or ethnic features, a community in which citizens may be able to spot the marks of common political values and beliefs.[8]

1	Protect citizens against concentration of power at EU level.	11	Representatives of EP Committees, Commission, Council, EPP-DE, GUE/NGL, Verts/ALE.
2	The Charter won't replace national jurisdictions in fundamental rights protection/will be subsidiary to national courts	9	Representatives of EP Committees, Commission, Council, EPP-DE, Verts/ALE, GUE/NGL.
3	To give the Union a clearer identity and profile.	7	Representatives of EP Committees, Council, EPP-DE, GUE/NGL, Verts/ALE.
4	To respond to new challenges, i.e. bio and communication technologies.	6	Representatives of EP Committees, Commission, PSE, GUE/NGL, Verts/ALE.
5	To strengthen the Treaties' constitutional character.	4	Representatives of EP Committees, Verts/ALE.
	Others (≤ 2)	8	

Table 2: Reasons for the CFR in order of frequency.

The substantive reasons can be spotted in the "protection of citizens against the concentration of EU power". MEPs intend to give a genuine contribution to the enhancement of fundamental rights in the European space. The response to the advancement of communication and biotechnologies is a means to this end. At the

7 See Emma De Angelis's contribution to this volume.

8 As to the "constitutional patriotism" as a component of EU constitutionalisation see Paulo Barcelos's contribution to this volume.

same time, restrictions of biotechnologies and privacy protection are generally undisputed, and engender no particular conflict amongst MEPs.[9] In the first plenary, symbolic and substantive motivations hold all in all the balance, albeit the latter are far more fragmented than the former.

Symbolic reasons	17	Identity; Constitutionalisation; Legitimacy; Building a post-national community.
Substantive reasons	19	Protection of citizens' rights in the EU legal space; Bio- and communication technologies; Enlargement; Guarantee of fundamental rights inside MS.

Table 3: Symbolic and substantive reasons for the Charter, 14 March 2000.

Safeguarding member states: what the Charter was not supposed to achieve

Potentially more controversial and less obvious are some *caveats* that insistently accompany the debate. These concern the relation between the Charter and national jurisdictions. It is evidently not by chance that in the plenary of 14 March 2000 representatives of Council, Commission, and various EP Committees hasten to assure that the Charter will not replace the priority of national jurisdictions in fundamental rights protection, being instead a "surplus". Various EPP-DE representatives join in this assessment.

This warrant on the preservation of the pre-eminence of national institutions as the citizens' first addressees in cases in which the respect of fundamental rights is at stake is meant to defuse a claim made by opponents of the Charter as to its disruptive effects

9 A ban on human cloning, eugenics, and the commodification of the body, as well as a right to give or refuse consent to medical treatment, will finally be accommodated in Art. 3 of the Charter, while an agreement on generic "data protection" will be entrenched in Art. 8.

on the independence of national institutions. The Charter is indeed supposed to provide control of the legitimacy and constitutionality of legal acts of EU institutions, and of member states only inasmuch as they implement Union's *secondary* law. The Charter is however not meant to serve as a yardstick for measuring the respect of fundamental rights in the member states in general.

Doubts as to the scope of the Charter seem, however, to spread well beyond those who see in it just a further attempt to undermine national sovereignty, as is obviously the case for representatives of the nationalist and Euro-sceptic groups. It is Remarkable, moreover, that some of the more federalist-minded MEPs underscore how much a Charter is needed in order to regulate relations among member states and between these and EU law. Thus, among the reasons mentioned in the plenary session of 14 March in favour of drafting a Charter there is a concern for the endangerment of fundamental rights within member states, as Seixas da Costa says in representation of the Council. This seems to refer to the prospective Eastern enlargement, rather than the Austrian case of the same year.[10]

Widespread worries arise indeed with regard to the candidate countries' newly acquired, and therefore still unstable, democratic institutions and "diverse" political cultures (indeed, the enlargement will remain one of the topics most often mentioned in the subsequent debates until the end of the fifth term, after which the issue looses its momentum, the Eastern enlargement being now accomplished).[11] The fact that the obligation to preserve democratic values even within the long-standing members is mentioned shortly

10 See below.

11 "The enlargement of the European Union to cover new countries, which is an ethical imperative and an essential strategy for stability and peace in our continent, will unite us with states which have very diverse political cultures and which, in many cases, have young and untried institutions and structures. Both for these states and for those among them that are fighting for fundamental principles that will structure their contemporary societies, it is becoming important for these principles to be incorporated into a body of Community legislation to which they will remain linked after accession" (Seixas da Costa, 14th March 2000).

thereafter points out how one of the possible outcomes of the Charter is to establish a formal basis to legally assess the state of the respect of fundamental rights in the member states in general.

This timidly mentioned, and yet plausible, expectation, more than the Charter's political value, delivers the Charter to the criticisms of the less integration-friendly groups. Euro-sceptic speakers air the fear that the Charter may marshal in a European superstate,[12] claim the Charter's uselessness due to the sufficient protection of fundamental rights at national level, and show themselves worried as to limitations on actual fundamental rights protection that the Charter may bring about as a consequence of the further weakening of national sovereignty and the increasing distance between European citizens and institutions. These worries are overwhelmingly voiced by members of UEN.

All other EP groups however welcome the Charter as an instrument that is not expected to substantially change the EU institutional framework, except as regards police and judicial cooperation. The two plenary sessions of the year 2000 anticipate, however, a theme that will more potently come to the fore in the following years: the Charter's contribution to further European political integration and transmission of sovereignty from the member states to the Union. All in all, MEPs seem more keen to converge on uncontroversial issues, such as biotechnologies and data protection, in order to promote the Charter as a common interest of Parliament in its role of citizens' "champion", than to go to the bottom of the different models of Union and citizenship they support. Indeed, the role of Parliament as representative of the European peoples (as a counterpart to the Council as representative of the European governments) runs along the whole track that the Charter makes in parliamentary debates. Such a role is in fact repeatedly mentioned in a number of documents.[13]

12 A similar criticism is also issued by a GUE/NGL MEP during the debate of 3 October 2000.

13 See for instance EP *Resolution on the establishment of the CFR* (B5-0110/1999 of 16.9.1999); EP *Resolution on the drafting of a EU CFR* (A5-0064/2000), § 4, which concludes the first plenary.

The Parliament as guarantor of citizens' rights

In the plenary session that occurred on 3 October 2000, after the draft Charter has been tabled, two issues are scheduled for discussion: the impending IGC at Biarritz and the Charter itself. However, several speakers barely mention the Charter at all, and a simple look at the frequency list of the words used in the debate shows how the Charter is overshadowed by references to the "balance of power" among EU institutions. Considering the impending drafting of new treaties this is certainly not surprising.[14] The key topic of the session is, instead, the choice between strengthening what the then President of the European Commission Romano Prodi repeatedly addresses as the "communitarian method" as opposed to the pre-eminence of the intergovernmental level. This will indeed be the topic upon which MEPs, in close alliance with the Commission President, will mostly insist when addressing Mr. Moscovici as the Council's representative.[15] In the second plenary, the adoption and legal status of the CFR is arguably seen as a symbolic and political issue that is chiefly played

14 The following is a list of the first twenty nouns and adjectives used in the entire debate: "European" (203/0.739%); "Charter" (182/0.662%), "Rights" (130/0.473%); "Union/European Union" (124/0.451%); "Europe" (105/0.382%), "Council" (93/0.339%), "Commission" (86/0.313%), "Fundamental/fundamental rights" (71/0.258%); "States" (71/0.258%); "Member/member state(s)" (65/0.258%); "Nice" (60/0.218%); "Convention" (57/0.207%); "Future" (56/0.204%), "Parliament" (53/0.193%), "Biarritz" (52/0.189%); "Time" (49/0.178%), "Need" (48/0.175%), "Citizens" (46/0.167%), "Intergovernmental" (43/0.157%), "People" (43/0.157%).

15 In an institutionally correct way, Moscovici grants to the Charter almost half of his time (42%), the other half being devoted to the Biarritz meeting. Prodi will be the one to underline the most the importance of the Biarritz meeting and the subsequent IGC for the future of the Union. All in all, half of the session is devoted to the Charter (appr. 40% of the periods). Text attribution is performed by means of a count of the periods in which the Charter or the drafting Convention are explicitly mentioned, to which the periods are added that display a deictic reference to either the one or the other.

in the context of a criticism of the intergovernmental level of governance.

The references to the "method" that was used to draft the Charter are indicative of the nature of the controversy. The drafting Convention, which united representatives of the EP as well as of national and communitarian institutions, has indeed proceeded to an extensive consultation with associations from civil society, and marked thereby a distance from the "bargaining behind closed doors" that is typical of the intergovernmental level of EU governance (Schönlau 2005: 107–111).[16] In the plenary, "method" is thus associated with "inclusiveness", "communication", "civil society", and "citizens' representation", and indicates a consensual and inclusive model of decision-making as opposed to the clash of member states' particular interests characteristic of Council's meetings and intergovernmental conferences. The Charter plays an indeed relevant role in this struggle, as MEPs seem to equate the constitutionalisation of the Union to an overall strengthening of the communitarian level of governance.[17] Indeed, the great majority of MEPs still press for the Charter's acquiring a binding character and being included in the Treaties, whereas Council's representative uses more careful words and assures its solemn proclamation in consideration of the lack of unanimity among member states.

16 The experiment was deemed successful and repeated at the Convention on the Future of Europe (Schönlau 2007). For a supportive assessment of the method that the Convention adopted see Deloche-Gaudez (2001).

17 The method and the Charter's legal status account for half of the statements devoted to a general appraisal of the Charter. General assessments attract six times as many statements as those that MEP dedicate to the content of the Charter (62 vs.11), which indicates what the discussion is actually about.

1	CFR should be binding and included in the Treaties	19	EPP-DE, PSE, Verts/ALE, ELDR, GUE/NGL, NI
2	Prizing the method	12	Council, EPP-DE, PSE, Verts/ALE, ELDR, GUE/NGL
3	Further favourable appraisals	27	Council, Commission, EPP-DE, PSE, Verts/ALE, GUE/NGL
	CFR gives the EU a clearer identity and profile	4	
	CFR represents an advancement towards political integration beyond the common market	2	
	CFR represents a step forward towards European citizenship	3	
	CFR is important for enlargement	3	
	CFR is a reference point for EU values	2	
4	Critical appraisals (CFR is poor/useless)	3	TDI, UEN, EDD

Table 4: Topics of EP debate of 3 October 2000 in order of frequency.

The wider audience of European citizens stands finally out as the main addressee of the draft.[18] In the words of both the MEPs and the representatives of Council and Commission, the Charter is finally meant to respond to:

- A lack of legitimacy of the European institutional system;
- A lack of citizens' identification with European institutions.

As in the session of 14 March 2000, it is again reiterated that the Charter is not meant to add anything substantial to the national protection of fundamental rights, nor is it aimed to alter the balance between national and EU competence in this respect. Least of all is it meant to break new ground for formal entitlements of EU citizens.

These points seem to gather substantial support from all parliamentary groups – excepted the integration-sceptic, so much so that controversies on politically qualifying aspects such as social rights remain in the background and consensual issues are again emphasised. In the face of the main controversy between the EP, as a champion of transparent governance, and the intergovernmental

18 Remarkable are in this respect also the commentaries of those that highlight the Charter's accessibility for non-experts: 3 entries concern statements that underlines how "well-written" the Charter is. See also the final Resolution of 14 March 2000, 1.

institutions such as Council and IGCs, as embodiments of national interests and scarce communal spirit, matters of content are, however, a minor issue. With only 11 direct references, they receive in the second plenary even lesser attention than in the first. The fact that the Charter is itself caught in the whirl of confrontation between the intergovernmental and the supranational-communitarian level of governance adds much to the support that it receives from MEPs.

Moreover, at this point MEPs still see the CFR as

1. An instrument of "symbolic politics", inasmuch as it holds up to citizens a set of common values;
2. An instrument of foreign policy, inasmuch as it represents an "identity card" to show to third countries;
3. A standard to hold up to candidate countries;
4. A measure to gauge and shape EU internal policies, especially in the Area of Freedom, Security and Justice.[19]

Further developments show how much a certain short-sightedness as to the Charter's consequences on European governance affected these initial debates, the more so, as its substantial impact on fundamental rights control in the European space were actually foreseeable, as some interventions underscore. Thus, a MEP of ELDR insists that the Charter should be complemented by means of legal enforcement on member states.

An ambiguous instrument: the Charter's unclear scope of application

From the start, the actual legal scope of the CFR is shrouded in uncertainty. Although it is meant to apply to Union's institutions and to member states only while implementing EU law, early assessment of its legal impact draw a far more blurred picture. Thus, a Report issued by the Committee on Constitutional Affairs as the

19 EP *Resolution on the drafting of a EU CFR* (A5-0064/2000), 1.

drafting process was still going on (A5-0064/2000) clearly points out the difficulty lurking behind the attempt to clearly circumscribe in advance its real scope of application. If it is indeed cumbersome to implement the principle of subsidiarity in EU policies generally, this is all the more the case when fundamental rights are involved, as the Report highlights. Thus, the introduction of a code of fundamental rights at EU level "alters the paradigm of European integration [and] *redefine[s] where power lies*",[20] inasmuch as such a code necessarily ends up affecting the distribution of competences between the Union and the member states.

In the light of such a clear assessment on the part of the Committee before any debate takes place at Parliament, it is utterly remarkable that any more detailed discussion of the topic is avoided. Worries are clearly present that the joining Eastern European countries may represent a discontinuity with the Western European tradition of fundamental rights protection, especially as minorities are concerned, but with an eye on fundamental freedoms generally. This seems to imply that the Charter ought indeed to serve as a legal means of Europe-wide fundamental rights enforcement on member states – a prospective that is partly obscured by the as well widespread conviction that, despite the Austrian controversy of the year 2000, fundamental rights protection in member states of long standing is a settled issue or at least a matter deserving minor attention. Subsequent developments will however show how illusory such a conviction indeed was.

Indeed, the years that follow the Charter's "solemn proclamation" show an important evolution in the way the EP deals with both the Charter and fundamental rights. At first, old patterns of interpretation of the Charter's role and significance persist, as new facts have not yet emerged to alter them. Thus, the assessment of the Charter's impact performed and debated in 2002 is still framed according to the functions initially ascribed to it. While underlining that the Charter has become, as expected, a "reference point" for the ECJ as well as for national courts, MEP Andrew Duff, the draftsperson, highlights that the Charter does not add

20 A5-0064/2000, Explanatory statement, 9, emphasis added.

anything to EU competences (A5-0332/2002). Inasmuch as it applies to Union's acts only, it does not alter, let alone undermine, the usual functioning of fundamental rights protection in the member states.[21] The report also reiterates the well known arguments commending the Charter: it increases the Union's legitimacy and the citizens' sense of belonging. The text adopted in the subsequent plenary (P5_TA(2002)0508) underscores the respect for national diversities alongside the development of common values, reaffirms the principle of subsidiarity, and insists upon the Charter applying to EU institutions and to member states only insofar as they implement Union's legislation.

As an instrument of control over fundamental rights respect at Union's level, the Charter seems nevertheless to play only a minor role in parliamentary proceedings. Instead, member states remain in the spotlight to a far larger extent than EU institutions. It is only in 2005 that the Commission attempts to satisfy the requirement that its own activities be benchmarked against the norms of the Charter. The Commission issues a paper concerning the internal scrutiny of its own initiatives in order to assure compliance of its legislative proposals with the Charter's provisions (COM(2005) 172). In it, it affirms the need to promote a fundamental rights culture, but underscores that the internal benchmarking is also intended to grant visibility to its own fundamental rights monitoring in the eyes of European citizens, to enhance its credibility and authority before the European public, and to promote an image of the Charter as conveying a civic identity based on common values. Moreover, as a guardian of the Treaties, the Commission advocates to itself the role of checking on the fundamental rights-adequacy of the overall legislative activity, which includes Parliament and Council as the two legislative branches.

Parliament reacts with a claim for a public, instead of a merely internal, scrutiny of the Commission's activity. As an elected body

21 See along the same lines the working paper on *The future of the Charter and Institutional Arrangements for the protection of fundamental rights in the member states* (AFCO 102 EN) commissioned by Parliament and issued in November 2002.

representing the peoples of Europe and in the face of the limited individual access to the ECJ, the EP vindicates for itself the main role of a defenders of fundamental rights in the European political space (CRE 14/3/2007 – 16; P6_TA(2007)0078). Thus, the Charter is again put to the service of the internal struggle for visibility and legitimacy among EU institutions. Its scope of application remains thereby uncertain in the perception of most MEPs. Thus, higher representatives of EU institutions recall its real scope whenever the occasion arises, as in the debate of 28 November 2007 on the *Approval by the EP of the CFR of the EU* in the perspective of its solemn proclamation, in which Wallström, as the representative of the Commission, as well as several voices from all the major political groups remind their colleagues that the Charter applies to the Union's institutions and to member states only inasmuch as they implement EU law. Such interventions also seem to represent a response to the Polish and British opt-out, as both countries had contended the unclear scope of application of the Charter. Scepticism as to the legal impact of the Charter upon fundamental rights protection at national level, as well as serious concern as to its consequences for the relations among European partners are, however, well rooted in the way the Charter's provisions had been made reference to along the years from the most diverse actors. Indeed, a wide range of issues had come to be formulated in terms of fundamental rights, as covered by the Charter's provisions.[22] Such a practice develops strongly inside the EP, and is occasioned by the Parliament's decision to exert a yearly scrutiny of the state of fundamental rights respect in Europe.

22 MEP Wojciechowski's reaction to the "encouragements" addressed at Poland to refrain from their opt-out tells a lot of the uncertainty caused by such a rhetorical and political use of the Charter: "In august 2007 the President of this Parliament [...] stated that the source of the right to homeland should be sought in the right to dignity. [...] The right to dignity is enshrined in the first article of the Charter. [...] The German association of displaced persons laments the fate of people resettled from Poland. What would happen if the German lament and specific interpretation of human dignity were applied to Alsace and Lorraine?"

Widening the scope of fundamental rights assessment: the limits of subsidiarity

During the first plenary debate on *Human rights in the world and EU fundamental rights* (4 July 2001), with which a yearly scrutiny of the state of fundamental and human rights both inside and outside the Union's space on the basis of the Charter's provisions begins, MEPs discuss the matter mainly according to the three functions that the Charter has been elaborated for: delivering a standard for EU foreign policy, enlargement, and EU legislative activity, with a marked emphasis on the first two. However, a further topic emerges: the assessment of the state of fundamental rights in the member states *independently of whether the latter are or not implementing EU legislation*.

The Report at the basis of the debate (A5-0223/2001) encourages to widen the scope of the debate inasmuch as it carries through an assessment of the state of fundamental rights respect within the Union's space in general. However, such an assessment was formulated in mild terms in the attempt to avoid to "brand this or that state", in MEP Cornillet's – the draftsperson's – own words. The "naming and shaming" of member states will, however, become common practice in the subsequent years. From the start, the assessment's desired outcome is, indeed, that legislative, regulatory, or administrative action be taken at EU level whenever a breach of fundamental rights is discovered inside the Union, as the draftsperson underscores.

Such a development is hardly made thematic as such. Thus, it is only a few speakers (namely 4) that underline such a shift in fundamental rights assessment and to encourage a more outspoken control on member states in fundamental rights matters,[23] whereas even less (namely 2) express their concern. The text

23 See for instance Buitenweg: "Although the Charter itself was only supposed to relate to the actions of the Union, that is, the European institutions, the member states themselves are now being tested".

adopted (A5-0223/2001) raises a claim to general monitoring irrespectively of whether member states are implementing or not EU legislation, and invokes Art. 6 and 7 TEU as the corresponding legal basis: since member states would have acknowledged that the respect for their common tradition of fundamental rights is the ground on which their Union rests, a monitoring on the part of the EP as representative of the peoples of Europe is due. A dialogue with member states' parliaments and further national and supranational institutions acting for fundamental rights respect is repeatedly called forth as a main goal to be pursued. Remarkably, except Directive 97/66/EC on interception and storage of data no further legal basis is given. In the absence of further substantial provisions in secondary law, EU primary law seem to MEPs sufficient to buttress their claim. Inasmuch as the text enters into details, it covers mostly, but not exclusively, areas to which EU legislation applies, such as the recognition of judicial decisions in criminal matters, privacy protection in data treatment, and fundamental rights respect or disrespect by police officers. Recommendations to specific member states with regard to areas not covered by EU legislation are nevertheless not dispensed with, such as for instance the recognition of conscientious objection to military service in Greece (P5_TA(2003) 0012, 52), recommendations as to national housing policy in relation to Roma people (82), calls on member states' Parliaments to ratify international conventions, etc. More encompassing recommendations are issued also for topics that are heatedly debated at Parliament, such as the recognition of same-sex relationships (84). Censorship of member states for specific failures in the application of EU law is, on the other hand, rare. The two texts adopted in the subsequent year (P5_TA(2003)0012 and P5_TA(2003)0376) follow the same path.

The plenary debate of 21 October 2002 confirms this trend towards an encompassing monitoring of fundamental rights respect in member states beyond the implementation of EU law. With a perspective on the drafting of the *Treaty establishing a Constitution for Europe*, the Charter's legal status, its political importance and contribution to EU legitimacy are, again, the topics the attracts the bulk of MEPs attention. Voices expressing concern with regard to the Charter's impact on the balance of power between member states and the Union become nevertheless louder. Besides George Berthu's (NI) minority opinion on the report and his speech in the plenary, three MEPs from UEN, EPP-DE, and GUE/NGL warn of an extension of the scope of the Charter's application in order to put the member states under tutelage (a point on which Queiró, UEN, also touches a year later).

A growing scrutiny of member states independently of whether they are or not implementing EU legislation is a *fait accompli* at least from 2003 onwards. In the debate of 13 January 2003, Cornillet affirms on behalf of the EPP-DE group that the yearly discussion on fundamental rights gives Parliament "an opportunity to go beyond the strict application of the Charter with regard to the legislation of the Union" as well as to "acquire power to control the actions of the States". Overall scrutiny becomes such an obvious practice that in the 2004 debate on the state of fundamental rights in the EU MEP Swiebel affirms that MEPs "have a Charter which explicitly states the human rights obligations of the member states".[24] The initial intent of the Charter to be applicable to member states only while implementing EU legislation is again disregarded.[25] Questioning the policies of national governments beyond the scope of the Charter is raised to a political strategy in the words, of Commission's vice-president Barrot, who in the debate of 17 december 2008 affirms that

24 *Fundamental Rights in the European Union* (2003), 31 March 2004. Notably, the same speaker also utters the need of further clarification as "to what extent the human rights problems in one member state are actually an issue for the European Union as a whole".

25 Thus, a MEP feels safe in mentioning in one leg fundamental rights control in relation to the European arrest warrant, which falls under the provisions of the Area of Freedom, Security and Justice, and the French ban on headscarves as two fundamental rights issues of equal standing.

> There are also situations in which we go beyond Community competences. These are political moves that may prove necessary in certain circumstances, where we do not have the option to use national mechanisms.[26]

The EP's oversight on fundamental rights respect in member states occurs in form of a "moral suasion" or, in more acute cases, by means of a public naming and shaming, and has in both cases no immediate legal consequence. The EP issues, in fact, recommendations. Naming and shaming is, moreover, a controversial topic. Thus, draftsperson Wyn's opinion on behalf of the Committee on Culture is rejected by those who would like to avoid Italy being named and shamed in relation to Prime Minister Berlusconi's conflict of interest, mainly in virtue of the opposition from the EPP-DE group, as Cornillet emphasises in the plenary.

Perhaps as a reaction to the continuous controversies on the range of fundamental rights covered by European law, and also as a mirror of the member states' recalcitrant attitude towards fundamental rights monitoring at EU level, references to a circumstantial legal basis increase from 2008 onwards, also due to an increasing coverage in secondary law. Thus, in the text adopted in 2009 (P6_TA(2009)0019) a list of directives is mentioned alongside Art. 6 and 7 TEU by way of a justification, and the aim to enhance the fundamental rights culture in the European space is reiterated. The text also punctually replies to objections from the part of member states. Detailed remarks to specific issues in member states are, indeed, systematically covered by as many detailed references to Directives. Like the former, also the Resolution of 15 December 2010 on the effective implementation of fundamental rights under the Lisbon Treaty (P7_TA(2010)0483) distinguishes between areas covered by EU law and topics that would imply an extension of the EU legislation. Both in 2009 and in 2010 the Parliament does not refrain, however, from issuing recommenda-

26 He explicitly mentions Poland, Romania, and Bulgaria as countries subjected to pressures in relation to doubtful handling of fundamental rights in specific cases, whereas Art. 7 was used as a "threat". Speaking on behalf of the EPP-DE group, Gál confirms that several topics addressed in the Report fall under the competence of national governments.

tions on a wider range of fundamental rights-related topics far beyond actual EU law, such a the linguistic protection of minorities, an enhancement of the rights of disabled persons, etc. Some of the topics are highly controversial inside the EP, and reflect the groups' political platforms rather then the entire EP's duty of monitoring (a corresponding articulation in the structure of the documents in areas covered by EU law and areas that are not, but are nevertheless judged as relevant for fundamental rights, can also be viewed as an attempt to keep both functions apart).[27]

Parliament attempts to entrench the Union's control on fundamental rights straightforwardly. Thus, Gál's 2010 Report (A7-0334/2010) ponders the instatement of a "freezing mechanism" that the Commission could enforce on member states' policies whenever the latter are suspected of infringing on fundamental rights, which would in fact imply a thorough reversal of the relation of sovereignty between member states and the Union. However, the suggestion receives support from ALDE and Verts/ALE only.

Targeting member states: the final breakthrough?

Although a control of fundamental rights respect in member states seems at first not to lie at the top of the reasons that motivate the entrenchment of fundamental rights in the EU's primary law, it soon imposes itself as an important point in Parliament's agenda. There is no lack of occasions to call on the bench specific member states. In the following, four debates are singled out for analysis:

27 Thus, in the chapter on equality of opportunities it "Calls on the member states to disallow the invoking of custom, tradition or any other religious consideration to justify any form of discrimination, oppression or violence against women or the adoption of policies which might be put their lives in danger", which is a highly controversial topic even inside the EP, as it refers to abortion, unmarried couples, etc.

the rise to the government of the Austrian People's Party (ÖVP) in 2000, the 2004 debate on freedom of expression in Italy, the French government's Roma policy in 2010, and the Hungarian media law and constitutional revisions in 2011-2.

Austria

The debate on Austria of 2 February 2000 is utterly remarkable inasmuch it concerns an external control on what in previous times would have been considered as a country's exquisitely sovereign affairs: the formation of a governmental coalition. It is preceded by a number of steps taken by the then 14 other member states, and announced by the Portuguese Presidency, in the attempt to prevent the ÖVP to share in the Austrian government. Measures included the suspension of bilateral contacts and the refusal to support Austrian candidates for posts in international organisations. The 14 announce likewise that Austrian ambassadors would be received "only in the formal sense" as a way of penalising the alleged antisemitism, xenophobia, and demonstrations of sympathy towards national-socialism that the ÖVP's leader Jörg Heider had uttered along the years. The 14 fear that Austria might stray away from the "common European values", enact discriminatory policies towards foreigners, and endanger the credibility of the EU democratic values in the face of the prospective Eastern enlargement.

The Council is fully aware of the seriousness of the measures taken against Austria. In the session of 2 February 2000, Seixas da Costa in representation of the Council affirms that "the rules for protecting minorities and combating racism, xenophobia and intolerance are no longer issues to be discussed purely within a country". He stresses likewise that Europe as a "community of values and principles" requires that Austria's "international commitments" be taken as a yardstick against which its government's behaviour be scrutinised by the European partners. Notwithstanding a considerably more careful formulation, Commission President Romano Prodi strengthens this position by affirming that the Commission "will bear down heavily on even the slightest breach of the rights of individuals or of any minority".

In the text adopted on 3 February 2000 (B5-0101, 0102, 0103, 0106 and 0107/2000) the EP joins in the governments' reprimand, and underlines the importance of living up to the standards that the Union asks of candidate countries. Remarkable is that at that moment Austria could not be blamed for any specific contravention to EU law, as the Austrian coalition is still in the debate and the government has not yet taken office. There being no room for legal action, Art. 6 and 7 TEU are invoked in the text as a *political* foundation of the Union. Parliament likewise maintains that (preventive) vigilance is called for on the side of EU institutions. Such a vigilance clearly goes beyond the guardianship of the Treaties in the strictly technical sense, and opens up the way towards a *political* control on compliance with, and fidelity towards, the "common European values".

The text reflects the position of groups on the left of EPP-DE, while the latter, notwithstanding the numerous criticisms levelled against the ÖVP and its leader, attempts by and large to downplay the risks in the light of the fact that the ÖVP's coalition partner is the EPP-affiliated FPÖ. Remarkable is nevertheless that, besides some integration-sceptical voices from UEN and EDD, no MEP contends the legitimacy of Parliament's or Council's concern with the Austrian situation. The discussion is, moreover, highly politicised, dominated as it is by the sharp confrontation between MEPs from EPP-DE on the one hand, and PSE, Verts/ALE, GUE/NGL, and ELDR, on the other.[28] The first rejoins indeed that the Left is taking issue with the Austrian government mainly in order to put blame on the EPP-DE. Despite the diverging assessments on the merits, the right to take issue with a country's political choices goes, however, generally unquestioned and is indeed strength-

28 The Spanish delegation to the EPP-DE registers its disappointment with the group's position, while announcing to align with the resolution against Austria. MEPs from other national EPP-delegations also express sharp criticism of the FPÖ. On the relation between national delegations and transnational EP groups see (Smith 1995: 72–73).

ened in the words of most MEPs who take the floor. Even those representatives of EDD and UEN who lament the interference with a country's internal affairs, reaffirm the common values and admit that serious breaches of fundamental rights ought to be monitored at European level.

Italy, 2004

As in the Austrian case, also the debate on the *Risk of violation in the EU, and especially in Italy, of freedom of expression and information* is set on thin legal ground, but mobilises considerable political energies. The matter revolves around the influence that the Italian Prime Minister Berlusconi exerts on the Italian media landscape both in virtue of direct ownership and through his parliamentary majority's control on public broadcasting. The debate is set off by a motion of a number of MEPs (B5-0363/2003), at which the Committee on Citizens' Freedoms and Rights, Justice and Home Affairs drafts a Report (2003/2237 INI) with the contribution of Opinions from the Committees on Legal Affairs; Culture, Youth and Education; and Constitutional Affairs.

Both the Report and the Opinions reflect a highly politicised climate, in which the members of EPP-DE (with the Italian delegates at the forefront) engage a hard struggle to fend off a foreseeable unfavourable result for the Italian Prime Minister and parliamentary majority. Italy stands indeed decidedly in the focus of both the Committees' proceedings and the plenary debate. In fact, the Reports rely on a number of arguments that relate directly to the Italian debate, and support or opposes the stances of the Italian parliamentary majority, according to the degree of influence that Italian MEPs are able to exert on the proceedings.[29] The whole plenary session will indeed be almost entirely an Italian affair, with fifteen out of twenty-one speakers, not counting the President, being of Italian nationality.

29 Whitaker (2011: Ch. 7) presents an interesting study of the influence of national delegations on the Committees' proceedings.

Based on a considerable set of rulings of the Italian Constitutional Court, which Italian governments had left unattended over the years, as well as on a number of various observations from NGOs and international research institutes, but also in the face of an admittedly scarce legislative support from EU law, the Committees (with the only exception of the Committee for Legal Affairs and the Internal Market, which supports the stances of the majority in the Italian Parliament) detect a risk of fundamental rights violation in Italy, and invite the Commission to take up the issue with adequate legislative initiatives to fill the existing legal gap.

For lack of sufficient coverage from EU secondary law, to which Commissioner Patten openly admits to in the plenary, numerous MEPs justify the EP's initiative by calling on primary law, and especially on Art. 6 and 7 TEU as well as on the not yet binding CFR. The Committee on Citizens' Freedoms and Rights argues indeed that the Charter is in itself an instrument that lends sufficient support to a scrutiny of member states' internal affairs for the sake of the protection of common principles and values. It sees a more encompassing scrutiny as required in order to implement European citizenship (as of Art. 17–22 TEC), in particular due to the EU citizens' right to stand for, and vote in local elections and the EP in any member state. Moreover, it asserts that on the basis of the Treaties of Amsterdam and Nice, the protection of fundamental rights has become a UE task. This is a clear step beyond the careful assessments of the role of the Charter and of fundamental rights protection by EU institutions that had come out of the debates in previous years. With a more circumspect wording, the Committee on Constitutional Affairs asserts that the Charter is *politically,* although not legally, binding.

The final Resolution asserts indeed that "the EU has a political, moral and legal obligation to ensure within its fields of competence that the rights of EU citizens to free and pluralist media are respected" (P5_TA(2004)0373: 1). However, the issue at stake is indeed the very definition of its fields of competence, as the following paragraph, calling for the definition of EU-wide criteria for pluralism while guaranteeing respect for cultural and geographical differences, makes utterly clear.

Remarkable is also that the subsidiarity argument, the claim for protection of national and cultural specificities, and finally the autonomy of member states in setting the rules for areas not directly covered by EU law becomes loud both in the Opinion of the Committee for Legal Affairs (whose position is the most friendly for the Italian government) and in the course of the plenary at the hand of MEPs from the EPP-DE. Noteworthy is also the practice to let mainly MEPs of the country concerned take the floor, as had already happened, although to a lesser extent, in the debate on Austria. As in the latter, also in the session on Italy does the EPP-DE stand firmly behind their Italian members, who are engaged in the defence of their own government and of the legislative initiatives of their parliamentary majority at home.

France, 2010

The debate on the *Situation of the Roma people in Europe* of 7 September 2010 ends up being in fact a heated debate about the French government's decision to deport as well as to offer financial incentives for Roma people of Romanian and Bulgarian to leave the country. Contrary to the aforementioned, this controversy rests on a more precise, although still controversial, legal basis, and illustrates a serious test for the Parliament's attempt to vindicate its universal vigilance on fundamental rights within the Union inasmuch as a founding member states is called for to justify its policies in such a sensible field as immigration and internal security.

The decision to proceed with large scale expulsions had been taken in the aftermath of an attack on policemen for which a group of Roma citizens had been indicted. Several voices, including the one of Commissioner Viviane Reding, raise themselves to express concern for the decision of the French government on grounds of ethnic discrimination and in virtue of a varied legal basis that includes the provisions of the now binding CFR as well as Directives for non-discrimination (a principle that rests on EU primary law since the introduction of the new Art. 13 TEU in the

Amsterdam Treaty). A wide political basis, such as the Stockholm Programme, is also mentioned, and strong references to the common values and principles are reiterated throughout the session. The final resolution (P7_TA(2010)0312), which reflects the motion jointly set forth by S&D, GUE/NGL, ALDE, and Verts/ALE (B7-0493; –0500; –0503; –0504/2010, respectively), expresses concern for the conduct of public officials of several member states, including Italy and France, with respect to the values of ethnical non-discrimination towards the Roma, condemns the expulsions of Roma citizens enacted by the French government, and reiterates the duty that EU institutions have to secure the respect for citizens' fundamental rights on the part of member states. Remarkable are the references to the EU's primary law, such as the CFR and the Treaties, in order to buttress the limited support that secondary law is once again capable of delivering to support criticisms of France's conduct. Citizens from Eastern countries are in fact excluded from the application of the Free movement Directive until 2013, so that the expulsions or repatriation of Roma citizens by the French government can be questioned in legal terms only on the basis of Directive 2000/43/EC.

However, the relatively vague and often misplaced use of legal references in the course of the session makes it sufficiently clear that MEPs call on secondary legislation in order to buttress political, instead of primarily legal, claims (contrary to what applies to Committees' documents, it is indeed doubtful whether a sharp distinction between the two can be assumed in the case EP plenary sessions). Most MEPs seem not to be aware of the fact that the Free movement directive (2004/38/EC) is all but the best support to lean on in order to condemn the practice of massive repatriation of Eastern European citizens. The goal that MEPs pursue with their criticism of France seems on the other hand to be the defence of the equal implementation of fundamental rights all over the Union, the latter's authority over member states, and Parliament's legitimate scrutiny as representative of the European peoples. Hence the defence of "common values" as enshrined in primary law and the willingness to enforce them even on a founding member state such as France.

As in the two debates analysed previously, also the debate on France's expulsions policy is characterised by a clear confrontation between the Left, which levels heavy criticism at the Right-wing French government, and the Centre-Right of EPP-DE, to which the French governmental coalition is affiliated. Despite the controversial legal basis, both sides accept, however, the EU's supervision on fundamental rights. Arguments are exchanged on the merits of the controversy, but remain well clear of the question of the competences, and no distinction between the legal and the political aspects can be detected except in the words of Commissioner Reding and a handful of MEPs.

Hungary, 2011-2

The Hungarian file is considerably thicker and more complex than the aforementioned. It illustrates the attempt to take influence on nothing less than a member state's constitutional process. The government of Prime Minister Viktor Orbán, whose administration enjoys a two-thirds majority support in the Hungarian Parliament, comes under the fire of international critique first in occasion of a revision of the media law in 2010–11, then a year later as a consequence of a broad constitutional revision that raises widespread concerns as to his country's democratic stability. His Fidesz party rules in a coalition with the Christian Democrats.

The EP dedicates a session to the media law in Hungary on 16 February 2011 (CRE 16/2/2011–13). The Commission had raised a number of issues both on the basis of the Audiovisual Media Services Directive (2010/13/EU) and of Art. 11 of the CFR regarding freedom of information. Neelie Kroes, Vice-President of the Commission, announces the Hungarian government's willingness to amend the media law on that basis. Parliament, however, finds both the steps that the Commission had taken against Hungary and the opening of the Hungarian government unsatisfactory, inasmuch as both would be related to mere technical details instead of tackling the real issue at stake, which would concern nothing less than the overall independence of the media in Hungary. The text adopted on 10 March 2011 (B7-0191/2011) with the votes of S&D, ALDE, Verts/ALE, and GUE/NGL, and under opposition from the EPP-DE, admonishes therefore the Hungarian authorities to "restore the independence of media governance", and registers once again the inadequacy of EU law for the protection of media pluralism, thus calling for a more adequate EU policy. Once more, a proper EU fundamental rights policy is solicited from the Commission. The motion tabled by MEPs from EPP-DE (B7-0099/2011), which is withdrawn before the vote under reference to the assurances given by the Hungarian government, laments the "manipulative and politically motivated" attacks from the Left (some MEPs see raise the same allegation against Council and Commission, whose preposterous attacks at Hungary would be motivated by this country's scarce pro-European attitude rather than its legislative provisions; indeed, other Eastern European countries, such as Poland, would not suffer any comparable criticism despite displaying similar provisions in their fundamental laws).

The situation repeats a year later upon the constitutional laws passed in the Hungarian Parliament. During the debate of 18 January 2012 on *Recent political developments in Hungary*, both the Council and the Commission exert sharp criticism on the Hungarian government and show themselves considerably less prone to compromise than a year earlier. The situation is judged so serious that Nicolai Wammen, Council's President-in-Office, announces that "action is being taken" to ensure compliance with EU law. Such an action takes the form of infringement procedures on three topics: the independence of the national central bank, the retirement age of judges, and the independence of the data protection authority.

Despite the fact that both the Commission and the Council see the very values enshrined in the Treaties as being endangered, the measures taken do not reflect the whole range of fundamental rights infringements that the Hungarian constitutional laws are suspected of. Instead, they seem more directed at deflecting worries that several MEPs see more directly related to Hungary's shattered financial situation. Only a few weeks earlier, negotiations with the IMF and the EU had been discussed in order to obtain financial assistance. As a matter of fact, the financial situation is indeed the topic on which Commission President José Manuel Barroso's opening statement lays more emphasis. President Barroso adds, however, that further issues are on the table that go beyond the strict implementation of EU law, such as "the quality of democracy in Hungary". The importance of the session is underlined by the presence in the Chamber of Hungary's Prime Minister Viktor Orbán, who takes the floor to strengthen his government's allegiance to "European values and principles".

Unlike the Commission President, MEPs are again not willing to draw too careful a distinction between matters covered by EU secondary or primary law. Indeed, the text adopted with the votes of S&D, Verts/ALE, ALDE, and GUE/NGL (B7-0095/2012) calls on primary law for denouncing the risks that the new Hungarian constitutional laws imply for the independence of the judiciary, religious freedom, and freedom of information, The text also expresses criticism of the limitations to legislative scrutiny by the Hungarian Constitutional Court, and reproves the decision to enshrine in the Hungary's primary law a number of policies, such as the fiscal, that usually belong into secondary law in the attempt to shield them from shifting majorities in the future. The EPP-DE lends its support to the Hungarian majority by means of a resolution (B7-0050/2012/rev.) in which the Hungarian constitutional sovereignty is stressed and the risks for democracy in Hungary are belittled. In the end, this is yet another episode in the confrontation between political families at the EP.

Monitoring fundamental rights respect in the member states: reasons and justification

As mentioned above, MEPs do not dwell too long on the reasons why member states ought to be subjected to control on the side of the Union. In the course of the debates on the state of fundamental rights in Europe, 37 speakers out of 138 who participate in the debate take stance on the topic. The bulk of the statements focuses on two reasons. The reason the most often mentioned concerns the avoidance of double standards when Union's agents, and in particular the EP, cast a look on the state of fundamental rights beyond the Union's borders, be it to discuss foreign policy issues or to examine candidate or associated countries. The second most often mentioned reason concerns the "right to monitoring" that would descend from Art. 6 and 7 TEU. A more interesting pattern emerges from the debates on specific member states in relation to which risks of breaches are feared: there, the respect for "common values" as a reason to carry out a serious monitoring is put forth from all integration-friendly groups (alongside 2 out of 8 MEPs from EPP-DE), while national sovereignty is defended from less integration-friendly and right-wing groups (Table 5).[30]

Sub-sets of debates	*Reasons for monitoring*	*N*
Debates on FR in Europe	No double standards	23
	Right to monitoring ex Art. 6 & 7	10
	Others	4
Debates on specific MS	Common values	31
	National sovereignty	14
	Others	3

Table 5: Reasons for monitoring MS respect of FR.

However, neither the principles that justify the EP's monitoring nor the presence or absence of a solid legal basis are on top of MEPs' thoughts when it comes to subjecting specific member states to scrutiny or to lamenting possible or current breaches (Table 6).

30 Both reasons may be formulated with different wordings, such as "democratic values", "a community of values", or "national autonomy", "people's sovereignty", etc.

EP Groups	ALDE/ ELDR	GUE/ NGL	EPP-DE/ EPP	PSE/ S&D	Verts/ ALE	NI	EDD	IND/ DEM	EFD	ECR	TDI	UEN	Tot
N of speak. mentioning reasons/Total N of speak. p/group													
Debates on FR in EU	4/11	2/16	5/33	10/29	4/10	0/9	1/3	0/1		1/1	0/3	0/7	37/123
Debates on specific MS[31]	6/17	2/11	10/66	16/43	7/15	6/12	1/1		4/9	3/7	1/3	2/4	58/188

Table 6: N of MEPs uttering reasons for monitoring MS.

The reasons that MEPs adduce for monitoring or censoring member states when breaches are suspected relate mostly to the fundamental principles of the Union. Likewise, the legal basis they mention, as far as any is explicitly indicated, draws mostly on EU primary law (Table 7).[32] This is lastly due to the fact that the primary law is certainly more extensive than secondary law, but on the other hand MEPs do not seem overly interested in legal aspects. Instead, they are keen on making a political point.

Primary Law	29	Left = 17; EPP = 3
Secondary Law	2	
No breaches detected (no law applies)	7	EPP,UEN, TDI, EDD
No legal basis/Not EU competence	5	UEN, NI, EFD, EPP, S&D
Tot./MEPs speakers	*43/189*	

Table 7: Legal basis for MS scrutiny in Sub-set 2.

31 Figures refer to statements to the principles or the legal basis that justify the EP's interest in monitoring a country or taking steps against it.

32 What at EP sessions is usually referred to as "monitoring" is an informal activity consisting of collecting information on the state of fundamental rights protection in a member state. The Treaty of Nice includes, however, formal steps for a procedure by means of which EU agencies ought to ascertain whether breaches have been committed or are likely to happen. Parliament is part of such a formal "early warning" mechanism (Art. 7.1). However, references to Art. 6 and 7 TEU occur in Parliament mostly as a "moral suasion" to make known to a country that MEPs intend to take issue with some policies or specific governmental actions. Only in the case of Hungary do some MEPs threaten with the constitution of a commission to be sent into the country for closer, formal observation ex Art. 7 TEU.

Likewise, MEPs do not overly embark on a legal or political justification for monitoring member states. A generic reference to the Union's fundamental principles or to primary law seem sufficient for Parliament to proceed. This is certainly due to Parliament's interpretation of the "early warning" mechanism that ought to prevent serious breaches of fundamental principles by member states, but it also rests on the attempt to increase the role of Parliament in championing citizens' rights throughout the Union as a means of self-promotion. Paradoxically, integration-sceptic groups are relatively more keen on questioning the legal basis in order to reduce the scope of EP's monitoring, but as far as the integration-friendly groups are concerned, the right to exert a control is taken almost for granted on the basis of the Treaties' provisions. Justifications occurs by means of an almost ritual reminder to the Union's general political and ethical principles.

Nevertheless, three findings still wait for explanation:

1. The EP subjects member states to a far closer scrutiny than MEPs themselves foresaw (and seemed to welcome) at the beginning of the decade of 2000, and does so in the absence of a shared understanding of which fundamental rights ought to be protected at EU level, and to what extent;
2. MEPs do not normally distinguish between EU and national competences,[33] nor do they pay overly attention to the legal basis for scrutiny or action;
3. Although the CFR (and EU primary law generally) was not expected to make a substantial difference in the way EU institutions dealt with fundamental rights policies (despite some contradictory statements as to its scope and innovativeness), several policy areas that clearly fall outside the Union's competence become the object of the EP's activity in the subsequent years.

33 On the other hand, the EP traditionally raises issues beyond the strict scope of EU competence (Hoskyns and Newman 2000/2007: 109–112).

Besides the scarce justifications that some MEPs utter in this respect, some patters emerge from the debates that may cast more light on the factors that played in the development of MEPs' attitudes towards fundamental rights scrutiny in Europe.

Explaining the EP's debates on fundamental rights

In order to go to the bottom of the progressive extension of fundamental rights control on the side of the EP, three hypothesis can be formulated:

1. Political groups see in EP debates a chance to foster their own fundamental rights agenda with no regard to whether the topic they address is, in legal terms, of EU competence. Most MEPs pass over the distinction or either they claim a European policy to cover the claims they raise. Especially those parties that are in the opposition in their own country show more interest in taking their issues up to the European stage. This accounts for the fact that the periodical check of the state of fundamental rights in Europe rapidly trespasses the boundaries set to European competences at the beginning of the decade, as the CFR was being discussed.
2. Likewise, European concerns with member states are easily accompanied by an interest on the side of national minorities to take issue with their national majorities, and readily receive support by their fellow-MEPs of the same political family.
3. Finally, the reasons initially set forth for promoting the entrenchment of fundamental rights in EU primary law emancipate themselves from the original setting and gain force as a justification of an ever more active role of the EP in monitoring member states, as corresponds to this institution's long established interest in promoting its own role in the concert of European institutions (Toussaint Report 1988, PE 111.236/fin.1; Smith 1995: 83; Kreppel 2002: 87).

The scarce relevance of nationality

A statistical analysis of the debates discussed thus far confirms scholarly findings as to the relative little impact that nationality has on MEPs' behaviour. With very few exceptions, neither the debates on the state of fundamental rights in Europe nor the sessions devoted to specific countries show any relevant correlation between nationality and the predisposition to exert criticism or either take the defence of a member state. Thus, being a national of a specific member state is, at least in general terms, not a good indicator for one's propensity to defend one's own country. However, the debates on the state of fundamental rights in the European Union also show that MEPs have little propensity to defend a country other than one's own. The only notable exception to this rule is represented by the engaged defence that Romanian MEPs take of their country in the controversy concerning the French government's expulsion policy in 2010. Although Romania had not been subjected to open criticism in the course of the session, the French repatriation practice was aimed at sending back foreigners, and especially Roma, to Romania (and, to a lesser extent, also Bulgaria) as their country of origin. French authorities had expressed concern at the easiness with which the Romanian authorities had let their nationals expatriate. In this debate, Romanian MEPs stand unite behind their own country independently of their political affiliation. This is, however, the only case in which nationality impinges on the stances that MEPs take in the debate.[34]

34 These findings are in line with recent knowledge about the importance of nationality on MEPs' behaviour. Andeweg (1995) and Moravcsik (1998) have suggested that EP groups would split along national interests as soon as the latter were at stake. Hix, Noury e Roland (2007) show, instead, that groups' cohesion has increased in time, so that MEPs tend now to follow the indications of their own national delegation to the detriment of their EP group's cohesion only when a serious conflict is given between the two, although Kluger Rasmussen (2008) extends the possibility of disagreement to a number of policy areas. Noury (2002) had already pointed out the relatively scarce importance of national belonging in MEPs' behaviour. Such conflicts would, however, seldom occur. Maurer (2007) shows how increas-

In the debates concerning the state of fundamental rights in Europe, criticisms of member states account for less than a half of the statements, the rest consisting of general assessments as to the opportunity and the forms to subject member states to Parliamentary or EU scrutiny. The bulk of the speakers express themselves in favour of a general scrutiny of member states, while few of them, i.e. less than one fifth, draw any distinction between countries implementing or not EU law.

Methodology
For the debates on the state of fundamental rights in Europe (A), the speakers' attitude towards the countries singled out for criticism has been recorded. In particular, it has been registered whether MEPs exert criticism or either defend their own or a different country. In the case of the debates in which specific member states stand in the focus of MEPs' attention, such as the debates on Austria, Italy, etc. (B), the behaviour of the nationals of the countries involved has been observed. In particular, it has been counted how many nationals defend and how many subject their own country to criticism. The data have been collected in a 2×2 contingency table. The results are as follows:
(A) Fisher Exact Probability Test (one-tailed) = 0.029;
Despite the test's positive result, nationals show little more willingness to defend than to criticise their own country (60% v. 40%), while they are more keen to criticise than to step in to defend a foreign country. Figures are, however, very small, amounting to as few as 44 overall (foreigners criticising or defending another country being as few as 9!).
(B) Phi = –0.23 (Pearson's $Chi^2 = 8.19$; P = 0.0042; OR = 2.69). The association between nationality and the attitude to defend or criticise a country is present, but weak, nationality being thus only to a minor degree a factor protective protecting from criticism. Foreigners are only little more prone to criticise than to defend another country (63% v. 37%), and nationals are only slightly more incline to defend than to criticise their own country (62% v. 38%).[35]

---

ing group's cohesion goes along with growing EP's powers. Earlier findings also confirmed that the EP is increasingly characterised by a competitive party system in which positions on policy issues tend to map onto the left-right axis, while groups tend to be increasingly cohesive. See Kreppel and Hix (2003) as well as Thomassen and Schmidt (2004).

35 These figures have been calculated not taking into account utterances in which countries are criticised for breaching EU legislation, as long as exact reference has been made to secondary law.

Advocating scrutiny of MS (no specific country mentioned)	32
MEPs criticising own country	21
MS criticising foreign country	9
Attempts to limit or defend MS from scrutiny (no specific country mentioned)	5
MEPs defending own country	14
MEPs defending foreign country	0
Criticisms of MS while implementing EU law	20
No MS should be scrutinised	1

Table 8: Attitudes towards MS in Debates devoted to assessments of FR respect in the EU.

Government and opposition: national minorities and the European Parliament

While nationality is not a good indicator of MEPs' attitudes towards member states, the fact to criticise a country administered by a member of a political family different than one's own is thoroughly relevant. There is in fact a direct correlation between the political colour of the a country's government and MEPs' attitudes towards it. Indeed, both in the sessions devoted to the state of fundamental rights in Europe and in the ones devoted to the assessment of single member states' compliance, MEPs whose national parties find themselves at the opposition in the country of origin are considerably more likely to express criticism of their own country. In general, MEPs are considerably more likely to express criticism of countries governed by a different political family than one's own. Conversely, they are less likely to step in to defend an "unfriendly" government, but do frequently defend a "friendly" one. In particular, in the debates taken into account groups to the left of EPP-DE express criticism of member states' governments ruled by parties affiliated to the EPP-DE.

Methodology
A speaker can critically address or either defend a government that is ruled by parties that belong to one's own political family or to a different one. These two variables (criticism/defence; government/opposition) give rise

to two 2×2 contingency table: one for the debates on the state of fundamental rights in Europe (A), and another for the debates in which specific member states are targeted. The data have been collected in a 2×2 contingency table to which the Phi coefficient of correlation has been calculated. The results are as follows:

A) Fisher Exact Probability Test = 0.00011. Proportions are significative: 69% of those who defend a government happen to belong to the EP group kindred to it, and 95% of those who exert criticism happen to belong to oppositional groups. This confirms the first impression according to which an oppositional position to the criticised government is decisive in determining the MEPs' attitudes. As in the case of nationality figures are, however, relatively small, amounting to 43 cases only.

B) Phi = 0.84; Pearson's Chi^2 = 105,34; P < .0001. Proportions are, again, way more significant than for nationality, as MEPs who step in to defend a government happen to be mainly of the same political colour (89% v. 11%) and, conversely, MEPs who criticise it belong to or are allied with groups whose delegation from the corresponding country opposes the government in the national parliament (90% v. 10%).

For both samples, EP groups behave coherently with their position with respect to the colour of the government under criticism inasmuch as MEPs are more likely to criticise a government that is ruled by a party that belongs to an different political family than their own, and are more likely to defend a government that is ruled by their own national delegation or affiliated national delegations. Nationality is only a minor factor in determining the MEPs' attitudes.

In both cases, the distinction is coextensive with the Left-Right contraposition, as it is mostly parties to the left of the EPP-DE to criticise governments supported by parties affiliated with the latter group. The figures show that it is indeed the opposition, which in the countries subjected to criticism happens to be in the opposition, to be particularly prone to raising the critical issues at the EP.[36]

Thus, the EP becomes a forum in which parties that homely electoral results put to a disadvantage in relation to the opposing political family have a chance to get a more international hearing for their platforms. MEPs from EPP-DE (from 2009 onwards EPP

36 The figures encountered show that groups of the left display a higher rank-and-file behaviour than the EPP-DE, which is also in line with recent findings (Kreppel and Tsebelis 2002).

only) accuse "the Left" of using the debates to bend the issues at stake in favour of their own political cause, while in the discussions of the Austrian and the Hungarian case MEPs from PSE (later S&D), GUE/NLG, and Verts/ALE criticise the EPP-DE for lending support to government pursuing policies opposed to the Union's common values. However, MEPs from EPP-DE believe to have more reasons for complaint (Table 9).

Criticising the Left	29	Mainly EPP-DE
Criticising EPP-DE	7	PSE/D&S
Criticising the Right	3	GUE/NGL; Verts/ALE
Total N of speakers	201	

Table 9: Criticism of EP groups in debates concerning fundamental rights in specific member states.

The fact that member states are criticised according to the national patterns of government and opposition may seem unsurprisingly as long as serious shifts in a country's political balance occur, as is the Austrian and the Hungarian case, or when a government's actions are suspect of making a difference in the way public issues of fundamental importance are dealt with, as is the case in Italy in 2004 and France in 2010. In particular, the first case represents the acute example of a country finding itself in a situation of prolonged illegality in a key-area such as the right to information and media freedom, after ten years of heatedly conducted national debate have failed to yield a satisfactory solution to the conflict of interest. However, the same reproduction of national political cleavages surface even when the issues at stake do not bear so heavily on a country's democratic life, and is actually a marking characteristic of all the debates analysed. In the debates on the state of fundamental rights' respect in Europe figures are, however, far smaller. These debates are indeed better characterised by a different kind of Left-Right clash: the one concerning which fundamental rights policies are to be shaped at European level (see below).

"Going European": fundamental rights and political polarization

As emerges as early as in the debates on the Charter, fundamental rights are the object of a Left-Right clash throughout the decade.[37] During the session of 14 March 2000, the left, in particular GUE/NGL and (although to lesser extent) the PSE, insist on the need for the Charter to include social rights, whereas MEPs of EPP-DE are the only ones to mention the protection of the family among the Charter's priorities. Likewise, in the plenary of 3 October 2000 opinions are clearly split among those who find the Charter weak on social rights (GUE/NGL in the first place and also, although to a minor extent, PSE and Verts/ALE), and those (mostly from EPP-DE) who express satisfaction with the Charter as it is. Immigration soon turns out as a particularly controversial topic, as shown by the clash on the extension of fundamental rights protection to residents, and not only to member states' nationals, with the Left advocating, and the Centre and Right opposing it.[38] In the context of the debate on the Charter this is nevertheless a minor point, and figures are correspondingly small (Table 10). An abstract interest in the innovative nature of the Charter and its inclusion of rights concerning data protection as bio-technologies, which are widely consensual topics, overweights the interest in the Charter's further content. These topics are indeed meant to make the Charter to a more up-to-date, and therefore also more "attractive", document than national bills of rights, and matches therefore with the "institutional" interest of Parliament in enhancing its image of champion of EU citizens' rights. Hence the tendency throughout the debate to emphasise consensual issues.

37 For scope and limits of bipartisanships at the EP see Kreppel (2002: 171).

38 A similar controversy inflamed the Convention's proceedings (Schönlau 2005: 93).

1	CFR should include new rights[39]	7	Commission, EPP-DE, PSE, Verts/ALE
2	CFR should include social rights	6	Commission, EPP-DE, PSE, GUE/NGL
3	Fundamental rights protection should be extended to residents	5	Commission, PSE, Verts/ALE, GUE/NGL
4	CFR should protect family	3	EPP-DE
5	Others	4	

Table 10: Statements on CFR's content in order of frequency.

Controversy sparks, however, as soon as the yearly scrutiny of fundamental rights in Europe takes off, also fanned by the decision to assign the yearly Report to a representative of a different political group every year. Such a rotation spurs groups to use the chance to bring to the fore their own fundamental rights platform. Several MEPs warn of such a dubious practice. Thus, in the 2001 plenary Haarder (ELDR) calls attention to the "tendency in this Parliament to make every conceivable subject from the party programmes into human rights issues".[40] Such a widespread "opportunistic" attitude goes along with a substantial neglect for the distinction between legal and political claims, so that any policy that is found unsatisfactory is often construed as a fundamental rights issue without paying attention to whether the claim can be put on a solid legal basis. As MEP Marinho (PSE) declares after defending his own country from (apparently quite groundless) allegations of entrenching gender discrimination in its legal framework: "We all want to ban breaches, but there are no political breaches of rights – there are legal or practical breaches, and these either exist or they do not."

39 A debate flared up at the drafting convention, and spilled over to the EP, as to whether the CFR should merely sum up the rights that were already part of the common constitutional tradition of the member states or contain "new rights", instead (Schönlau 2005: 81–91).

40 Terrón i Cusi (PSE) downheartedly underscores that MEPs are "capable of deciding on a weekly basis what the human rights problems are in any corner of the world, but we are not capable of agreeing once a year on what standards should be complied with within the EU in relation to fundamental rights."

Despite these warnings, the debates on the state of fundamental rights in the EU become a stage in which different political platforms are opposed to one another. In particular, MEPs from EPP-DE lament that "the Left" is attempting to frame its favourite stances on individual rights in terms of terms of fundamental rights. Thus, Sylla's 2003 Report is branded as "an ideological wish list of the left-wing ideologies" (Pirker, EPP-DE). The EPP-DE rejects the report because of its insistence on the promotion of a EU fundamental rights policy that includes expansion of the right to asylum, recognition of same-sex relationships, etc.[41] The 2008 Report receives similar criticisms. In the words of Ignasi Guardans Cambó, draftsman of the opinion of the Committee on Culture, it "suffers from trying to resolve everything, not just human rights issues, but every social problem that currently exists in Europe" (CRE 17/12/2008–14).

A closer look at the sessions concerning the state of fundamental rights in Europe highlights indeed that political groups see in them a chance to foster their own (fundamental) rights agenda. Thus, of the 138 speeches held in the plenaries devoted to the state of fundamental rights in Europe, 65 speakers take the floor to claim a Europe-wide promotion of fundamental rights. Significantly, the issues the most lively and frequently debated bring in topics that belong to EU competences only to a limited extent. These are family policies (20 entries) and immigration (15 entries) (speakers from GUE/NGL also underscore social rights).[42] Family policies include the rights of unmarried couples,

41 See also Hermange's statement (EPP-DE), according to which "imposing a particular set of moral values on the entire European Union is contrary to the principle of respect for diversity, which, moreover, enshrined at the very heart of [...] the CFR [...]."

42 Since the Amsterdam Treaty, immigration partly belong to the policies to be covered at EU level. Nevertheless, a clash is evident between two different understandings of immigration policies: common immigration policies as a way to dam up the influx of immigrants, in the understanding of the Right, or as a way to add to the rights of immigrants, in the understanding of the Left. Therefore, parliamentary debate is actually about the scope, meaning and extension of a common immigration policy.

gay marriages or gay unions, and "reproductive rights", i.e. access to medical assistance. Further 13 speakers advocate a fully fledged European fundamental rights policy generally (i.e. without making explicit reference to any specific policy area). The fronts are clearly split between the Left, which claims "permissive", and the Right, especially EPP-DE (in virtue of the size of its delegation), which aims to maintain "restrictive" policies. These happen to be controversial policies at national and EU level. As far as family policies are concerned, MEPs attempt to forward their (national) claims by seeking the attention of a supranational forum or even by "europeanising" the issues. As far as immigration policies are concerned, the struggle sparks around the rights to be granted to immigrants (including the regulation of their influx). The important finding is that MEPs are once again not interested in distinguishing what falls under EU competences. Political platforms are forwarded independently of the question as to what ought to be regulated at EU level. This concerns especially the Left, which is interested in gaining ground for its own (fundamental) rights policies due probably to the difficulty of promoting them in their home countries, whereas the Right, and especially the EPP(-DE) struggles for preserving the current limitations in both family and immigration policies.

Conclusions

The way the EP has dealt with fundamental rights over the past ten years shows a remarkable trend towards a growing scrutiny of fundamental rights respect in the member states as well as an increasing pressure from Parliament for the inclusion of ever more numerous policy areas in EU secondary law. And yet, when the Charter was being discussed MEPs did not seem to expect or look forward to an increase in EU competences or to any change in fundamental rights protection in Europe, nor was any deep change in the Union's capacity to interfere with the member states' internal fundamental rights policies being envisioned. The decision to draft a CFR and to make it legally binding seemed more a symbolic and political response to a lack of legitimacy than a tool for straightforward institutional innovation. Besides the will to set a landmark to make explicit what the Union's political principles are in the face of citizens' growing scepticism towards the political nature of the Union and the still weakling political culture of the Eastern candidate countries, what lies behind the EP advocating the Charter is the intention to gain ground over the Council in a time in which the Treaties had to be rewritten and the constitutional balance of power in Europe rediscussed. In giving the Charter a legally binding character the EP spotted a chance to endow the Union with a political identity of its own, and in this it was in accord with the European "main narrative" of the 1990s. Such a step implied a significant upgrading of Parliament's importance in the eyes of European citizens as the champion of citizens' rights against the overweight of the intergovernmental level of European governance. The idea that the Charter's binding nature would grant citizens direct access to the Courts, which was the only true innovation that some envisioned at the time, was but a short-term dream. Despite the uncertainty that shrouded the Charter's legal consequences, MEPs do not seem to reckon with a substantial impact on institutional equilibria inside the EU.

Nonetheless, the following years are characterised by an increasing scrutiny of fundamental rights in Europe, including the monitoring and censoring of member states. Three factors may contribute to explaining such a development:

- The tendency to reproduce national political fronts and their respective controversies inside the EP, and
- The tendency to formulate controversial policies that involve individual rights in terms of fundamental rights;
- The tendency to reproduce at the EP national controversies on individual rights, especially when national stand-offs block a solution to the problem, as is the case for family rights.

These factors seem to account for the europeanisation of fundamental rights policies and for the progressively closer scrutiny of member states. Indeed, at EP sessions national struggles are re-staged and issues are debated that belong to the groups' own (fundamental) rights platforms independently of whether they belong to EU competences. Thus, topics that are highly controversial at national level, such as family policies, or in relation to which different understandings of the desirable scope of EU coverage are given, such as immigration and asylum policies, are brought up at the EP in order to get a larger audience and forge European alliances for issues that cannot be settle at national level.

Moreover, whenever specific member states are singled out for debate, it is mostly national oppositional groups that increase the pressure on their national counterpart by taking issue with their own national governments at the EP. With very few exceptions, EP groups usually stand behind their national members and allies. However, the bar for questioning specific member states is usually set considerably high, as only serious, although always controversial, concerns for fundamental rights respect motivate a debate at the EP. This is independent of the normative basis on which a country can be legally blamed for or become suspect of breaches. The political sensibility for what is important from a democratic point of view widely trespasses the legal aspect. National impotence of the domestic parliamentary minority (due for instance to the sheer size or solidity of the parliamentary majority at home, as in Hungary or Italy, to the recent disappoint result of national elections, as in Austria, or even to the interest that the EP can have in discussing a given topic, as in the French case) can be more of a reason to address the EP.

Whenever fundamental rights policies are discussed, the bar is set, on the other hand, relatively low. MEPs only need to be dissatisfied with a country's (mostly their own) legislative tools in a given fundamental rights area to raise the issue at the EP. In such cases, no distinction is usually made as to the scope of European competences. Political criteria of relevance or a felt need for action are sufficient for a topic to be found worth of MEPs' attention. This regards in particular family policies and gay marriages, which are both highly controversial issues in the 2000s in several

EU countries. It is, again, in particular the Left that attempts to breach subjects that are controversial at national level. Thus, the clash between the Left and the Right and the dichotomy government-opposition account for a good part of the MEPs' behaviour in the debates examined here.

Surely, the reasons that MEPs give for questioning member states and claiming broader EU policies in matters of fundamental rights, although scarce, also have to be taken in due account. Since the Amsterdam Treaty, the EU has endowed itself with means to ensure that member states comply with a set of broadly defined fundamental principles of democracy and fundamental rights. Art. 6 and 7 TEU, which are the only legal means available to sanction a member state that commits serious breaches of fundamental EU values and principles, are equivalent to a political and institutional "atomic bomb", in that they allow to take measures when serious breaches have already been committed, and sanctions consist of the marginalisation of the violator from decision-making. Parliament can therefore easily justify its interest in a member states's "internal affairs" as being part of its activity of monitoring as an extensive interpretation of the "early warning" mechanism that is foreseen since the Treaty of Nice (Art. 7.1). Further justifications address the "indivisibility" of fundamental rights and the need to forward their protection in the EU as a whole as part of European citizenship.

Exerting a control on member states' respect of fundamental rights is, however, an irksome undertaking with respect to the perception that citizens of targeted countries may have of EU intervention. This emerges with notable clarity during the debates on Austria and Hungary due to the fact that both issues concerned the legitimacy of governments or governmental actions at constitutional level, whereas the governments in question had been clearly legitimated by electoral results. Several MEPs, and in particular the groups' spokespersons at the end of the debate, hasten to stress their sympathy with the people of Austria and Hungary and attempt to distinguish between criticising of a government and questioning a people's sovereign will. The distinction is nevertheless awkward. In fact, it comes natural to most MEPs to refer themselves to the countries instead of the governments. Moreover, according to EU law sanctions are directed at states.

The debates analysed above show that the EP has come to claim an ever larger role in the determination of the scope and content of fundamental rights in Europe in the course of the years, and has carried out a consistent "europeanisation" of fundamental rights issues. This seems only in part to be the outcome of a conscious strategy concerning the development of the European polity. The fragility of the institutional mechanisms aimed to ensure member states' compliance with the Union's fundamental principles, as foreseen in Art. 6 and 7 TEU, has surely motivated Parliament to deepen its own scrutiny. Likewise, the institution of an Area of freedom, security, and justice has certainly contributed to upgrading Parliament's fundamental rights competences.

And yet, despite all this, the reproduction of national political fronts and the groups' will to promote their own rights' agenda, while framing a great variety of issues in terms of fundamental rights, also account to a large extent for Parliament's growing interest and intervention in this field.

Some observers may welcome such an apparently unintended development as a "cleverness of reason",[43] but independently of one's own ideological preferences a new equilibrium between member states and EU institutions in the core field of fundamental rights seems, in the long run, in need to be found. In particular, a less occasional and opportunistic European debate on conception, rather than protection, of fundamental rights seems as necessary as to raise the question concerning the extent to which fundamental rights have to be homogeneously implemented and interpreted in the whole Union. Thus, the old question comes back as to how much we wish the Union to be a single polity with a unitary legal system and political principles, and how much room we wish to leave to national or regional differences and specificities.

---

43 See for instance the role that Colomer (2002) assigns to European political parties in furthering the European integration as opposed to member states' resistances, and De Giovanni's neo-hegelian attitude towards the European project (De Giovanni 2002).

References

ANDEWEG, Rudy (1995), The Reshaping of National Party Systems. In *The Crisis of Representation in Europe*, ed. by Jack Hayward. London: Frank Cass.

BELLAMY, Richard, and Justus SCHÖNLAU (2004), The Normality of Constitutional Politics: An Analysis of the Drafting of the EU Charter of Fundamental Rights. *Constellations*, Vol. 11, N. 3, 2004, pp. 412–433.

BRAVO, Teresa (2011), O reenvio prejudicial de urgência no contexto do espaço de liberdade, segurança e justiça. *Revista Portuguesa de Ciência Criminal*, Vol. 21, N. 3, pp. 355–394.

COLOMER, Josep M. (2002), How Political Parties, Rather than Member-States, Are Building the European Union. In Bernard Steuenberg (ed.), *Widening the European Union*. London: Routledge.

CORBETT, Richard (1998), *The European Parliament's Role in Closer EU Integration*. Houndmills-London: MacMillan.

DE GIOVANNI, Biagio (2002), *L'ambigua potenza dell'Europa*. Napoli: Guida.

DELOCHE-GAUDEZ, Florence (2001), *The Convention on a Charter of Fundamental Rights: A Method for the Future?* Groupement d'études et de recherches Notre Europe. Research and Policy Paper No. 15, November 2001.

HIX, Simon, Abdul G. NOURY and Gérard ROLAND (2007), *Democratic Politics in the European Parliament*. Cambridge: Cambridge University Press.

HOSKINS, Catherine, and Michael NEWMAN (2000/2007), How Democratic Is the European Parliament? In Eadem (eds.), *Democratizing the European Union*. New Brunswick and London: Transaction Publishers, pp. 93–116.

JUDGE, David, and David EARNSHAW (2002), The European Parliament and the Commission Crisis: A New Assertiveness? *Governance*, Vol. 15, N. 3, pp. 345–374.

KLUGER RASMUSSEN, Maja (2008), Another Side of the Story: A Qualitative Case Study of Voting Behaviour in the European Parliament. *Politics*, Vol. 28, N. 1, pp. 11–18.

KREPPEL, Amie, and George TSEBELIS (1999), Coalition Formation in the European Parliament. Comparative Political Studies, Vol. 32, N. 8, pp. 933–966.

KREPPEL, Amie, and Simon HIX (2003), From "Grand Coalition" to Left-Right Confrontation. Explaining the Shifting Structure of Party Competition in the European Parliament. *Comparative Political Studies*, Vol. 36, N. 1/2, pp. 75–96.

KREPPEL, Amie (2002), *The European Parliament and Supranational Party System. A Study in Institutional Development*. Cambridge: Cambridge University Press.

MORAVCSIK, Andrew (1998), *The Choice for Europe. Social Power and State Purpose from Messina to Maastricht*. Ithaca: Cornell University Press.

NOURY, Abdul (2002), Ideology, Nationality and Euro-Parliamentarians. *European Union Politics*, Vol. 3, N. 1, pp. 33–58.

RITTBERGER, Berthold (2003), The Creation and Empowerment of the European Parliament. *Journal of Common Market Studies*, Vol. 41, N. 2, pp. 203–225.

SCHÖNLAU, Justus (2005), *Drafting the EU Charter. Rights, Legitimacy, and Process*. Houndsmill Basingstoke: MacMillan Palgrave.

— (2007), The Convention Method. In Castiglione et al. *Constitutional Politics in the EU. The Convention Moment and Its Aftermath*. Houndsmill, Basingstoke: Palgrave Macmillan, pp. 90–111.

SMITH, Julie (1999), *Europe's Elected Parliament.* Sheffield: Sheffield Academic Press.

— (1995), *The Voice of the People. The European Parliament in the 1990s.* London: The Royal Institute of International Affairs.

WHITAKER, Richard (2011), *The European Parliament's Committees. National Party Influence and Legislative Empowerment.* London-New York: Routledge.

Multi-Level Rights Protection in the European Union. The Sub-national Dimension

JUSTUS SCHÖNLAU[1]

Multi-level governance and fundamental rights in the EU

A considerable part of the debate regarding fundamental rights in the European Union and their development focuses on the question as to which level of authority or governance is responsible for the protection of the individual rights. In a Union composed of member states with distinct legal traditions, which are moreover parties to international agreements and conventions in the domain of rights, it is clear that some kind of "multi-level" structure is required. Yet, there are at least two (distinct) understandings of the connection between the concept of "multi-level governance" and fundamental rights in the EU: In the legal debate and much of scholarly literature, the concept of multi-level protection of fundamental rights in Europe normally refers to the coexistence of different regimes of protection at different levels, most commonly the national, the European, and the international level. The interaction between these levels is subject to a great deal of legal debate both theoretically and in the practice, and the continuous development of the EU as an actor of fundamental rights protection in its own right has fuelled this debate (Fabbrini 2010). The key question in these discussions is how the

1 Advisor of the PES-Group in the Committee of the Regions.

different systems, notably national (constitutional) catalogues of fundamental rights, the EU Charter of Fundamental Rights (EUCFR), and the European Convention on Human Rights (ECHR) interact in what has been labelled "one of the most sophisticated systems for the protection of fundamental rights worldwide" (Fabbrini 2010: 3).

The second understanding of "multi-level rights protection" is developing at the EU level itself and focuses on a rather different question: namely the role to be played by different levels of governance in *implementing* fundamental rights within the EU. This debate is of particular interest to the sub-national levels of governance (i.e. regions, provinces, local authorities, etc.) who are increasingly conscious of the impact of fundamental rights on the exercise of their competencies. In this perspective, the EU is developing as a multi-level governance structure understood as a system of overlapping, interlocked, and interlocking levels of public decision-making in which different levels contribute both to the policy making and policy implementation, controlled by a hierarchical legal order (Jachtenfuchs 2006).

The protection of fundamental rights is relevant in this perspective as a crucial element of the legitimacy of the entire system, and as a way to develop and communicate the 'added value' of European integration to the citizens: on the one hand, fundamental rights can be shown to be protective boundaries against the excessive limitations of individual liberties by the higher levels of public authority (notably the national level), on the other hand they can be portrayed as protection against undue interference from the EU level, and therefore as an implementation of subsidiarity. Local and regional authorities have therefore a particular interest in the development of a multi-level system of fundamental rights protection in the EU. Rather than losing power in the ongoing process of Europeanisation, integration is seen to strengthen their position in many respects, opening new avenues for co-operation, both horizontally and vertically with 'their' member states. A successful and visible implementation of a high level of (EU-guaranteed) fundamental rights protection could be a vehicle to justify local/regional policy measures. The protection of fundamental rights is, in this view, both a pre-condition for the legitimacy of the European Union as a new system of governance, and of the local and regional level within this system.

This new and still rather under-developed rights-related understanding of multi-level governance is the main focus of this chapter. This topic will be approached through an analysis of the recently established co-operation at the institutional level between the Committee of the Regions (CoR) and the EU Fundamental Rights Agency (FRA), and the focus will be on the practical accessibility of those fundamental rights specifically granted by the EU Charter of Fundamental Rights (CFR), and the necessary contribution from local levels in providing information about these rights and, in some cases, also the public service structures necessary for their realisation. While this understanding may raise a number of legal problems in the concrete situation at the EU level with regard to the applicability of different fundamental rights regimes, it is being pursued for a number of political reasons, and it does follow its own coherent logic. If indeed the aim is the creation and dissemination of a European citizenship and a corresponding feeling of belonging which would be less in competition with existing loyalties to the national level than currently seems to be the case, then active policies of improving the protection of fundamental rights in cooperation in particular between the EU and the local levels seem *politically* appropriate. If the existing legal structures do not correspond to this aim, it may be them which have to be changed.

The chapter will therefore start from a short presentation of the concept of "multi-level governance" as it is currently applied to the European Union, not so much as an analytical theory, but rather as a prescriptive tool that also entered the political debate as a policy goal. The paper will then try to clarify the two understandings of "multi-level rights protection" set out above, i.e. the legal discussions around fundamental rights protection in the EU, which currently focus on the developments triggered by the inclusion, albeit as a protocol, of the EU Charter of fundamental rights in the Lisbon Treaty, and the ongoing debates around the role of sub-national levels of governance in 'realising' fundamental rights in the EU, focussing in particular on the activities of the Committee of the Regions in this domain in recent years. While the activities of CoR and FRA can only be a very first step and only form part of the wider efforts to create a genuine EU-specific fundamental rights culture, it will be argued, by way of a conclusion, that a bottom-up contribution of the local and regional level to the protection of fundamental rights is a pre-requisite for the development of a more active EU citizenship, which in turn is a *conditio sine qua non* for the future sustainability of the EU's legitimacy (Schönlau 2005).

Multi-Level Governance as an analytical prism to understand the reality of the EU

The concept of the emerging European (Union) polity as a system of multiple layers of 'interlocking' governance was developed in the mid 1980s in the aftermath of the 'grand debates' between intergovernmentalists and supranationalist, when the focus changed from the role of different actors in the European construction, to the functioning of particular policies (Jachtenfuchs 2006: 165). While the original application of the multi-level approach was focused in reality on two levels (i.e. the European and the member state), it was the study of the EU's regional and cohesion policies, which had been based since the mid 1980s on the principles of partnership and inter-level co-operation, which shed new light on the kinds of connection and interaction which European integration provoked between the different (territorial) levels of governance including the 'sub-national' (Marks 1993).

Beyond the question on who calls the shots in developing further integration, and whether the process of EU development will and should lead to a withering away of nation states, a Europe of the Regions, a European super-state or a re-emergence of the national level, the concept of multi-level governance has ever since then be applied to a large variety of different policy areas within the EU system and beyond (OECD, 2010). Moreover, the concept was directly taken up by the EU institutions in the internal debate about the future development of the Union, notably with the European Commission's White Paper of 2001 on the European Governance, which at the time of its publication sparked a lively debate both institutionally and academically inasmuch as it claimed to address some of the key problems of legitimacy, transparency, and implementation of EU policy. Coming, as it did, in the context of the failure of the Nice Treaty to solve fundamental institutional issues (2000) and of the ensuing debate about re-founding (re-constituting) the EU, the white paper was an important contribution to the debate about *how* to organise and run a multi-level system of governance, even though it did not give all the definitive answers and was in fact criticised by many as not going nearly far enough (see for example Joerges, Mény and Weiler 2001).

It is on this basis and with direct reference to the debates of 2001, that in 2008–09 the Committee of the Regions decided to present its own 'white paper' in an attempt to re-launch the debate in the interest of a stronger and more structured involvement of the sub-national level in EU policy making. The CoR explained its initiative with reference to

> [...] the 'Berlin Declaration' adopted by the Heads of State and Government on 25 March 2007, which mentioned the common challenges and tasks [...] *shared between the European Union, the member states and their regions and local authorities* (European Council 2007).

By drafting its White Paper (jointly presented by then CoR president Luc Van den Brande, EPP, and 1st Vice-President Michel Delebarre, PES) the CoR underlined its aspirations to contribute to the development of a functioning multi-level system which was defined by

> [...] coordinated action by the European Union, the member states and regional and local authorities, based on partnership and aimed at drawing up and implementing EU policies. It [MLG] leads to responsibility being shared between the different tiers of government concerned and is underpinned by all sources of democratic legitimacy and the representative nature of the different players involved (CoR 2009: 2–3).

While this definition as such is probably not contested, the key question is of course, as the CoR itself has admitted, what this means in practice in each policy area or with regard to any specific decision. Indeed, in the debate about multi-level governance it is frequently recognised from a local or regional perspective that most of the real problems in involving sub-national actors in policy making do not originate at the *European*-level, but occur in the member states. Whether due to constitutional structures that do not give much power to local communities or regions, or to executive arrogance, it is often the national governments which do not want to involve 'their' sub-national actors: neither in European, nor in domestic affairs. Paradoxically, given the principle of subsidiarity and the explicit recognition of the EU's respect for the 'member states' internal structures, including regional and local self-government' (TEU Art 4.4), there is very little that the European level can do to address this problem and strengthen the role of local and regional governments, apart, that is, from supporting the development of 'good' practices of concrete policy implementation which do bring local/regional authorities into the game in those policy areas in which the European level does have a say. Recognising this fact, the CoR has, in 2011, launched a follow up debate on how to build a genuine 'culture of multi-level governance' in Europe. To this end, the CoR proposes a range of ideas from setting up a 'multi-level governance observatory', to improving the involvement of sub-national actors in impact assessments on proposed EU legislation (CoR 2011). The activities of the Committee in highlighting the role of local and regional actors in implementing fundamental rights are a pertinent example of such an approach.

In this sense, multi-level governance is being used not just as a descriptive category in the analysis of European policy making, but has become a policy goal in its own right and has been 'adopted' by certain actors in the system. These two uses of the 'multi-level' label need to be distinguished, however, from the more specific application to the sphere of fundamental rights protection in the European Union. This additional dimension will be explored in the following section.

Fundamental Rights Protection in the EU: Overlapping regimes

As mentioned before, the term 'multi-level' in relation to European Union matters and fundamental rights is usually employed to describe the co-existence of at least three distinct judicial levels with competence of fundamental rights:

1. A national level, normally based on a catalogue of fundamental rights as defined at constitutional level, either explicitly in the constitutional document, or implicitly in case law;
2. A European Union level, based originally on the case law of the European Court of Justice and, since its proclamation in December of 2000 and with its subsequent inclusion as an Annex to the Treaty on European Union, on the EU Charter of Fundamental Rights;
3. An international level, based on the European Convention on Human Rights and its additional protocols.

In this understanding, these different systems, each with its own courts and a related, but not necessarily identical, set of fundamental rights, do interact in a variety of ways, and can therefore be jointly considered, alongside some additional but somewhat less institutionalised structure like the OSCE as a common but 'fragmented' regime of human rights (Brosig 2006: 9).

In such a situation, the interaction between the different levels is of course of key importance. Moreover, this complex of different systems which has its origins in the immediate post-World War II period, is in constant change both through deliberate institutional reform and through the development of legal practice and inter-system 'dialogue'. The notion of 'multi-level governance' understood as a system of "dispersion of authority over a complex, flexible, and fluid patchwork of overlapping jurisdictions" (Grant 2011: 1) is useful in this particular context because it highlights the non-hierarchical and therefore necessarily co-operative nature of the interaction between the different systems. Otherwise deadlock or even mutual 'destruction' seem inevitable. In terms of the interaction of different rights protection systems within the EU, at the latest since the German Constitutional Courts *Solange* Judgement of 1974,[2] it is clear that the different levels are condemned to take note of each other and find mechanisms to ensure consistency among their respective actions in order to avoid mutual destabilisation (Weiler 1999).

Yet, interestingly for the purposes of this investigation, this application of the MLG-concept to the fundamental rights domain is so far rather blind, it seems, to the role of the levels below the nation state. This may be due to the complex and fragmented, but all in all rather limited role of sub-national legal systems in the debate about fundamental rights in the member states, since even in the ones with strong regional levels and possibly their their own constitutions, including sometimes their lists of fundamental rights (for example Germany, Spain, Italy), a systematic dialogue about fundamental rights between the levels has not emerged, and "the relation between the national and regional level (or subnational level) is usually neglected on the grounds of a presumed homogeneity" (Delledonne & Martinico 2011: 16). Nevertheless, in any account of how fundamental, and in particular social, rights can actually be implemented, it would seem logical to include, a reference to the appropriate level of public authority in order to create the material and structural pre-conditions for the exercise of those rights. In this sense, whenever the concept of 'multiple levels' as an explanatory tool is in use, even the legal discourse about fundamental rights in the European Union should be expanded to cover the local and regional levels of authority, both as subjects to the rights in question and as actors in the processes of their application.

2 BVerfGE 37, 271ff, 1974.

Developing Multi-Level Rights Protection in the EU: marginal institutional activity?

Starting from these observations about multi-level governance in the domain of rights, we are now going to look at recent activities in precisely this direction by two actors in the EU institutional system that are generally considered to play only somewhat marginal roles: the Fundamental Rights Agency and the Committee of the Regions. Both bodies (neither of which are officially speaking EU "institutions") are relatively recent (CoR in 1991) or very recent (FRA in 2007) additions to the EU system, and are supposed to carry out advisory roles although in different contexts and on different bases. While the CoR has its basis as a consultative organ in the Maastricht Treaty and brings together locally and regionally elected representatives, the Fundamental Rights Agency is based on a EU regulation to set up a structure for national and EU level experts to "provide the relevant institutions and authorities of the Community and its member states when implementing Community law with information, assistance and expertise on fundamental rights in order to support them when they take measures or formulate courses of action within their respective spheres of competence to fully respect fundamental rights" (Council Regulation 168/2007, Art. 7). It is interesting to see how these two structures with their different remits and interests are trying to work together in order to promote the idea of an overall improvement of fundamental rights protection in the EU.

The development of the EU Fundamental Rights Agency on the basis of the previous European Monitoring Centre on Racism and Xenophobia, set up in 1997, has been a difficult process, and the current status of the Agency embodies in many respects many of the limitations of the EU in the fundamental rights area. Yet, at the same time the, the very existence of the agency may also be seen as "an institutional acknowledgement that the EU, at the dawn of the last century, has embarked on the journey of an EU-specific fundamental rights policy" (v. Bogdandy 2009: 1067). The Agency's mandate is clearly based on the Charter of Fundamental Rights and is subject to the same limitations, notably with regard to the 'scope' of the rights in question: like the Charter, the agency's mandate only covers the actions of EU institutions and bodies, and applies to member states only in as far as they are implementing EU law.[3] At the same time, and despite its narrow mandate, the Agency is an important part of the institutionalisation of what Stijn Smismans calls the "European Union's Fundamental Rights Myth" (Smismans 2010), because it contributes to the development of an EU Fundamental Rights narrative which has both legitimising function for the Union as a polity, and an effect on the practicalities of rights protection.

The Committee of the Regions (CoR) was originally created as a tool to give local and regional authorities access to, and information about, the EU legislative process, its focus clearly being at first on policy areas in which EU legislation directly affected regional competencies or had to be implemented at sub-national level. These were first and foremost the area of regional and cohesion policy, but also issues like transport, education, or the environment. Yet, once created, the Committee and its members, who have to hold an electoral mandate, also started to explore new areas of interest and to take an active part in the EU constitutional debates, including the drafting of the Charter of Fundamental Rights. In the Convention that drafted the Charter in 1999–2000, the CoR was represented by two 'observers', and adopted a number of resolutions concerning the elaboration of the Charter. Interestingly from early on, while the debate on the future scope and status of the Charter was still going on, the CoR adopted a position that clearly showed federalist leanings, and stressed the link between the Charter process and the development of a genuine, rights-based European citizenship to sustain

3 Von Bogdandy points out that the Agency's mandate is even more limited because it refers to "member states when they are implementing *EC* law" rather than *EU* law (emphasis added), in order to explicitly exclude (former) third pillar issues from the Agency's scope – but this distinction has been superseded with the entry into force of the Lisbon Treaty (v. Bogdandy 2009: 1047 and 1065–1068).

the emerging EU polity. The CoR resolution on "The Charter of Fundamental Rights of the European Union" (of September 2000) states in its second paragraph that the CoR

> stresses the *political* nature of the Charter and its major contribution as a pillar of European citizenship. In this connection, it notes the positive nature of the preamble and the author's desire to present all the rights of Union citizens under distinct, horizontal headings (CoR 2001/ C 22/01, emphasis added).

In the following paragraphs, the CoR also promotes some of its more narrowly defined 'self-interests'. Thus, in paragraph 3 it

> proposes that the principle of democracy be backed in the preamble by the principles of local and regional autonomy, as these play a part in guaranteeing the practical application of democratic rights. Reference should also be made in paragraph 3 to the principle of subsidiarity and to Article 6 of the EU Treaty in the following terms: "The Union contributes to the development of these common values while respecting the principle of subsidiarity and the diversity of the cultures and traditions of the peoples of Europe as well as the national identities of the member states and the organisation of their public authorities at national, regional and local levels; it ensures balanced and sustainable development through the free movement of persons, goods, capital and services" (CoR 2001/ C 22/01).

It is interesting to note that this text is only marginally different from the wording actually adopted in the Charter's preamble. The CoR also called for a specific recognition of the applicability of the Charter rights to member states "when they are implementing EU law at national, *regional or local level*" (CoR 2001/ C 22/01, paragraph 8, emphasis added), which it did not obtain. The CoR complained that the discussion at local and regional level about these rights had not sufficiently been taken into account (paragraph 13).

Interestingly for the purposes of this chapter, the CoR also offered its commitment and assistance in future information efforts on the new Charter which would help to "strengthen their [the citizens'] feeling of being a part of the European Union and will place the Union on truly democratic foundations." (CoR 2001/ C 22/01, paragraph 14). This observation and the understanding that, in order to improve the fundamental rights situation in the EU and realise the expected positive effects of the EU fundamental rights 'myth' in favour of the Union as a whole, a concerted communication and information effort at multiple levels would be necessary, has not changed in more than a decade, another Convention and a failed constitutional process later. Given this precedence and the numerous political statements not only in the CoR debates but also by other institutional players, it is actually quite surprising to note that in the official document setting out the mandate of the FRA, *no* specific reference is made to the local or regional levels, but just to the member states (EC Regulation 168/2007), and that the Agency is asked only in a very generic way to co-operate "as closely as possible with all relevant Union institutions as well as the bodies, offices and agencies of the Community and the Union" (paragraph 16). But at least this can be construed as a 'mandate' to cooperate also with the Committee of the Regions, and on this basis the two 'bodies' started to organise joint events in 2008.

The main focus of these cooperative events have so far been indeed questions of implementation and information of specific fundamental rights: in 2008 a joint seminar was organised between the CoR Commission CONST (Constitutional affairs and governance) and the Fundamental Rights Agency in Reggio Emilia, Italy, under the title "Multi-level protection of Fundamental Rights – A Europe of Rights: A system of rights and duties for citizens and institutions", during which the newly appointed director of the FRA, Morten Kjaerum, stressed the need to build a genuine culture of fundamental rights across different levels, with specific responsibilities of local and regional authorities. As an example of areas in which the latter's responsibilities become visible, he quoted:

> spatial planning (where the specific need of certain vulnerable groups needs to be taken into account); promoting diversity (local and regional initiatives to foster inter-cultural understanding and combat discrimination); responding to migration flows (providing housing, education and other rights for migrants, often before their final status can be determined); and healthcare, where the control and supervision of local health care facilities also needs to adopt a rights-sensitive focus (Kjaerum 2008: 2).

In a similar vein, in 2009, in the context of a joint CoR-FRA seminar in Gödöllö, Hungary, the focus shifted to "Implementing Citizens Rights at Local and Regional Level". Here the emphasis was very much on citizens' participation as a pre-condition for realising fundamental rights. Locally and regionally elected members of the CoR discussed with external experts (from university and NGOs), as well as among themselves, the practicalities and challenges of promoting knowledge about fundamental rights at local and regional level. In 2010, a joint seminar between the two institutions was organised in Vienna, preceded by a visit of the CoR members of the Commission on Citizenship, European Governance and External relations (CIVEX) to the offices of the FRA. The seminar focused on the implementation of fundamental rights after the Lisbon treaty and the elevation of the CFR to a legally binding status. In particular, the discussion centred on the role of local and regional authorities in *monitoring* fundamental rights (both on their own and in the context of different international networks and structures), and the need to develop reliable and easy-to-use indicators. A specific session looked at the situation in terms of fundamental rights of Roma, where local and regional authorities as providers of essential services have a particular role to play in ensuring equal access and fighting discrimination of vulnerable groups.

Despite these activities, however, it is still true that the Charter and its rights are not widely known at local and regional level, neither by citizens nor by local administrators. A small study which the CoR had commissioned in 2008 on the 'Implementation of the Charter of Fundamental Rights' found

> a low level of public awareness of the Charter, though in certain countries we have identified a limited campaign to promote the Charter, primarily in new member states, and usually in connection with the ratification of the Lisbon Treaty (CoR 2008: 11).

Moreover, even though many of the activities to promote rights and freedoms (many of which are now enshrined in the Charter) are actually being undertaken by local and regional governments, these are often

> carried out not in connection with the Charter, but for other reasons. [...] Thus, the level of activities underpinning and reinforcing the stated aims, objectives, and values enshrined in the Charter at the local and regional level is actually quite high. However, local and regional authorities are not explicitly linking their rights-based activities and initiatives to the European context (CoR 2008: 11–12).

The report also stresses a general need for local and regional levels of governance to be involved in disseminating information about fundamental rights (and the EU Charter in particular) as a precondition for their implementation. The report also lists a number of areas where LRAs have particular competencies or expertise in providing the conditions for the realisations of rights, such as childrens' rights (in particular migrant children); fighting discrimination and social exclusion (once more with a special focus on migrants and Roma); fighting racism and xenophobia and promoting diversity; informing citizens about their rights of participation in the European political process (electoral rights, organisation of consultation processes, etc.) through political education; protection of the right to a 'healthy environment' (Art. 37); protection of linguistic diversity (CoR 2008: 5–6).

One key problem in this respect remains however the limited scope of the Charter of Fundamental Rights in its current form, notably the restrictions of its application to EU institutions and bodies, and to members states only in as far as they are implementing EU law (Art. 51). These restrictions, which had of course been subject to extended debates not just in the Convention which drafted the Charter (Bellamy and Schönlau 2004), but also in the subsequent Convention and IGCs which prepared and drafted the Lisbon Treaty (including the UK and Polish limitation protocols), are bound to make it extremely difficult to communication with citizens about fundamental rights as an expression of the European community of values at a local or regional level. In fact, the EU suffers here from a self-inflicted expectation gap. The EU Commission acknowledged as much in its communication on a "strategy for the effective implementation of the Charter of Fundamental Rights by the European Union" (European Commission 2010), which states that increased information activities are particularly necessary to redress

> the difficulty of knowing which are the appropriate legal remedies and confusion about their roles, [which] may lead complainants to knock on the 'wrong door'. The Commission receives many letters about situations for which it has no competence under the Treaties because they are unrelated to Union law (European Commission 2010: 11).

It is interesting to note, however, that the Commission then immediately goes on, in a rather defensive tone, to

> point out that it is up to national authorities, including the courts, to rule on cases of alleged breaches of fundamental rights and that the Commission is not a court of appeal against the decisions of national or international courts (European Commission 2010: 11).

This statement is interesting both because of the lack of ambition or imagination in terms of potential information activities to be carried out by European institutions in order to promote fundamental rights, and because there is no reference in this paragraph (or anywhere else in the document, for that matter) to local and regional authorities and their key role in providing information. It is also to be noted that even the European Fundamental Rights agency is only mentioned on three occasions in the entire 13 page document, and only referred to as a tool for information gathering, not for information dissemination (European Commission 2010: 13). As a follow up to this strategy, and with a clear focus on its own internal procedures, the Commission produced a 'staff working paper' with "operational guidance on taking account of Fundamental Rights in Commission Impact Assessments" (European Commission 2011), but, again, the general direction is 'respecting' fundamental rights instead of promoting them, and the FRA is mentioned yet again merely as a useful source of data.

These omissions were noted when the CoR responded, in 2011, to the Commission's communication on the 'strategy' (CoR 2011): the main thrust of the original CoR document in response to this communication is referring to fundamental rights in a much broader context than the carefully legally circumscribed vision of the European Commission. The CoR

> notes that the strategy mainly addresses the institutions and more specifically what the Commission should and must do. The Committee [however] advocates taking a more strategic approach to implementing the Charter which will require the involvement of all authorities, including at local and regional level (CoR 2011: 3, point 11).

Moreover, the CoR underlines that the future development of the EU's fundamental rights' regime, composed of not just the Charter but of course also of the member states' internal systems for rights protection, as well as the ECHR, will occur "both through political action and judicial rulings" (CoR 2011: 3, point 12). The CoR points out its joint activities with the FRA as well as the role of local and regional authorities in providing citizens with information about fundamental rights, engaging them in a dialogue in order to develop a 'culture of multi-level promotion and protection of fundamental rights', and training officials of different levels of governance. The CoR also offers its help in developing and disseminating appropriate indicators in order to evaluate initiatives and measures to protect rights. These are, at the stage of writing, of course mere suggestions and proposals, and future concrete action still has to follow from these declarations.

Yet, the example of the European Commission's "strategy" for the implementation of fundamental rights and the CoR's response to it clearly reveal the dilemma in which the EU finds itself. While the three 'strands' of the strategy (i.e. that the EU must be *exemplary* in living and acting on its own fundamental rights standards; that *better information* to the public is needed; and that the Commission is going to issue *an annual report* on the state of the application of the Charter) are hardly contestable, they do not amount to a 'strategy' in the political sense of the word. And while the European Commission's cautious attitude is clearly based on existing legal constraints, it also reflects the divisive debates about the role of the European Union in the fundamental rights domain, in which member states are weary of what they see still as 'external' interference into domestic affairs. Recent controversies (in 2010–2011) regarding the situation of specific fundamental rights such as freedom of expression in the media, or the treatment of minorities such as Roma in particular member states, have also shown that in the currently difficult climate vis-à-vis the EU in general, there is even less appetite on the part of the Commission to make use of the Fundamental Rights Agency with the intend to take a strong political position in these debates.

For the local and regional level and its representative organ in the EU process, this means that no great leaps are to be expected any time soon. Instead a continuation of the small steps to build co-operation, improve the exchange of best-practices and highlighting particular problems is the way forward. The third edition of the 'annual dialogue' between the Committee of the Regions and the Fundamental Rights Agency in October 2011 followed this trajectory. Focussing on the specific issue of "Implementing fundamental Rights of irregular migrants" and bringing together representatives not only of FRA and CoR, but also the European Commissioner for Fundamental Rights, as well as representative of the European Parliament and of regional associations, the event highlighted once again that access to key fundamental rights as specified by the Charter such as health, education, protection of children and vulnerable individuals, depend on policies often developed, implemented and paid for by local or regional authorities. It remains to be seen whether this kind of events will lead over time to a more comprehensive understanding of multi-level governance in the domain of fundamental rights.

Conclusion: early days for real multi-level fundamental rights' protection

The examples of cooperation between the Committee of the Regions and the Fundamental Rights Agency quoted above are clearly only very first steps in the ongoing processes of building a more coherent and comprehensive fundamental rights regime in Europe on the one hand, and in the development of a genuinely *multi*-level polity, on the other. Both the CoR and the FRA are clearly only small institutional actors in the wider EU context, and their activity can only serve as a pointer for further investigations into this particular aspect of the process. Yet, the fact that there is a recognition that fundamental rights protection in the EU does need positive political action, and that this action may not only come from EU level institutions or member states but also from below, is rather important, given that both the EU and the national level seem to be currently rather weak and/or reluctant to move beyond a narrow, defensive understanding of fundamental rights as 'limits' to EU action.

In this context, some suggest that the greatest hope for further development of fundamental rights would lie in extending the 'open method of co-ordination' to fundamental rights, or at least in using its tools such as benchmarking, exchange of information, evaluation of experiences, identification and promotion of best practices (De Schutter 2005). This would allow and possibly promote the development of a more open 'EU fundamental rights culture' inasmuch as good implementation practices, but also negative experiences, would be shared and lay the foundation for collective learning at EU level, with a more coherent fundamental rights situation as a result. The choice on the side of the Commission to publish annual reports on the state of fundamental rights (since 2010),[4] but also the annual conferences organised by the Fundamental Rights Agency at highest political level,[5] are as many initiatives that follow this trajectory. Clearly, the subnational level(s) of governance could play a key part in such an approach, given that they are in large parts the holders of the information and experiences on the implementation of rights. Moreover a number of channels and mechanism already are already at place for them to exchange best practices. For instance, the work of the Fundamental Rights Agency on common indica-

4 Published in 2011 as Report from the Commission – *2010 Report on the Application of the EU Charter of Fundamental Rights*, Com (2011) 160.

5 The annual conference 2011 takes place on 21–22nd Nov in Warsaw and focuses on the fundamental rights of irregular migrants. The Committee of the Regions is represented by the chairman of its Commission for constitutional affairs, fundamental rights, European governance and external relations (CIVEX).

tors and in collecting and disseminating information, is of course of paramount importance in this regard.

Finally, it remains to be seen whether or not the eventual accession of the European Union to the European Convention on Human rights, which has become a concrete prospect with the entry into force of the Lisbon Treaty,[6] will give boost anew the debate on fundamental rights protection in the EU. While it will probably not change too much in terms of contents and current rights protection,[7] it will at least underline symbolically the need and desire for coherence of fundamental rights regimes which include an element of external 'supervision' not only of the member states but also of the EU as a whole. This would strengthen the multi-level concept of fundamental rights protection, which could in turn also encourage the sub-national levels of governance in their struggle for recognition of their contribution to the implementation of fundamental rights.

References

BELLAMY, Richard and Justus SCHÖNLAU (2004), The Normality of Constitutional Politics: An Analysis of the Drafting of the EU Charter of Fundamental Rights. *Constellations*, Vol. 11, N. 3, pp. 412–433.

BROSIG, Malte (2006), Human Rights in Europe: An Introduction. In Malte Brosig (ed.), *Human Rights in Europe – A Fragmented Regime?* Bern: Peter Lang.

COMMITTEE OF THE REGIONS (2008), *Making a Reality of the Charter of Fundamental Rights*. Available via the CoR web-site.

— (2009), *CoR opinion 'White Paper on Multi-Level Governance'*. CONST-IV-20, CdR 89/2009, Brussels.

— (2011), *CoR opinion on the Strategy for the effective implementation of the Charter of Fundamental Rights by the European Union*. CdR 406/2010 (adopted 11.10.2011), Brussels.

DELLEDONNE, Giacomo, and Giuseppe MARTINICO (2011), Legal Conflicts and Subnational Constitutionalism. *EUI Working Papers LAW 2011/03*.

---

6 "Draft legal instruments on the accession of the European Union to the European Convention on Human Rights" were published by the Council of Europe on 19.07.2011 as CDDH-UE (2011) 16.

7 See Teresa Bravo's and Teresa Violante's contributions to this volume.

De Schutter, Olivier (2005), The Implementation of Fundamental Rights through the Open Method of Coordination. In O. de Schutter and S. Deakin (eds.), *Social Rights and Market Forces: Is the Open Coordination of Employment the Future of Social Europe?* Brussels: Bruylant.

European Commission (2010), *Communication: Strategy for the effective implementation of the Charter of Fundamental Rights by the European Union.* COM (2010) 573 final, 19.10.2010, Brussels.

— (2011), *Commission Staff Working Paper, Operational Guidance on taking account of Fundamental Rights in Commission Impact Assessments.* SEC (2011) 567 final, 06.05.2011, Brussels.

Fabbrini, Federico (2010), The European Multilevel System for the Protection of Fundamental Rights: A Neo-Federalist Perspective. *Jean Monnet Working Paper* 15/10, New York.

Grant, Wyn, Multi-Level Governance, *Oxford Dictionary of Politics.* Available at: http://www.answers.com/topic/multi-level-governance (last accessed October 11, 2012).

Kjaerum, Morten (2009), *Opening Remarks for the Seminar 'Multi-level Protection of Fundamental Rights'.* Available at: http://fra.europa.eu/fraWebsite/material/pub/speeches/Dir_speech_ReggioEmilia19092008_en.pdf (last accessed October 11, 2012).

Jachtenfuchs, Markus (2006), The European Union as a Polity II. In K. E. Joergensen, M. A. Pollack, B. Rosamond (eds.), *Handbook of European Union Politics.* London: SAGE.

Joerges, Christian, Yves Mény and Joseph Weiler, eds. (2001), Mountain or Molehill?: A Critical Appraisal of the Commission White Paper on Governance. *Jean Monnet Working Paper* No 6/01. Available at: http://www.eui.eu/DepartmentsAndCentres/RobertSchumanCentre/Research/Archives InstitutionsGovernanceDemocracy/MountainorMolehill.aspx (last accessed October 11, 2012).

Marks, Gary (1993), Structural Policy and Multilevel Governance in the EU. In Alan W. Cafrunny and Glenda G. Rosenthal (eds.), *The State of the European Community – The Maastricht Debate and Beyond.* Harlow: Longman.

Schönlau, Justus (2005), *Drafting the EU-Charter: Rights, Legitimacy and Process.* London: Palgrave-Macmillan.

Smismans, Stijn (2010), The European Union's Fundamental Rights Myth. *Journal of Common Market Studies,* Vol. 48, N. 1, pp. 45–66.

Von Bogdandy, Armin, and Jochen von Bernstorff (2009), The EU Fundamental Rights Agency Within the European and International Human Rights Architecture: The Legal Framework and Some Unsettled Issues in a New Field of Administrative Law. *Common Market Law Review,* Vol. 46, pp. 1035–1068.

Weiler, Joseph (1999), *The Constitution for Europe: 'Do the New Clothes Have an Emperor?' and Other Essays on European Integration.* Cambridge: Cambridge University Press.

Section III
Consequences of Constitutionalisation: Legal Dilemmas, Legal Conflicts

Legal Certainty in Europe. Legal Pluralism and Argumentative Practices of the European Court of Justice

GIOVANNI DAMELE[1]

Dialogue between Courts in Europe and comparative atmosphere

The subject of this article, the relationship between the national courts and the European Court of Justice (ECJ), is in itself neither new nor original. However, this well-known and deeply-analysed issue is here considered from the point of view of legal argumentation and interpretation.[2] Under these terms, the main question is to see how the plurality of levels of legal protection from the national courts up to the ECJ influences, if it does indeed influence, the practises of legal argumentation. Thus, the main question is the (possible) comparative nature of legal argumentation in this context. The multilevel protection has led to rulings inspired by a comparison between the legal traditions of different countries and different sources of fundamental rights. Some authors have metaphorically described this state of affairs as "comparative atmosphere" characterised to a certain degree by "consonance" or "polyphony". This conception of multilevel legal protection presupposes

1 The author is researcher at the Institue of Philosophy of Language, Faculty of Social Sciences and Humanities, Universidade Nova, Lisbon. His research is made possible by a scholarship of the Fundação para a Ciência e a Tecnologia.

2 Here I am using the locutions "argumentation" and "interpretation" in a more or less equivalent sense, since every interpretation "*in mente interpretis* [in the mind of the interpreter]" is justified, and made therefore intersubjectively available, through argumentations.

the possibility to give a "harmonic" interpretation of the relationship between the national and the supranational level. In order to grant legal certainty, the different legal sources and traditions should be amenable to a consistent and coherent whole. However, this may be based on a misrepresentation of this system as well as of the harmonizing potential of legal argumentation. Such coherence would indeed be possible if the courts would take comparison "seriously", i.e. as a true tool to intentionally harmonize these different sources and traditions. Instead, it is possible to show that comparison is often used "rhetorically" in the attempt to achieve a ad-hoc justification of legal rulings. As a matter of fact, legal arguments always display an intrinsically rhetorical face. However, the specific feature of the current legal multilevel governance consists in the overhand that ad-hoc rulings have taken over the attempt to forge an enduring Europe-wide legal tradition. It is in this respect that common forms of legal arguments such as comparison should give us some deeper concern.

The question as to how the plurality of levels of legal protection influences the practises of legal argumentation obviously implies a series of more general theoretical problems relating to the very nature of legal interpretation. It is not possible to go into these in detail here. However, it hardly needs to be emphasised that, if we leave aside every reductionist conception of legal interpretation, every flatly "logicist" or "formalistic" approach, what appears clearly is that legal interpretation is based, ultimately, on judgements of value. This is especially true in the area of constitutional interpretation, within which the technique of balancing of principles plays a fundamental role, that is, an activity which takes shape through the creation, on the part of the interpreter, of an axiological hierarchy among the principles, a hierarchy, in fact, based on a judgement of value and, therefore, a hierarchy which is radically subjective. The same, however, can be said for judicial interpretation in general, since every interpretative proposition is not a cognitive act but the result of an act of will and, as such, therefore, necessarily suggests a judgement of value.

This bond between judicial argumentation and judgements of value appears to be even clearer in the case of analogical argumentation which, especially when understood as "argumentation starting with principles" *(analogia iuris)*, in fact, implies a high level of discretion on the part of the judge and, more generally, reveals the rhetorical dimension of judicial argumentation very well. Now, it is exactly this type of interpretative technique, this type of "directive" or "canon" of judicial interpretation – "analogical reasoning" or "analogical arguments" – which one expects to be typical of a phenomenon like the so-called "judicial dialogue" between national and supranational courts. A phenomenon, that is, which is referred to by many of the law theorists and philosophers who deal with European law when they speak of "transjudicial communication", "constitutional dialogue" or, making use of an even more metaphorical language, "judicial cross-fertilization". These phenomena, and the interpretative activities which they imply, are based, in fact, on a new concept of sovereignty.

It goes without saying that the process of European integration is a new challenge for the traditional concept of "legal order". It is sufficient to refer to what we may consider to be the most founding of the decisions of the ECJ, *van Gend en Loos*, in which the Community is described as

> a new legal order of international law for the benefit of which the states have limited their sovereign rights, albeit within limited fields, and the subjects of which comprise not only member states but also their nationals.[3]

Starting from its own point of view, the ECJ itself clearly stated what the consequences of this "new legal order" would be, in another founding case, *Costa vs. Enel*:

> *the law stemming from the treaty, an independent source of law*, could not because of its special and original nature, be overridden by domestic legal provisions, however framed, without being deprived of its character as Community law and without the legal basis of the Community itself being called into question.[4]

3 See Case 26/62 NV Algemene Transporten Expeditie Onderneming van Gend en Loos v. Nederlandse Administratie der Belastingen [1963] ECR 1.

4 Case 6/64, Flaminio Costa v ENEL [1964] ECR 585.

This means, firstly, that European community law intervenes decisively in the internal relations of the member states, and, secondly, that it considers itself to be the holder of an original authority, that is, authority which is not delegated.

What are the consequences of this for our discourse? Apparently, such an affirmation of superiority of European law over internal law leaves very little room for the comparison between national and continental standards. On the other hand, if we admit, following a large part of the doctrine, that the ECJ in some way "dialogues" with the legal systems of the member states, this dialogue should take shape as analogical arguments or, in any case, as arguments with a comparative tenor.

The use of analogical reasoning with a comparative tenor arose, clearly, within the comparison between national law and foreign law. As Emilio Betti, commenting the work of Ernst Zitelmann, has emphasised, every reference made by the judges to foreign law may be considered as a "creation", within the national legal order, of "something new" which did not exist before, making one legal order so relevant for another legal order, that is, the laws of another State, which would otherwise be irrelevant or non-effective (Betti 1925: 53; quoted in Repetto 2011: 32). In this sense, the judges create new law through the interpretation of foreign law, of laws of foreign countries. It follows that the incorporation – or the reception – of foreign law and its interpretation are two indistinct and indistinguishable processes. In the same way, when a legal decision is incorporated (that is, interpreted), it has a sort of "dialectic exchange": an exchange which seems, apparently, to be communicative, in the sense of an acquisition of information.

This idea of a "dialectic exchange" may be transferred to the area of European law, and seems to adapt itself very well to the already-mentioned theories on "judicial dialogue". It seems to adapt itself, for example, to the intriguing image of Poiares Maduro of a "contrapuntal" or "polyphonic" law (Maduro 2003). This metaphor, which is very revealing, is well known to scholars of European law. The counterpoint, as Maduro rightly says, is a method for harmonising different melodies. Using this practise, musicians are required to follow certain fundamental musical rules, on the basis of which different melodies played simultaneously combine to form musical harmony. Similarly, according to Maduro, it is always possible to obtain a harmony from two contradictory "constitutional narratives". The two narratives (in this case, the national sovereignty and European integration narratives) are mutually exclusive but, following certain fundamental rules, it is always possible to avoid conflicts. These rules are:

1. Recognise the existence of different legal orders, and the possibility, at least, of different points of view on the same question (pluralism);
2. Entertain a vertical and horizontal discourse between the courts, in order to increase the level of consistency, which means at least considering the point of view of the court belonging to the respective legal order;
3. Only use arguments which may be used by the other participants in the dialogue (universalisability).

From our point of view, what is interesting is above all how the national and supranational courts develop this idea of a "vertical and horizontal discourse". Recent studies have dedicated much attention to European supranational jurisprudence and its relations with legal systems and national jurisprudential decisions. However, in many cases, the focal point of the attention was placed on the "institutional connections" between national and European courts, examining, for example, techniques such as the "reference for a preliminary ruling". Authors like Fontanelli and Martinico (2008), among others, have taken into consideration the characteristics of what they have defined as "strategic interaction" between European and national courts, as it appears in a sort of "struggle for interpretive power". In this sense, the increase in the influence of the ECJ has been underlined, emphasising its authority and the effects of its decisions. In the wake of similar research, expressions like "common constitutional law" (for example, the "regulatory ideal of a *common constitutional law*" which "coexists with the actual plurality of national constitutional laws") or "constitutional synthesis", "dialogue between judges" or "between courts", "constitutional pluralism" etc., have become quite common in works dedicated to European law. One of the first impressions, however, is that the novelty of the phenomena which these expressions are used to identify is, at times, rather overestimated.

A "vertical and horizontal discourse", or polyphony in law: *nihil sub sole novi*?

The idea of a "vertical and horizontal discourse" between national and supranational courts is one of the key points of Maduro's metaphoric image of a "contrapuntal" or "polyphonic" law. It is interesting, as a mere intellectual curiosity, to note that this importing of musical terminology suggests an intriguing parallelism. In fact, the counterpoint, within Western musical tradition, has been a highly elaborate musical technique since the Late Middle Ages which flourished in the Renaissance and Baroque Ages, falling somewhat into disuse in the second half of the 18th Century (curiously, at the dawn of the so-called "age of codifications").[5]

In the same way as the counterpoint, at least in its original version, is mainly a phenomenon of the Late Middle Ages and of the modern age, the pluralism and the "harmonic complexity" of legal orders have been a main characteristic of the European *ius commune*, theorised in great depth by jurists of the Middle Ages and the modern age. Take, by way of example only, the relations between *ius commune* and *iura propria*, *ius civile* and *ius canonicum*, *ius strictum* and *aequitas*, *ius* and *gratia*. In this situation, the theorists elaborate a large arsenal of *topoi* and *regulae* which can still be considerably productive nowadays (Hespanha 2005).

In fact, many "commonplaces" or commonly-used terms (*ad absurdum*, *a simili*, *a contrario*, *ex materia*, *ex effectu*, *ex coniunctis*,

5 This process began in the eighteenth century, with the (few) preliminary projects of codes, aimed at systematizing and classifying a disordered and frequently contradictory congeries of dispositions (Tarello 1976; Bellomo 1995).

etc.) are still widely-used, being used to identify the premises or "places" *(topoi)* of the most common judicial arguments. These argumentative practises, over time, took shape as specialised knowledge based on models which can be referred to, collectively, with the term *"modi arguendi"* (Hohmann 1998). The analysis of these models, it is important to emphasise, was focused above all on the persuasive characteristics of argumentation, and traditionally and strongly associated with a rhetorical approach. Indeed, as Giovanni Tarello has emphasised in his works on interpretative arguments, these models themselves take shape as "schemes of persuasion" and "schemes of justification", and not as "schemes of inference" (Tarello 1980: 392). This means, roughly speaking, that justifications usually include non-deductive argumentative schemes, aimed, first of all, at persuading an audience. It is in this very sense that we can state that they have an eminently "rhetorical" nature, in the Aristotelian sense of the counterpart of dialectic. And it hardly needs to be said that these arguments or "models" or "schemes" also include, obviously, the analogical argument or *"argumentum a simili"*, of which a peculiar case is represented by what Vico, in his *Institutiones oratoriae*, defined as *"argumentum a comparatis"* (Vico 1711–41/1989: 131).[6]

What has been said in this brief aside, in any case, intends to go beyond historic reference or an ancient curiosity. The mainly rhetorical nature of judicial arguments, in fact, throws some initial light on certain characteristics of a dialogue which should take shape through these arguments. A dialogue which could be presented, consequently, as being based more on a persuasive than on a communicative colouring. Firstly, however, we must ask ourselves what is the role of these arguments, and of the comparative argument in particular, within this so-called inter-judicial dialogue.

6 See Repetto (2011: 93). The typical case is that of a legal gap, when, in the absence of a specific legal provision, the argumentation starts from "similar" or "analogous" legal texts. More in general, the "comparative argument" offers a "reservoir" of alternatives and allows the jurist to select differences and similarities between cases and provisions.

Polyphony through comparison?

If the key point is primacy in the interpretation of the law, every type of "constitutional synthesis" carried out by the courts, every type of "constitutional dialogue" must naturally be based on techniques of judicial interpretation and argumentation. In particular, among these techniques, a central role should be played by analogical reasoning and, in particular, by comparative argument. Even so, however, the question of the *way* in which national courts and the supranational courts (in this specific case, the ECJ) make use of comparative argument, and if this use encourages the formation of a common European law or not, would remain open. Apparently, the answer is obvious: the courts make use of the comparative argument and this practise encourages the formation of a common European law.

A preliminary step, necessarily, consists in stating what "comparative argument" means. We can take into consideration a standard definition: comparative argument is the argument through which an interpreter attributes to a legal text, or a part of it, the same meaning attributed by unanimity, by the majority or by the "best" doctrine and/or judicial authority of another legal system. This is what we could call, more precisely, "authoritative-comparative argument". Apparently, this is exactly the type of technique which should be adopted by the ECJ. As M. Hilf (1986: 566) has claimed, European integration cannot become a reality except within a "comparative atmosphere", within which the jurisprudence of the ECJ should play a role of "harmonisation".

Authors like Balaguer Callejón have emphasised the difficulties that this "harmonisation" actually encounters in reality, connected essentially to the fact that the two jurisdictions express themselves in different languages: the language of constitutional law and the language of European law. This difference is caused, above all, by "structural conditions" which may also have a procedural nature, as in the case of the use or not of the instrument of the "reference for a preliminary ruling" (Balaguer Callejón 2006), but also by substantial questions, that is, the absence, indeed, of a "common language". This does not mean that there is not, necessarily, a physiological alignment of the two perspectives, but that the presence, in any case, of a certain level of incommunicability prevents the creation of a "productive dialectic relationship", given the absence of a "language of European law", which the Lisbon Treaty has not yet managed to create. Indeed, from the European side of the question, that is, from the side of the ECJ, it has to be asked if such "harmonisation" is really taking place in the form of a "comparative atmosphere" which, in this case, would mean taking into consideration the work of the national constitutional courts, their work methods and their jurisprudence.

In a recent and very-well documented text, Giorgio Repetto (2006) analysed the presence and the use of comparative argument in European supranational jurisprudence. The point of view, in this case, is not totally sceptical and, indeed, takes into consideration the considerable transformations within the systematic framework of inter-judicial dialogue, starting with a conceptual re-elaboration of the laws as structurally-open principles which would configure an essentially topical use of them.[7] The use of comparative argument could, in that case, constitute a common language among the courts, based on the compatibility and the relationality between the value choices and the cultural directions lying behind the various models (Repetto 2011: 270). A "reasoning around the principles" (271), in other words, with regard to which the author emphasises, rightly, that the judges cannot be asked to make the same use of comparative argument made by jurists.

On the other hand, a thorough and detailed analysis of the cases of the ECJ, as Repetto himself emphasises, does not make it possible to trace a "detailed comparative method which can allow the interpreter, starting from certain premises, to foresee on which results the decisions on future cases may be orientated" (Repetto 2011: 309). On the other hand, in relation to community

7 The reference here is to the topical use of the principles of interpretation (see Dann 2005: 1463).

jurisprudence, one would be more inclined to feel "that the rare references to comparative data are nothing but a screen for hiding decisions already taken on the basis of other factors, which is felt to be best left in the background of the argumentation". The best example is, in this case, what is claimed by the well-known *Hauer*[8] sentence relating to the limiting of property law, admitted by the constitutions of three of the then nine member states (Germany, Italy and Ireland) for the purposes of the "general interest". As is known, this latter notion, which Repetto defines as "composite and dense in terms of value", is used to safeguard, more modestly, the purposes of the common agricultural policy in a specific case, that is, the "common organisation of the wine market" (Repetto 2011: 211), that is, to guarantee the "uniformity [and the] guarantee of the community law" (222).[9]

This reveals, then, a much more instrumental use of the so-called "comparative atmosphere", that is, use aiming to "ensure the effectiveness of supranational law within internal law" (Repetto 2011: 269).[10] On the other hand, as pointed out by the author himself, in the experience of the *ius commune,* foreign *leges* were (also) used in accordance with their persuasive potential (Repetto 2011: 307). Now, it is also here that we can ascertain the traces of that difference between the use of comparative argument which can be made by judges and jurists. And it is interesting, with regard to that, to look at the long reference made by Repetto to a text of De Vergottini, in which De Vergottini emphasises that, however widespread the claim that the European courts make use of a comparative method, "in reality, these judges usually act with total discretion, using the law of the member states which is seen to be most suitable for resolving the cases submitted to them", so that,

---

8 Judgment of the Court of 13 December 1979. – Liselotte Hauer v Land Rheinland-Pfalz. – Reference for a preliminary ruling: Verwaltungsgericht Neustadt an der Weinstraße – Case 44/79

9 For this interpretation, the author refers to I. Pernice-F. Mayer, Art 6 EUV, p. 35. and Craig-de Búrca (2003).

10 In this case, the author refers to G. Benos (1984: 253), Hilf (1986: 556–557), and Lenaerts (2003: 106, 123).

> within the jurisprudence of the Court of Strasbourg and the Court of Luxembourg, there is no, as might be felt at first sight, systematic comparison between the different constitutions, legislations and jurisprudence of all the member states (Der Vergottini 2010: 195).

In this case, we should not even talk of comparison because, in this latter case, the “interpretative and decisional process” should make it possible to “identify comparative reasoning as intrinsic to the *ratio decidendi* (De Vergottini 2010: 193; Repetto 2011: 309). Or perhaps, indeed, we should speak of a (not surprisingly) rhetorical use of comparative argument, useful for “masking decisions taken elsewhere, to enrich the reference legal terms which lead to the decision” (De Vergottini 2010: 159; Repetto 2011: 310–311).

We can, then, once again recall Balaguer Callejón (2006) and recognise that the major difficulty in creating judicial dialogue between the national European constitutional courts and the ECJ is the fact that this “multilevel” structure runs the risk of appearing too much as a juxtaposition of different spheres of legality which appear to be difficult to reconcile and which can put into play, each from their own point of view, equally different strategies. In this case, the best solution could be a kind of “judicial heterogenesis of ends or heterogenesis of purposes” or also what Cass Sunstein has defined as “incompletely theorised agreements”, a kind of temporary coagulation of an irreducibly heterogeneous body of rules and principles, around a single case and a single solution. In this case, the possible solution is not the best interpretation nor the most generalisable interpretation, but simply “to make possible to obtain agreement where agreement is necessary, and to make it unnecessary to obtain agreement when agreement is possible” (Sunstein 1995: 1733). This, in other words, is a temporary compromise guided by the circumstances, in which it can be imagined that every eventual use of the comparative method is at the service of teleological interpretation, that is, of the interpretation of the law in light of its ends: an interpretation which, by its very nature, goes beyond the search for a common denominator, possibly subjecting it to the identification of the objectives of the (community) law. In these terms, the parallelism identified by much theoretical literature between the reconfiguration of the political space in Europe and, on the other hand, a judicial dialogue interpreted as "transjudicial communication", "judicial cross-fertilization", "constitutional dialogue", will appear more as a legal reconstruction (fully legitimate, obviously), than a description of the reality.

But can a sequence of "incompletely theorised agreements" configure if not "consonance" (Repetto 2011: 270) at least a quasi-harmonisation? Comparison activity within a very articulated and pluralist context, made even more fragmented by the versatility, not to mention the vagueness and imprecision, of the legal principles, can present a further element of complexity, that is, that the problem is not only harmonising the different lines of melody, but resolving the dissonance present in each of them.

Polyphony and dissonance

It is curious to note how the analysis of the jurisprudence of the European courts leads to mass importing of musical metaphors and terminology. The idea of the ECJ as a "dodecaphonic" court which "emancipates" the dissonance and then tries to resolve them comes, for example, from an article by Alexander Somek (2010). Moving beyond a complete analysis of the considerations contained in this dense and interesting article on theory of law, which cannot be made here, it may be interesting to consider, for the sake of metaphor, the idea of legal "dissonance". This is a phenomenon which, according to Somek, would take place firstly when a court reaches a conclusion which appears to be difficult to support on the basis of the traditional methodological standards of legal interpretation. Somek presents an example of "emancipation" of the dissonance (and the attempt to resolve it) on the part of the ECJ, starting with the renowned Advisory Opinion on the European Economic Area. The well-known context is the clash between the EEA agreement and the E(E)C Treaty. In this context, the ECJ has claimed: "In contrast, the EEC Treaty, albeit concluded in the form of an international agreement, none the less constitutes the constitutional charter of a Community based on the rule of law". According to Somek's reconstruction, the dissonance resides, within this claim, in the fact that it is not immediately or intuitively easy to see the connections between a treaty and a constitution. The attempt to resolve the dissonance, on the other hand, lies in highlighting the characteristics which make the EEC Treaty more like a constitution than an international treaty:

> The Community treaties established a new legal order for the benefit of which the States have limited their sovereign rights and the subjects of which comprise not only member states but also their nationals. The essential characteristics of the Community legal order which has thus been established are in particular its primacy over the law of the member states and the direct effect of a whole series of provisions.

The dissonance, however, again according to Somek, only disappears at a superficial level, as the peculiar characteristics which the Court attributes to the Treaties are the fruit of an especially creative interpretation. This is, in Somek's words, a case of "liberal use of legal reasoning", or of loss of authority for the traditional methods of legal interpretation. In other words, and this is the key to the metaphor, the traditional methods of legal interpretation would be superseded here in the same way as dodecaphonic music superseded the traditional tonal keys. The positions held by Herzog and Gerken, cited by Somek, return here, according to which

> the ECJ consciously and systematically ignores central principles of judicial legal interpretation, sloppily underpins decisions, overrides the will of the legislator, or even turns the latter upside down, and invents legal principles, on which it can in turn base later decisions (Herzog and Gerken 2008; quoted in Somek 2010: 28).

In brief, to continue with the musical metaphor, the melody which should give the tone for the subsequent harmonisation, that is, the subject of this hypothetical legal canonical fugue, with which the reply and the subsequent counter-subjects of the other voices should collate, by means of comparison, takes initial shape as a "judge-made law" elaborated by a court which seems to act as an interpretative "free-rider". An aspect which, combined with the growing tendency to interpret on the basis of *analogia iuris*, rather than *analogia legis*, given the significance attributed to the "balancing of principles" but also, reluctantly, the different characteristics of the judicial and constitutional systems in play, contributes, in reality, to making the co-ordinates of every possible use of comparative argument even vaguer. At the same time, we can perhaps foresee here, again, the characteristics of that distinction between use of comparative argument by "jurists" and "judges", relating the vagueness of the latter to its eminently rhetorical and persuasive nature.

In the form of a (provisional) conclusion

It is worthwhile to go back to the origin of this quite disorganised series of musical metaphors, that is, Poiares Maduro's image of a "contrapuntal" law. In many cases, metaphors are perhaps more interesting because of what they do not say, but suggest, rather than what they do say. Often, in fact a metaphor, once used, may even escape the limits in which it had been apparently confined, and suggest unforeseen elements of comparison. The key characteristic of a metaphor, we know, is that they can never be definitively paraphrased.

What image of polyphony is created by the many voices aiming to give life to a common European legal space? When we think of the "counterpoint", the first idea which may come to mind is Baroque "canonical" polyphony. But this particular musical technique was based on a strictly mathematical form, and was determined by a series of quite rigid rules. This does not seem to be the case here. However, there might be other examples which suit our case more. Starting from the 1950's, a chance composition method was developed, based on a creative collaboration between the composer and the interpreter or interpreters, who become, so to speak, co-creators. This musical current is represented well in Italy by the 'Nuova Consonanza' Association and, in the words of one of its founders, Franco Evangelisti, has as a reference point a new musical form which "opposes, with its special manner of being totally, or partly, 'vague', the development of serial music, which is totally determinate". In other words, this is no longer just an "emancipation" of the tonality, but a musical form which takes it moves from a minimal scheme of the composer, reduced to a very few essential indications, on which the interpreters are free to act in an almost independent manner, giving life to "open" works related to momentary forms. Maybe this example, at least in its possible polyphonic interpretations, is the most suitable example for rendering Poiares Maduro's metaphor. Of course, we must be aware that the result of this particular musical technique is based on uncertainty and unpredictability.

References

BALANGUER CALLEJÒN, Francisco (2006), *Le Corti costituzionali e il processo di integrazione europea.* Associazione Italiana Costituzionalisti: Convegno annuale – 2006. Available at: http://archivio.rivistaaic.it/materiali/convegni/aic200610/Balaguer.pdf (last accessed October 12, 2012).

BELLOMO, Manlio (1995), *The Common Legal Past of Europe.* Washington, D.C.: Catholic University of America Press.

BENOS, George (1984), The practical debt of community law to comparative law. *Revue hellenique de droit international,* Vol. 37, pp. 241–254.

BETTI, Emilio (1925), Ernst Zitelmann e il problema del diritto internazionale privato. *Rivista di diritto internazionale,* Vol. 17, pp. 33–72.

DANN, Philipp (2005), Thoughts on a Methodology of European Constitutional Law. *German Law Journal,* Vol. 6, N. 11, pp. 1453–1474.

FONTANELLI, Filippo, and Giuseppe MARTINICO (2008), Alla ricerca della coerenza: le tecniche del 'dialogo nascosto' fra i giudici nell'ordinamento costituzionale multi-livello. *Rivista trimestrale di diritto pubblico,* N. 2, pp. 351–387.

HERZOG, Roman, and Lüder GERKEN (2008), Stoppt den Europäischen Gerichtshof. *Frankfurter Allgemeine Zeitung,* 8 September 2008.

HESPANHA, António M. (2005), *Cultura juridica europeia. Síntese de um Milénio.* Florianópolis: Fundação Boiteux.

HILF, Meinhard (1986), The Role of Comparative Law in the Jurisprudence of the Court of Justice of the European Communities. In Armand De Mestral et al. (ed.), *The Limitation of Human Rights in Comparative Constitutional Law* (Cowansville: Y. Blais), pp. 549–574.

HOHMANN, Hanns (1998), Logic and Rhetoric in Legal Argumentation: Some Medieval Perspectives. *Argumentation*, Vol. 12, No. 1, pp. 39–55.

LENAERTS, Koen, Interlocking Legal Orders in the European Union and Comparative Law. *International and Comparative Law Quarterly*, Vol. 52, pp. 873–906.

MADURO, Miguel (2003), Contrapunctual Law: Europe's Constitutional Pluralism in Action. In Neil Walker (ed.), *Sovereignty in Transition.* Oxford: Hart.

REPETTO, Giorgio (2011), *Argomenti comparativi e diritto fondamentali in Europa. Teorie dell'interpretazione e giurisprudenza sovranazionale.* Napoli: Jovene.

SOMEK, Alexander (2010), The Emancipation of Legal Dissonance. In Henning Koch et al. (eds.), *Europe: Tee New Legal Realism.* Copenhagen: Djof, pp. 679–713.

SUNSTEIN, Cass (1995), Incompletely theorized agreements. *Harvard Law Review*, Vol. 108, N. 7, pp. 1733–1772

TARELLO, Giovanni (1976), *Storia della cultura giuridica moderna: Assolutismo e codificazione del diritto.* Bologna: Il Mulino.

— (1980), *L'interpretazione della legge.* Milano: Giuffrè.

VICO, Gian Battista (1989), *Institutiones oratoriae.* Napoli: Istituto Suor Orsola Benincasa.

The Unbearable Lightness of Fundamental Rights in the European Area of Freedom, Security, and Justice

Teresa Bravo[1]

Structural changes in contemporary constitutionalism

Modern constitutionalism did not follow a homogenous historical route. It has been the result of breakthroughs and setbacks as well as of historical, cultural, social, and economic circumstances that have affected Europe since the beginning of the 18th century. Paradoxically, the first moment of modern constitutional history was represented by the Virginia Declaration of Rights, proclaimed in June 1776. This document combines, for the first time, the principles that structure modern constitutions:

> These are the responsibility and accountability of government, the right 'to reform, alter, or abolish it,' the separation of powers, the 'trial by an impartial jury,' and the inherent idea that constitutional government is by its very nature a limited government (Dippel 2002: 5).

The advent of modern constitutionalism goes therefore along with a twofold achievement: the civil and political individual rights, and the limitation of governmental powers. Through the drafting of constitutions these rights found practical consecration and achieved binding status both in the public and private

1 Teresa Bravo is PhD candidate at the Faculty of Law of the Universidade Nova, Lisbon, researcher at the Centro de Investigação & Desenvolvimento sobre Direito e Sociedade and judge at the Tribunal do Trabalho de Lisboa, Portugal.

spheres of citizenship. These constitutional pillars are currently undergoing profound structural changes as a result both of the weakening of traditional sources of sovereignty and of the empowerment of new supranational and sub-national entities (Slaughter and Matli 1993; Mancini 1998; Alston and Weiler 1999; Zagrebelsky 2008).

The contemporary legal landscape is indeed in constant transformation both at national and supranational level, as the law making process oversteps the physical and geographic boundaries of the nation-state. Legal frameworks are traditionally regarded as a product of statehood. In transnational settings, these legal frameworks are increasingly shaped by the reciprocal interaction of different organs, both vertically and horizontally connected. These new institutional actors are engaged in continuous mutual dialogue and co-operation, but are at the same time fully self-sufficient and often beyond the reach of the sovereign state's intervention (Slaughter 2004: 150–190).

State institutions take part in the shaping of legal orders at supranational and sub-national or regional levels. They contribute to the creation and maintenance of international institutions such as the United Nations and the International Criminal Court, and branch off into a plurality of sub-national institutions and legal sub-orders. Due to the emergence of pluri-normative and supranational legal orders, the leading role played by the institutions of the nation state is getting weaker.

The existence of regional and supranational normative order, based on general legal principles with their own axiology and their own jurisdictional bodies, defies the traditional concept of the legal system as a rational and hierarchical model that peaks in the Kelsenian *Grundnorm,* the basic norm or Constitution (Kelsen 1978). Normative blocs at regional and international level constitute, metaphorically, the *network society*.

The concept of *network society* describes the interpenetration of economies as well as the technological and financial flows that fragment power and account for the emergence of a new worldwide "ruling class": one unelected body made of technocrats, lawyers, business executives, and judges. Such a "ruling class" promotes meetings, seminars, and debates, fosters a worldwide exchange of ideas, defines common action strategies through informal channels, and shapes itself as an axis of power with an ever increasing aptitude for social and political intervention (Slaughter and Zaring 2007). These networks operate in an informal, but very effective manner: judges exchange points of view during conferences or seminars about cases they are reviewing, and apply jurisprudential models and rhetoric stemming from other countries and legal traditions; police forces from different states operate in joint investigations and create protocols of police cooperation to expedite investigations transnationally; business executives participate in international networks in order to foster their common economic interests; journalists receive information from numerous news agencies and share this information informally. The process of European legal integration has been a prime example of such an activity, inasmuch as the formation of a transnational network of legal practitioners has a significant impact on legal frameworks and jurisprudence.

In the European legal space, the normative status of fundamental rights no longer emanates exclusively from the state. In recent years, the whole of the European normative structure regarding human rights has been expanded through the creative and law-creating activity of the judges of the European Court of Justice (ECJ). This so often misconstrued "judicial activism" (Manacorda 2005) has been one of the most dynamic drivers of integration, filling in the gaps of political power and overcoming, through case-law, the opposition of member states.[2]

2 On the role of the European Court of Justice in shaping fundamental rights in the EU see Lenaerts and Bray (2006) and Lenaerts (2010) a. o.

Pluralism and Internormativity in the European Union

European constitutional law is a legal order that creates rights applicable not only to the member states but also to individuals. It is regulated by autonomous bodies. It includes both national and supranational competences, and is bound by legal principles, such as those incorporated in the fundamental rights tradition common to member states, and the principles of subsidiarity and social cohesion.[3]

And yet, European constitutional law is still a utopia under construction. Since Europe is not a constitutional state, its consolidation is hindered both by state sovereignties and by the fact that its creation depends very much on political will:

> [...] two causes have, for a long time, blocked any pathway to a common European constitutional law: the first is the national absolute state and the second is the notion of sovereignty still prevalent in the 20th century [...] (Häberle 1993: 12).

Nevertheless, despite difficulties and stalemates, it is indeed possible, according to Häberle, to discern the emergence of common European constitutional principles, i.e. of the so-called *ius commune constitutionale europeum.* Such a *ius commune* rests on a shared, embryonic legal culture that manifests itself in the approximation among the constitutions of the member states and in the case-law of its courts, namely the European Court of Human Rights (ECHR) and the European Court of Justice (ECJ), whose rulings have helped to consolidate a common European legal heritage. Objective indicators, such as the norms incorporated in the Treaties, European jurisprudence and doctrine, reveal the legal principles upon which these organs base their rulings, particularly in matters of fundamental rights. These indicators also re-

3 The constitutionalist doctrine attempts to explain the legal nature of this entity through two contradictory formulations: the nationalist or "constitutionalist/patriotic" perspective on the one hand, and the "Europeanist/federalist" view, on the other (Canotilho 2003: 1373).

veal a wider collective project, a European Constitution, whose roots are enshrined in the Preamble to the Statute of the Council of Europe of 1949, in the Preamble to the European Convention on Human Rights of 1950, in the case-law of the Court of Justice of the European Communities, and in the Single European Act of 1986.

This European constitutional project was clearly defined as one of the fundamental objectives of the Convention on the Future of Europe, resulting from the Laeken Declaration in December 2001. This Convention on the Future of Europe was the result of an open, transparent and democratic procedure whose members were representatives of national parliaments.

These elements reveal the emergence of an European legal culture characterised by democratic government, pluralism, and the respect of human rights, all of which are enshrined in the Charter of Fundamental Rights of the European Union (CFREU), which has now acquired a binding character with the ratification of the Treaty of Lisbon.

The principles of the Western constitutional state have made this development possible, as they include a common set of values such as democracy, pluralism, fundamental rights, the separation of state powers, and an independent judiciary (Häberle 2002: 257).

Although the construction of a common European constitutional law is grounded *prima facie* on political and legislative decision-making, the role of the courts cannot be overlooked for two reasons. On the one hand, the co-existence of several jurisdictional bodies within the European legal sphere paved the way to several rulings that shaped this process. On the other hand, the jurisdictional interpretation of legal principles fosters and strengthens the construction of the *ius commune constitutionale europeum* (Duarte 2006; Conway 2008). Moreover, modern constitutional law shows a dynamic character, an open and universalist texture that allows it to incorporate the influence of concepts that are alien to its original ontogeny. Zagrebelsky points out this flexibility of contemporary constitutional law as the central quality of the plural legal realities of the present day:

> [...] it is to this 'open' concept of the Constitution, which has progressively (if not straightforwardly) gained ground in Europe, to which can be attributed the merit, if it is indeed a merit, of allowing the member states to open up [...] to the organisation of a European authority and union [...] (Zagrebelsky 2008: 14).

For Zagrebelsky, such a ductility stems from the coexistence of a diversity of values and principles that claim neither a hegemonic nor an absolute status, but allows instead for a compromise. In this scenario, the courts will have to bring these different principles into line and work out solutions in order to diffuse conflict without neutralizing the pluralism and the diversity of values that coexist in modern societies.

The notions of pluralism, normative, and constitutional ductility, as well as the role conferred on courts regarding the interpretation and application of legal principles clearly flout the vision of the legal universe as an ordered and hierarchical system of norms and principles characterised by legal certainty and imbued with homogenous content. A corollary of these dynamics is the concept of the *co-operative constitutional state* (CCS) as it results from the evolution of the constitutional state. The CCS engages in institutional forms of co-operation with other states as well as with national and supranational entities (Häberle 2002: 259).

Normative integration designates a continuous movement of progressive penetration of EU law into the national legal orders of member states. The varied European legislative production in areas such as the economy, the environment, education and immigration policies, justice and security, has the purpose of bringing into line the normative contents of internal legislations. This challenge to the integrity of national legal orders is at the same time a challenge to state sovereignties, and constitutes a "strategic Europeanisation" (Maduro 2006: 34) that goes beyond the aim of transferring competences from member states to the EU. It is, instead, a more profound and complex phenomenon, which is a direct result of the "competition" and interaction between several institutional and non-institutional actors, such as national courts and the ECJ, governments, private citizens, and enterprises. These actors maintain a mutual contact and dialogue in the network society, oftentimes independently of formal mechanisms and institutionalised protocols (Slaughter 2004; Neil 2002: 317), and their aim is to align and (re)define the course of national and European policies according to their rights and expectations.

The judicial matrix of the European system of fundamental rights

Dynamism and controversy are the two main features of the construction of fundamental rights in the EU. Issues of sovereignty as well as the different constitutional identities and traditions of each of the European nations have hampered the legislative production of a binding core of fundamental rights in the EU. Thence the controversial nature of their constriction in the European legal space, in particular since the Maastricht Treaty.

Historically, European countries have always exhibited cultural, linguistic, and political differences. Nevertheless, such disparities cannot belie a common ground, which consists in the legacy of Hellenistic rationality, shaped by the Roman *res publica* and appropriated by the Judaeo-Christian worldview (Enes 2004: 17). This legacy is expressed in the preamble of the Lisbon Treaty, in which the "cultural, religious and humanist heritage of Europe" is adopted as the source of inspiration and axiological grounding for European integration (Duarte and Lopes 2008: 13). Human Rights emerge as an important aspect of these common beliefs (Barreto 2004: 24; Spielmann 2001).[4]

The importance and originality of the European Convention on Human Rights (ECHR) results from the rights it incorporates, and above all from the institutional weight it acquired, since it establishes provisions for any individual who considers to have suffered an infringement of its rights to bring the case before the

4 On the CFREU see also Sudre (2008), Tinière (2007), Tulkens and Callewaert (2002).

European Court of Human Rights. This grants an effective protection which transcends the boundaries of state sovereignty and endows an external judicial body with the power of judicial review as well as with the capacity to "sanction" the conduct of states in relation to citizens.

The creation of the Council of Europe on the 5th May 1949 represents the commitment of public powers towards the defence of fundamental rights, as is foreseen in Article 1 (a):

> the aim of the Council of Europe is to achieve a greater unity between its members for the purpose of safeguarding and realising the ideals and principles which are their common heritage and facilitating their economic and social progress.

The last few years witnessed a profusion of public and political discourses on the importance of fundamental rights that culminated in the proclamation of the CFREU at the Nice Council of 2000. The Charter was the product of a Convention, not of intergovernmental bargaining. Its genesis reveals its dual nature as a normative instrument, which some authors see as the product of a true constituent process, and therefore as the founding element of a new European constitutional order, whereas others see it as a way to consolidate fundamental rights that are merely derived from the European ideological legacy, as well as a means to prevent courts from creating new rights.

Nonetheless, the resistance and fierce criticism with which the proclamation was met thwarted at first the effort to endow it with binding force. In Portugal, Jorge Miranda has been quite outspoken in his disapproval, asserting that the proclamation represented a step towards European constitutionalisation and federalisation, thus leading to the abrogation of national constitutions.[5]

The drafting of the Charter was characterised by considerable transparency and publicity. Maria Luísa Duarte points out that the ontological originality of the Charter is not a product of self-proclamation (as was the case during the French revolution), but

5 http://app.parlamento.pt/site_antigo/destaques/anteriores/cartaUE/par_un_lisboa.html (last accessed October 11, 2012).

of an institutional and formal process (Duarte 2006: 132). The participants in the deliberative process were, noticeably, members of national parliaments and of the European Parliament, experts, and other independent personalities selected on the grounds of their technical expertise. This was quite a different approach from the intergovernmental method, in which deliberations are formulated as a rule by political representatives of the member states and of their national interests (Maduro 2006: 302).

However, despite any consideration regarding the role that the Charter is to play in the future constitutional development of the European Union, it sets a limit to the judicial creation of fundamental rights. Indeed, the fact that the Charter consecrates a set of rights and includes an addendum of explanations that was prepared under the authority of the Praesidium shows how much the European legislators intended to limit the interpretative authority of judges by binding them to a written text. This aspect is absolutely decisive, since it represents the reassumption of political control over the judicial control on European integration (Maduro 2006: 305).

Nevertheless, the EU is the result of an inter-normative process. As such, it encompasses different legal sources that stem from distinct normative orders. The coexistence of a variety of normative sources demands an intense effort of interpretation in order to accommodate such a diversity. In recent years such an effort has been mostly undertaken by the judiciary. Indeed, the European system of fundamental rights has been grounded on judicial interpretative work. In fact, until recently, the founding treaties did not provide for specific norms of fundamental rights and did not even include a general reception clause that would explicitly mark out the criteria to identify relevant sources.

However, this situation might be overridden in the near future through the incorporation of the now binding CFREU into the constitutional *acquis* of the EU. Consequently, we can argue that the political history of fundamental rights in the EU is the narrative of a struggle towards the recognition of the binding force of legal provisions. This has been the case both in 1989, when the Social Charter (Charter of the Fundamental Social Rights of

Workers) was created, and in 2000, with the advent of the Charter of Fundamental Rights of the European Union.

Swift changes in the EU system of protection of fundamental rights were caused by the introduction of European Union's citizenship, which grafted a set of provisions related to the legal status of European citizenship onto the EU Treaty. This regards the free movement of people, the right to vote and to stand as a candidate in elections to the European Parliament in the member state of residence, the right to complain to the European Ombudsman, and the right to petition the European Parliament.

As previously pointed out, it was up to the Community Courts to identify, through case law, the rights to be protected. Maria Luísa Duarte (2006: 74) remarks that, whereas case-law was not exactly a source of rights in itself, it was nonetheless a vehicle for the fleshing out of rights that resulted from sources such as the CFREU, as well as from the common principles of the constitutional traditions of the member states. Fundamental rights thus represent a "legal core", i.e. an "ethical-normative minimum", of values that are immanent to the normative system independently of hierarchy and legal sources. This legal core is binding for both the EU and national decision-makers.

It is important to notice how much the establishment of an Area of Freedom, Security and Justice (AFSJ) challenges the "legal core" of fundamental rights inasmuch as justice and police co-operation still belong to the most problematic aspects of the integration process.

The creation of the Area of Freedom, Security and Justice

One of the key elements of European integration was the creation of an Area of Freedom, Security and Justice, whose purpose was to make easier police and judicial co-operation in criminal matters. This set of policies goes back to the 1970s, as their idea was ushered in by French president Valéry Giscard d'Estaing at the 1977 European Council meeting, and gained momentum with a wave of terrorist attacks which hit Europe during the 70s and 80s. Subsequently, it received further impulse with the incorporation of the Schengen Convention in the European *acquis* with the ratification of the Treaty of Amsterdam.[6] The agreements aimed at expediting co-operation in criminal matters by simplifying procedures of notification, extradition, and direct contact between police and judicial authorities.

Three elements are constituent to the concept of an Area of Freedom, Security and Justice. Besides its territorial dimension, the AFSJ includes an axiological-normative dimension, in which different legal systems coexist within a spirit of close co-operation and shared objectives and values.

As defined in the Amsterdam Treaty, the AFSJ relates to territory in the same way as citizenship relates to nationality, and expresses the fundamental concept of the free movement of persons within an expanded geography. In fact, the Communication from the Commission to the Council dated 14/07/1998 (Com. 459) had already clarified its features:

> The concept enshrines [...] our democratic traditions and what we understand by the rule of law. The common values underlining the objective of an area of freedom, security and justice are indeed longstanding principles of the modern democracies of the European Union. [...] The three notions of freedom, security and justice are closely interlinked. Freedom loses much of its meaning if it cannot be enjoyed in a secure environment and with the full backing of a system of justice in which all Union citizens and residents can have confidence.[7]

---

6 The Schengen Agreements were celebrated on 14th June 1985 and supplemented by the Convention Implementing the Schengen Agreement on 19th June 1990. The treaties were originally signed by five states alone (France, Germany, Belgium, The Netherlands and Luxembourg), but were progressively expanded to include states such as Iceland and Norway, Switzerland (12th December 2008), Estonia, the Czech Republic, Lithuania, Hungary, Malta, Latvia, Poland and Slovenia.

7 http://eur-lex.europa.eu/LexUriServ/LexUriServ.do?uri=COM:1998:0459:FIN:EN:PDF (last accessed October 11, 2012).

"Freedom" means more than the free movement of persons across member states. It relates to the freedom to live in a law-abiding environment in which both national and EU authorities employ their competences to combat and prosecute crime while respecting fundamental rights.

The notion of "security" was introduced by the Treaty of Amsterdam,[8] and concerns the creation of an institutional framework for the development of common actions in the fields of police and judicial co-operation in criminal matters, namely, to combating organised crime and drug trafficking.

Finally, "justice" aims to shape a "European public order" based on shared fundamental goals in order to overcome the differences among national legal systems. The prevailing differences between legal orders justify the introduction of instruments that allow for the judicial systems to act more effectively and satisfactorily, thus ensuring a sense of equality to EU citizens in legal matters.

The Treaty of Lisbon brought about significant changes to the AFSJ, namely by abolishing the pillar structure and merging the areas pertaining to the third pillar into Title V, Part Three, of the Treaty on the Functioning of the European Union (TFEU). Judicial co-operation in criminal matters is detailed in Arts. 82 *et seq*. At institutional level, the new Treaty also introduced a number of innovations regarding the intervention of the European and national parliaments in the legislative procedure, as of TFEU's Ch. 4. Art. 19 of the TEU, and Arts. 267 and 344 of the TFEU, expanded the jurisdiction of the ECJ, which is now able to review all the measures taken regarding police and judicial co-operation in criminal matters, with the exception of operations carried out by police or other law enforcement services on any matters relating to internal security.

In the next chapter I will focus on the role of the ECJ in the AFSJ, so as to ascertain whether the case-law produced by this body encroaches on an eminently political area, and consequently violates the principle of the separation of powers.

---

8 See in particular Title IV of the EC Treaty in its post-Amsterdam version, which covers Visas, Asylum, Immigration and other Policies related to free movement of persons, as well as Title V of the selfsame Treaty.

The Judiciary as a protagonist of European integration: the ECJ's role in the context of the AFSJ

The norms set out in the criminal constitution of a political community tend to mirror the dominant values and the fundamental rights of citizens. Ideally, they ought to represent the optimum balance between social expectations of crime prevention and the safeguards of rights and freedoms. Judicial and police co-operation are traditionally part of the "core business" of state sovereignty.

Before the approval of the Lisbon Treaty, the ECJ's competences with regard to the Area of Freedom, Security and Justice were specified in Article 35 of the TEU, which set the legal basis of the ECJ's jurisdiction regarding the validity and interpretation of framework decisions, decisions, and conventions. However, these competences were limited and subordinate to two other conditions or prerequisites:

- The declaration of acceptance of its jurisdiction by member states;
- The specification, in the declaration of acceptance, of the courts or tribunals that were allowed to ask for the intervention of the ECJ.

In this respect, until 1997 the ECJ had occupied a marginal position, for its remit was limited to the evaluation of any conventions that might be adopted in the advancement of the objectives of the already established measures of police and judicial co-operation. Indeed, the system of judicial review was originally conceived to guarantee the competences and functions of the European Community regarding the First and Second Pillar, and was only extended to the third Pillar after the Treaty of Amsterdam.

If we compare Article 35 TEU to Article 230(4) TEC, a fundamental difference emerges: according to art. 230(4)

> Any natural [...] person may [...] institute proceedings against a decision which, although in the form of a regulation or a decision addressed to another person, is of direct and individual concern to the former.

This is in contrast to what was the case in Title VI. As a consequence, member states that did not accept the jurisdiction of the ECJ (such as the United Kingdom and the Republic of Ireland) deprived their citizens of an effective European judicial protection, which, in practice, led to formal and substantial inequalities. Such an opt-out was of the utmost importance, since it denied the access to European justice to nationals of these member states and opened the door for divergent interpretations of European legislation concerning the third pillar.

However, the general trend of the EU legal system develops towards increasing integration. Through famous rulings such as *Watson and Belmann* (1976), *Costa v. ENEL*, *Simmenthal*, and *Van Gend en Loos,* a.o., the ECJ has established since the 1970's a profusion of innovative case-law regarding the community pillars, thus contributing to the consolidation of the principles of primacy and conforming interpretation of community law. Through case-law, the Court of Justice has been able to build community law as a legal system, and paved the way to the constitutionalisation of the Treaties (Maduro 2006: 58; Conway 2008).

The ECJ has always maintained that the Community's legal order is autonomous from the legal orders of member states. Its enforcement should, therefore, take precedence over the latter, so as to assure the uniformity of implementation of community law. The Court bases these conclusions on the belief that member states have already transferred part of their sovereignty to the Union. As a consequence, the legitimacy of the Community's legal order is grounded on both state sovereignty and European citizenship, as citizens are the ultimate basis of political power.

In the above mentioned rulings, the ECJ sets forth a functional argument to justify the primacy of community law: if member states are able to unilaterally adopt measures contravening community law, the very subsistence of the European legal order would be compromised (Prechal 2006; Michaeau and Masson 2009: 117). The ECJ's case-law output eventually reveals a federalist perspective, as it has played a key role in promoting integration by placing community law at the top of the legal pyramid as a sort of *Grundnorm*.

The ECJ's creative law-making process has, however, encountered strong resistance. Several authors have levelled fierce criticism at the Court, accusing it of judicial activism (Manacorda 2005). The ECJ has been criticised for assuming the role of a European legislator despite the fact that this was not the original scope of its intervention. Conversely, the supporters of the ECJ's case-law contend that the Court has been the main force behind European integration, filling in the *lacunae* of legal texts, as well as resolving institutional conflicts.

The ECJ and the "creation" of a criminal policy for the European Union: the Pupino case

The principle of legality is one of the structuring elements of the democratic rule of law, in which power is exercised and legitimised in order to guarantee that the legal system pursues two essential ends of the political community: certainty and equality (Canotilho and Moreira 2007).

In the Portuguese legal system, the Parliament has the power to define criminal sanctions, while the government can only legislate on criminal matters if it is granted an authorisation to do so, as of Art. 165 (1) (c), of the Portuguese Constitution (CRP). The principle of legality also excludes common law as a source of definition of offences or of criminal punishment. According to Art. 8(4) of the CRP, international and European criminal norms take precedence over Portuguese internal law, within the constraints that derive from the fundamental principles of a democratic state based on the rule of law.[9] As such, the provisions of

9 Constitutional Law no. 1/2004 (6th revision) of 24th of July, published in *Diário da República,* No. 173, 1st series of 24/07/2004.

the European treaties and EU norms take precedence over Portuguese law, including the Constitution.[10]

Criminal law tends to be a barometer of the constitutional order. Consequently, one may ask if the case-law developed by the ECJ under the Third pillar did in effect pave the way to a progressive Europeanisation of criminal law. In this regard, one of the most emblematic rulings is commonly known as the *Pupino* case, and was delivered by the ECJ on 16th june, 2005 (Case C-105/03).[11]

In the Pupino case, criticism was raised against the ECJ on the grounds that the Court allowed the principle of conforming interpretation to be applicable in the context of the Third pillar. The question that the ECJ had to review was whether member states courts were bound to taking into account norms and, more specifically, framework decisions, produced by European decision-making organs in Third pillar matters. Previously to the approval of the Lisbon Treaty, Article. 34(2)(b) TEU stated that framework decisions did not entail direct effect, and an internal legislative act of implementation was needed.

In this particular case, the Italian court was required to interpret its internal law according to the wording and the purpose of the framework decision so as to attain the result which the decision envisaged. This reasoning was defined as the principle of *conforming interpretation*.[12]

10 Before the Treaty of Lisbon came into force it was questionable whether the EU had any criminal competences, for no such provision was present in the Treaties (Vernimmen 2000; Flore 1999; Sevenster 1992: 35).

11 This case was a reference for a preliminary ruling by the judge in charge of preliminary enquiries at the Tribunale di Firenze (Italy) regarding the interpretation of Arts. 2, 3 and 8 of the Council Framework Decision 2001/220/JHA of 15th March 2001 (OJ 2001 L 82/1), on the standing of victims in criminal proceedings. The question asked by the Italian court was: "[...] given the Framework decision regarding the standing of victims in criminal proceedings, could a national court allow small children to testify in criminal proceedings by alternate means that would ensure an adequate level of protection (i.e. outside the court room and during the pre-trial period)?"

12 See Press Release No. 59/05 of the 16 de June de 2005, Judgment of the Court of Justice in Case C-105/03, available at http://europa.eu/rapid/pressReleasesAction.do?reference=CJE/05/59&format=HTML&aged=1&language=EN&guiLanguage=en, (last accessed October 11, 2012).

In its judgement, the ECJ considered that Arts. 2, 3 and 8 of the Council Framework Decision 2001/220/JHA, of 15th March 2001 (OJ 2001 L 82/1) on the standing of victims in criminal proceedings

> must be interpreted as meaning that the national court must be able to authorise young children to give their testimony in accordance with arrangements allowing those children to be guaranteed an appropriate level of protection, for example outside the trial and before it takes place

which is to say that

> [...] the national court is required to take into consideration all the rules of national law and to interpret them, so far as possible, in the light of the wording and purpose of the Framework Decision.[13]

The principles upon which the ECJ based its ruling were as follows:

a) Remarking that the same mechanism for requesting preliminary rulings applied in both articles, the ECJ argued that the provisions of Art. 234 TEC were applicable to those of Art. 35 TEU, so that the jurisprudence established by the former shall equally apply to the latter;
b) The court claims that the wording of Art. 34(2)(b) TEU is based on the norm of Art. 249(3) TEU regarding Community directives, and that such a similar wording entails that the binding character of framework decisions confers on national authorities and, particularly, national courts, an obligation to interpret national law in conformity to them;[14]

---

13 The text of this judgment is available at http://curia.europa.eu/juris/document/document.jsf?text=&docid=59363&pageIndex=0&doclang=EN&mode=lst&dir=&occ=first&part=1&cid=48218 (last accessed October 11, 2012).

14 Art. 34 (2) TEC (included in the above mentioned Title VI of the Amsterdam Treaty) states "that the Council shall take measures and promote cooperation with a view to contribute to the pursuit of the objectives of the Union, namely through the adoption of framework decisions for the purpose of approximation of the laws and regulations of the Member States. [...] Framework decisions shall be binding upon the Member States as to the result to be achieved but shall leave to the national authorities the choice of form and methods."

c) The principle of loyal co-operation, set out in Art. 10 TEC, applies to the provisions of Title VI, since such a principle is a vital prerequisite to the creation of an ever closer union among the peoples of Europe and the development of judicial and police co-operation in criminal matters.

The Court's reasoning faced fierce opposition from the majority of the member states. The counter-arguments they submitted emphasised substantial differences between intergovernmental and community pillars both in terms of their objectives and of the legal instruments used by the Treaties to pursue them.

The main argument offered by the Italian government in order to prevent the principle of conforming interpretation from being applied to the Pupino case was that it considered framework decisions and community directives to be substantially different and separate sources of law. Along the same lines, the French government claimed that an interpretation of internal law according to a framework decision would not be possible, since framework decisions cannot have direct effect. Moreover, the TEU contains no such obligation as the one laid down in Article 10 TEC (Weyembergh 2007: 175; Baileux and Van Meerbeeck 2007: 158).

It is important to point out the differences between the concept of direct effect and the principle of conforming interpretation.[15] The principle of conforming interpretation is based on the primacy of community law and on loyal co-operation between member states. Its starting point is the analysis of the aims and purposes of the legislative instrument in question. It has two limitations: on the one hand, the principle that national law must be given a conforming interpretation cannot lead to an interpretation

15 Direct effect is the principle which confers the right to individuals (both natural or legal persons) to bring an action before the national and community courts when community legal texts result in specific rights and/or obligations for the citizen, regardless of the pre-existence of any national law or transposition texts. This principle, which has a jurisprudential origin in the *Van Gend en Loos* and *Franz Grad* rulings, both reinforces the effectiveness of European law and the safeguard of the rights of individuals.

that is *contra legem*; on the other hand, its practical application cannot lead to a violation of fundamental rights.

In the Court's view, the extension of conforming interpretation to framework decisions would enable an expansion of judicial and police co-operation in criminal matters, as it would enable an increasingly uniform application of European law by member states' courts without depending on the previous incorporation of framework decisions into national law.

The consequences and the impact of the Pupino judgement went largely beyond the legal issues being reviewed in this particular case, and acquired an unprecedented political and institutional significance that redefined the trajectory of European integration.

The Amsterdam Treaty foresaw that:

- The decisions taken with regard to the Third pillar presupposed the unanimity of Council (Art. 34(2) TEU);
- The member states and/or the Commission had legislative initiative;
- The European Parliament did not participate in the decision-making process, restricting itself to delivering an opinion;
- The legislative instruments (Decisions, Framework Decisions, and Conventions) did not entail direct effect (Art. 34(2)(b) TEU);
- The ECJ could merely give preliminary rulings on the validity of decisions, framework decisions, and conventions, if member states accepted its jurisdiction by means of a declaration to this effect (Art. 35(1),(2) TEU).

Thus, the general framework inherited from the Amsterdam Treaty confirmed the strong intergovernmental bias of the Third pillar, the democratic deficit of the decision-making process, and the lack of judicial review mechanisms to ensure fundamental rights, particularly in criminal matters.

The Pupino ruling was in this respect innovative and to a certain point revolutionary, inasmuch as it established that by means of preliminary rulings individuals could challenge framework decisions in criminal proceedings that took place in any member state. Thus, the Court created a mechanism of supervision of fundamental rights which had heretofore not been directly or expressly provided for in the Treaties. On the other hand, this ruling was a decisive step in the broadening of the European criminal area, since by applying the principle of conforming interpretation of internal law to European law it contributed to a peaceful (interpretive) harmonization of European legislation under Title VI.[16]

Finally, and from an institutional viewpoint, this ruling consecrated the ECJ as the upholder of European citizens' rights, freedoms, and guarantees to the detriment of the role of other institutional organs, such as Commission and Council, both of which are strongly dependent upon the political initiatives of member states.

Judicial empowerment and the Treaty of Lisbon: the current state of legal affairs in Europe

Two further landmark decisions were those delivered in cases C-176/03 and C-440/05, respectively on the 13th September 2005 and 23rd October 2007.[17]

In the first, the Commission brought about an action for annulment of the Council's framework decision 2003/80/JHA (OJ 2003 L29/55), on the grounds that this framework decision encroached upon the competences of the Commission by legislating in matters regarding the protection of the environment through criminal law.

In the second, a similar action was brought about under Article 35(6) TEU regarding the Council's framework decision 2005/667/

16 Bailleux and Van Meerbeeck (2007) criticised this ruling on the grounds that it extended the scope of the victim's protection without baring in mind that it would worsen the position of the accused.

17 See http://eur-lex.europa.eu/LexUriServ/LexUriServ.do?uri=CELEX:62003J0176:EN:HTML and http://eur-lex.europa.eu/LexUriServ/LexUriServ.do?uri=CELEX:62005J0440:EN:HTML (last accessed October 11, 2012).

JHA, which regarded the ship-source pollution (OJ 2005 L 255/164). In both matters, the ECJ decided to annul the framework decisions *in totum* as they were considered indivisible.

In the first ruling, the ECJ pointed out that, given both its aim and content, this legal instrument encroached upon the powers that Art. 175 TEC conferred upon the Community, endowing it with the competence to legislate on environmental protection, and infringed the provisions of Art. 47 TEU. In the second ruling the decision was identical, as the Court considered that the framework decision encroached upon the powers which Art. 80 (2) TEC conferred on the Community, endowing it with competence to legislate on matters of transport and maritime safety policy, thereby once again infringing Art. 47 TEU.

What was really at stake in case C-176/03 was the (re)definition of the distribution of competences in matters relating to the First and the Third pillar. The Commission petitioned for the annulment of framework decision 2003/80/JHA, adopted by the Council based on Arts. 29 TEU, 31(e) TEU, and 34(2)(b) TEU in their pre-Nice Treaty wording, since it considered that the purpose and the content of this framework decision were within the scope of the Community's powers on environmental legislation, as stated in Art. 175 TEC. The Commission's position was supported by the European Parliament. The recourse to criminal law became an essential measure available to Community bodies in the pursuit of the purposes of the Treaties, which was in this particular case the promotion of a policy of environmental protection as laid out in articles 3(1) (l) TEC, and 174 to 176 TEC.

Both rulings demonstrate the ECJ's clear commitment to break away from the prevailing legislative model. Its case law anticipated to a certain extent the solutions subsequently provided for by the Lisbon Treaty. The Treaty's text now abolishes the distinction between the legislative instruments of the First and Third pillars and adopts a single nomenclature (regulations and directives).

In that it recognised the existence of Community competences in criminal matters, the ECJ paved the way to the erosion of the difference between the pillars. In the Lisbon Treaty, a nucleus of shared competences between member states and the Union indeed comes out as the AFSJ.[18]

The ECJ's pioneering case law was grounded on two postulates: the recognition of implicit competences of the Commission in criminal law matters, and the importance of these competences in order to pursue community policies (Labayle 2006: 1; Flore 2003: 14).

The complexity of the European legal system as well as its indeterminacy in some fields has made room for the creative role of the ECJ. The ECJ is not just a mere legal body with technical competences. On the contrary, it is an institutional actor engaged in the prospective evolution of the system by anticipating solutions that only political will and compromise could be able to reach.

The ECJ has filled in the normative gaps that the European legislator didn't dare to explore. Its case-law has a political dimension from the moment it forced, for instance, the elimination of the pillar structure and the establishment of a single nomenclature for legislative instruments. Regardless of the criticisms that might be levelled at the ECJ, the fact remains that its rulings were a response to the stalemates of political institutions.

The long absence of a European catalog of fundamental rights also allowed the ECJ to somehow monopolize the topic, since its application of community law, its reference to the general principles of law, and its interpretation of the constitutional traditions of the member states, addressed the doubts raised by complainants and filled the gaps left by the European legislators.

However, the aforementioned rulings raise a number of questions: what are the limits of the ECJ's scope of action? To which extent does its "judicial empowerment" remain within the boundaries of legal interpretation? To which extent does it spill over into politics? To which extent can it be said that such a judicial empowerment contravenes the democratic principle as well as the principle of the separation of powers?

---

18 See Arts. 2, 4(1) and 4(4)(j), as well as the cluster of articles 61(a), 69(E to L) of the Treaty of Lisbon.

It seems important to bear in mind that the historical process that led to the emancipation of judicial power or, in other words, the progressive distinction between *gubernaculum* and *iurisdictio*, was difficult, lengthy, and contingent on the historical, social and political circumstances of each age (Ferrajoli 2006: 586). The independence of judges is the product of the ideas regarding the separation of powers in the *civitas*.[19] Nowadays, we face a different question because it is no longer the institutional autonomy of the judiciary that is at stake, but rather its interference with the sphere of competence of the executive and the legislative branches of the state.

References

ALSTON, Philip, and Joseph H. H. WEILER (1999), An 'Ever Closer Union' in Need of a Human Rights Policy: The European Union and Human Rights. *Harvard Jean Monnet Working Paper 1/99*. Available at: http://centers.law.nyu.edu/jeanmonnet/archive/papers/99/990101.html (last accessed July 12, 2012).

BAILEUX, Antoine, and Jérémie VAN MEERBEECK (2007), Droits de l'homme, droit pénal et droit communautaire à Luxembourg: Enjeux, difficultés et paradoxes d'un ménage à trois. In Y. Cartuyvels, H. Dumont, F. Ost (eds.), *Les Droits de l'Homme, bouclier ou épée du droit pénal?* Bruxelles: Publications de l'Université de Saint Louis, pp. 111–174

BARRETO, Irineu Cabral (1995), *A Convenção Europeia dos Direitos do Homem*. Lisboa: Editorial Notícias.

CANOTILHO, J. J. G. (2003), *Direito Constitucional e Teoria da Constituição*. Coimbra: Almedina.

CANOTILHO, J. J. G., and Moreira, VITAL (2007), *Constituição da República Portuguesa – Anotada*, Vol. I. Coimbra: Coimbra Editora.

CONWAY, Gerard (2008), Levels of Generality in the Legal Reasoning of the European Court of Justice. *European Law Review*, Vol. 14, N. 6, pp. 787–805.

19 Initially devised out of the Lockean model of the separation between the executive and legislative powers (see *Two Treatises on Government*), it was subsequently reconfigured by Montesquieu in *L'esprit des Lois*, in which the judicial became a power autonomous from the other two branches.

Dippel, Horst (2002), *Modern Constitutionalism. An Introduction to a History in the Need of Writing*. Available at: http://www.uni-kassel.de/~dippel/justitia/proc/10%20Dippel,%20Modern.pdf (last accessed July 7, 2012), p. 5.

Duarte, Maria Luísa (2006), *União Europeia e Direitos Fundamentais no espaço da internormatividade*. Lisboa: AAFDL – Associação Académica da Faculdade de Direito de Lisboa.

Duarte, Maria Luísa, and Carlos Alberto Lopes (2008), *Tratado de Lisboa – versão consolidada do Tratado da União Europeia e do Tratado sobre o funcionamento da União Europeia*. Lisboa: AAFDL – Associação Académica da Faculdade de Direito de Lisboa.

Enes, M. F. (2004), Ideia de Europa e Construção Europeia: a propósito do 'preâmbulo' da Constituição. *Cultura – Revista de História e Teoria das Ideias*, XIX, II série pp. 13–36.

Ferrajoli, Luigi (2006), *Derecho Y Razón – Teoría del garantismo penal*. Madrid: Editorial Trotta.

Flore, Daniel (1999), Une justice pénale européenne après Amsterdam. *Journal des Tribunaux, Droit Européen*, Vol. 60, 7ème année, pp. 121–129.

— (2003), Introduction, Un droit pénal européen: hasard ou nécessité? In D. Flore, S. Bosly et al. (eds.), *Actualités de droit pénal européen*. Bruxelles: La Chartre, pp. 5–16.

Häberle, Peter (1993), Derecho Constitutional Comun Europeo. *Revista de Estudios Politicos*, Vol. 79, pp. 7–46.

— (2002), *Pluralismo Y Constitución – Estudios de Teoría Constitucional de la sociedad abierta*. Madrid: Editorial Tecnos.

Kelsen, Hans (1978, reprint), *Pure Theory of Law*. Berkeley: University of California Press.

Labayle, Henri (2006), Architecte ou spectatrice? La Cour de Justice de l'Union européenne dans l'espace de liberté, de sécurité et de justice. *Revue Trimestrielle de droit européen*, Vol. 42, N. 1 (Janvier–Mars), pp. 1–46.

Lenaerts, Koen, Piet Van Nuffel and Robert Bray (2006), *Constitutional Law of the European Union*. London: Thomsom, Sweet & Maxwell.

Lenaerts, Koen (2010), The contribution of the European Court of Justice to the Area of Freedom, Security and Justice. *International & Comparative Law Quarterly*, Vol. 59, Part 2, pp. 255–301.

Maduro, Miguel Poiares (2006), *Constituição Plural – Constitucionalismo e União Europeia*. Cascais: Principia.

Manacorda, Stefano (2005), Judicial Activism dans le cadre de l'espace de liberté, de justice et de securité de l'Union européenne. *Revue de Science criminelle et de droit pénal comparé*, N. 4, pp. 940–950.

Mancini, Federico (1998), Europe: The case for Statehood. *European Law Journal*, Vol. 4, N. 1, pp. 29–42.

Michaenau, Claire, and Antoine Masson (2009), La Cour de Justice des Communautés européennes: moteur de l'integration européenne. In S. Devaux, R. Leboutte, P. Poirier (eds.), *Le Traité de Rome: Histoires pluridisciplinaires –*

l'apport du Traité de Rome Instituant la Communauté économique européenne. Bern: Peter Lang.

PRECHAL, Sacha (2006), National Courts in EU Judicial Structures. *Yearbook of European Law*, Vol. 25, N. 1, pp. 395–428.

SLAUGHTER, Anne-Marie, and Walter MATLI (1993), Europe before the Court: a Political Theory of Legal Integration. *International Organization*, Vol. 4, N. 1, pp. 41–76.

SLAUGHTER, Anne-Marie, and David ZARING (2007), Networking goes International: an update. *Washington & Lee Legal Studies Paper No. 2007-12.* Available at: http://papers.ssrn.com/sol3/papers.cfm?abstract_id=960484# (last accessed October 11, 2012).

SLAUGHTER, Anne-Marie (2004), Disaggregated Sovereignty: Towards the Public Accountability of Global Government Networks. In *Government and Opposition.* Oxford: Blackwell.

WALKER, Neil (2002), The Idea of Constitutional Pluralism. *Modern Law Review*, N. 65, pp. 317–359.

SPIELMANN, Dean (2001), Jurisprudence des juridictions de Strasbourg et Luxembourg: Dans le domaine des droits de l'Homme: conflits, incohérences et complémentarités. In Philip Alston (ed.), *L'Union européenne des droits de l'Homme.* Bruxelles: Bryulant, pp. 699–812.

SEVENSTER, Hanna (1992), Criminal Law and EC Law. *Common Market Law Review*, Vol. 29, N. 1, pp. 29–70.

SUDRE, Fréderic (2008), *Droit Européen et international des droits de l'homme.* Paris: Presses Universitaires de France.

TINIÈRE, Romain (2007), *L'office du juge communautaire des droits fondamentaux.* Bruxelles: Bruylant.

TULKENS, Françoise and Johan CALLEWAERT (2002), Le point de vue de la Cour Européenne des Droits de l'homme. In J. I. Carlier, O. de Schutter (eds.), *La Charte des droits fondamentaux de l'Union Européenne, son apport à la protection des droits de l'homme en Europe.* Bruxelles: Bruylant, pp. 219–240.

VERNIMMEN, Gisele (2000), Le point de vue de la Commission. In *Vers un espace judiciaire pénal européen/Towards a European Judicial Criminal Area.* Bruxelles: Editions de l'Université de Bruxelles.

WEYEMBERGH, Anne (2007), L'espace pénal européen: épée des droits fondamentaux dans l'Union européenne. In Y. Cartuyvels, H. Dumont, F. Ost (eds.), *Les Droits de l'Homme, bouclier ou épée du droit pénal?* Bruxelles: Publications de l'Université de Saint Louis.

ZAGREBELSKY, Gustavo (2008), *El Derecho Dúctil – Ley, derechos, justicia.* Madrid: Editorial Trotta.

Judicial Function in Context: Contextualising *judicial activism* in the US Supreme Court and the European Court of Justice

TERESA VIOLANTE[1]

Introduction

The European Court of Justice (ECJ or Court of Justice) has been one of the primary actors in the construction of the "European project". Much has been written regarding its contribution to the creation of a common market as well as on the leadership it has assumed in the *de facto* constitutionalisation of the EU (Weiler 1994).[2]

The legitimacy of the ECJ and the methods through which it has taken upon itself such an incumbency in the absence of an unequivocal legislative mandate, have also been the object of considerable debate. The legal community (practitioners as well as some national, mainly constitutional, court), representatives of national political institutions and even of some of the EU's political representatives have occasionally levelled a great deal of criticism at the ECJ, its doctrine, and judicial philosophy. Accusations of illegitimate judicial activism, which see the ECJ as a *wild runner*, face on the other hand a permissive defence of its judicial

1 PhD candidate at Faculty of Law of the Universidade Nova, Lisbon, and Legal Clerk at the Portuguese Constitutional Court.

2 For a critical perspective of the landmark decisions, and in particular on direct effect, EU law supremacy, implied powers, and human rights jurisprudence, that set the roots for the "European legal order" see de Waele (2010).

practice based on the consideration that the ECJ is in an optimal position to decisively contribute to the consolidation of the EU's *acquis* by means of judicious hermeneutics. This latter view mainly includes descriptive approaches to the role that the ECJ has progressively taken in within the European framework, and chiefly focuses on integration through law.

An assessment of the existing literature reveals a significant propensity towards the acceptance of the main interpretive method that the ECJ has chosen. Such a method is based on teleological and *meta-teleological* considerations (Lasser 2004). However, such an acceptance rarely goes along with a systematic critical scrutiny of the ECJ's judicial choices. Instead, a considerable number of scholarly works justify this method with reference to the specificity of the political and institutional context in which the ECJ operates.

Nonetheless, accusations of judicial activism have been levelled with some frequency at the ECJ (Rasmussen 1986; Neill 1995). In order to cast more light on this topic I attempt a comparative contextualisation of the European and the US debates regarding the *activism* of the ECJ and of the US Supreme Court (USSCt or Supreme Court).

The role of the USSCt as constitutional adjudicator has been the object of in-depth analysis and discussion concerning *judicial activism*. The debate has yielded an extensive analytic output regarding the hermeneutical options available to the Court. Particular attention has been paid to its judicial legal reasoning in view of the role that the Court plays in the wider context of the three branches of constitutional power. This is a multifaceted analysis that comprises descriptive and normative accounts. Scholarly works range from eminently doctrinal and strictly internal (legal) perspectives to accounts that combine legal analysis with political science.

In the first section of this article, I review the essential aspects of the rise of the debate on judicial activism in the US and in Europe. In the second section, I focus on the need to contextualize analysis of the Courts in historical and political terms. In the third section, I review the essentials of American theories of constitutional interpretation and show the specific features of the European process of "constitutional interpretation" and its focus on *telos*. Finally, I show that in both debates specific *checks and balances* are brought up in order to justify judicial creativity in the face of *democratic inertia*. I claim that some discursive elements of the American case which are absent in Europe (such as the existence of dissenting or concurrent opinions) may ultimately affect the "persuasion pull" (Weiler 1994: 516) of the ECJ's decisions, requiring it to amend its current mode of reasoning.

Judicial activism

In this paper I am primarily concerned with the ECJ's role of constitutional adjudication. The premises underlying the comparison between the ECJ and the USSCt can be summarised as follows. Both courts are the higher instance of their legal orders, and both shoulder the responsibility of judicial review on the basis of founding documents. The fact that neither those founding documents nor any other constituent act bestows on them the whole range of competences that they have advocated to themselves has not hampered the development and broadening of their respective remits, which has happened in the end by jurisprudential means, not least because of the specific institutional and political contexts in which both courts operate. In particular, the review of national legislation has never been ascribed to the ECJ, as the review of federal legislation has never been ascribed to the American federal courts. Both in the American and in the European case, the activity of the courts led, or is leading, to the consolidation of the federalist process,[3] and gave, or are giving, a proactive impetus to it in the face of *democratic inertia*. More-

3 The doctrines of direct effect and supremacy of EU Law paved the way to a European "federal constitutionalism" as opposed to the traditional legal framework of an international organisation, devoid of any supranational character (Shapiro 2005: 210). On the constitutionalisation of the EU's legal order see in particular Eric Stein (1981) and Joseph H. H. Weiler (1999).

over, the specific context of checks and balances in which the courts operate requires an attentive scrutiny of what is, in practice, the margin of discretion of judicial activity.

The expression *judicial activism* has long crossed the boundaries of mainstream jurisprudence, and is now an integral part of everyday language. It is not, however, a mono-semantic concept, and the first hurdle that the debate had to overcome was the very definition of its own object: what is precisely meant by *judicial activism*? The strict delimitation of the concept is of key significance, for the loosely employed activist rhetoric is sometimes to be heard from different quarters with the purpose of condemning judicial rulings that one purely and simply disagrees with. In simplified terms, accusations of *judicial activism* can oftentimes be seen as a plain manifestation of disagreement towards an alleged replacement of exogenous criteria of adjudication by mere personal or internal preferences, based on political, moral or religious considerations.

A more elaborated approach focuses on the relationship between the judicial and the legislative branches, posing the question as to when the former should defer to the latter or practice self-restrain in view of the latter's margin of discretion. In other words, when should the judiciary intervene and overturn laws that are at odds with the fundamental norm from which all political power, in its wider sense, receives its legitimacy? The dominant operating classification sees, therefore, *judicial activism* as opposed to *judicial self-restraint*.

The judiciary and the other branches of power. The US American debate

The expression *judicial activism* has become commonplace since the second half of the last century. The debate regarding the relationship between the legislative and executive powers on the one hand and the judicial power on the other is, however, considerably older, and reaches as far back as to the origins of the US as an independent nation. This is due to the (judicial) development of judicial review, and to the interaction that it creates between the judiciary and the legislator.

In *Democracy in America* (1840), Alexis de Tocqueville described the American judge as being "vested with immense political power" (2004: 113) due to the authority bestowed on judges to review the constitutionality of laws. This task is antithetical to the Jacobin model of the mere *executive* or *declarative* judge who simply pronounces the law (Montesquieu 1995 [1748]: 164). Whereas this archetype relegates politics to the status of forbidden object within the judiciary field, the US model has, from its very inception, placed the judiciary within a sphere whose pursuits are as much political in nature as those of the legislative and executive branches of power. Whereas political power is exercised by democratically elected representatives with temporally limited tenures, Supreme Court justices are appointed to life tenures. These unelected appointees exert a counter-majoritarian function (Bickel 1986), which is central, to this day, to the debate on the legitimacy of the Court's role of constitutional interpretation.

As regards the principle of the separation of powers, the innovative feature in *Marbury v. Madison,* whose outcome consecrated in 1803 the Supreme Court's function of judicial review of federal legislation, is the fact that the USSCt's *dicta* in this area were implicitly imposed on both the legislative and the executive branches. Since the American Constitution establishes the equality of the three branches of government, it might be argued that all three would be granted equal powers of constitutional interpretation, and the interpretations of each of them should neither gain primacy nor be overturned by any of the other two. Judicial review raised the worry that the protection against "elected despotisms" of occasional majorities would ultimately result in the rule by a non-elected *aristocracy* (Hirschl 2004).

On the other hand, in *Federalist 78* (1788), Alexander Hamilton described the judicial power as "the least dangerous branch to the political rights of the Constitution." Such an innocuous nature would result from the fact that the Court did not possess any adequate mechanisms to secure the effectiveness and implementation of its rulings, depending in this respect on the goodwill of the executive branch. Hamilton's term was subsequently adopted by Alexander Bickel in his *The Least Dangerous Branch – The Supreme Court at the Bar of Politics* (1962). This latter work appeared at a moment when the USSCt civil rights case-law of the 1950s sparked intense debate about the justification of judicial review, due to the consolidation of the role and power of the USSCt that the Warren Court brought about.[4]

Bickel (1962) justifies judicial review as a defence against majorities and denies its anti-democratic nature. For Bickel, judicial review is first and foremost a defence of the Constitution. The democratic element is to be found therefore not only within the normal workings of the elected bodies, but also in the institution that guarantees the defence of the *people's* Constitution against majoritarian tyranny.

Similarly, Aharon Barak (2006: 238) underlines how much the role of the judiciary in current democracies lies essentially in the control of democratic majorities. The judiciary guarantees the observance of democratic values, in opposition to the legislative field if need be, but the latter retains the means to redress the balance. Thus the balance between self-restraint and legal interpretative discretion is maintained. Barak describes a constant dialogue between the judicial and the legislative powers.

The idea of a dialogue between the judiciary and political power is closely related to the US *doctrine of acquiescence*, according to which the legitimacy of jurisprudential advances may subsequently be confirmed when the legislator, when debating on the relevant matter, refrains from creating regulations opposite to that which had previously been defined by the court. Such legitimacy can be furthermore explicit, when legislative produc-

4 Mark Tushnet (2009: 138–139) sees in the *Cooper v. Aaron* ruling (1958) the exact moment at which the American system turned definitely into a *judicial supremacy*. In that ruling the Court stated that "the federal judiciary is supreme in the exposition of the law of the Constitution."

tion restates the content resulting from the court's ruling on a particular case.

In the US, *judicial supremacy* has been opposed by defenders of *departmentalism,* which contends that the equality between the three branches must be restored on the grounds that President and Congress would be equally entitled as constitutional interpreters. Thus, Edward Meese, President Reagan's Attorney-General, developed a strong defence of a *co-ordinate construction* theory. This theory implies that in case of particular constitutional disagreements each branch shall be granted its margin of interpretation, which should not be diminished by a different interpretation of another branch.

Several institutional means are available to restore the balance between the branches of power. These include the development of doctrines of self-restrain by the Court itself (such as the choice of the scrutiny level or the doctrine of political question), political mechanisms (such as the overruling of judicial decisions by federal legislation); the political appointment of judges, their impeachment, and the curtailment of the Court's appellate jurisdiction by Congress (Fischer 1988).

More than to formal mechanisms, the defence of a *co-ordinate construction* is more generally related to the theories of *constitutional dialogue,* which conceives judicial review as a sort of dialogue between the judiciary and the legislator. Notwithstanding the fact that the only formal mechanism that allows for a legislative overruling of a Supreme Court decision is the constitutional amendment, dialogue theories stress the existence of *informal* mechanisms that have allowed, in practice, such overruling without the need to resort such a cumbersome process.[5] These elements play a prominent role in the European debate.

5 See for instance Dahl (1957).

The legitimacy of the ECJ's activism: acquiescence

Accusations of judicial activism have also been frequently levelled at the ECJ. For many years, however, the law-making activity of the ECJ received little attention from the academic community. Although a few preceding studies on the topic do exist (Colin 1966; Stein 1978), the first major systematised study of the ECJ's influence on law and politics appeared no earlier than 1986, authored by Hjalte Rasmussen. Rasmussen claimed that the ECJ had pursued a federalist agenda by usurping powers that had not originally been conferred upon it by the founding treaties. For Rasmussen, *judicial policymaking* designates the courts'

> contribution to creating, conserving or changing public policies, or existing priorities among them, in areas of public policy which are subject to some sort of governmental regulation by binding rules of law (Rasmussen 1986: 4).

The *judicialization* of EU politics rests on two different mechanisms. Firstly, by establishing the direct effect of EU law, which binds both individuals and corporations, the ECJ has not only attracted the sympathies of vast and decentralised groups that support the enforcement of EU law, but also granted these a recourse which has now become an instrument to pressure national and European institutions (Dehousse 1998: 109–114). Nonetheless, the factor that most deeply impacted on the judicialization of European politics is perhaps the previously mentioned judicial review. In the ECJ case, however, this function is substantially different from its US counterpart. Whereas in the US the control of constitutionality has a counter-majoritarian function, in the European case it represents a mechanism in the service of the majority. As Maduro has pointed out,

> the European Court's constitutional activism was not faced with a traditional democratic representative body at EU level, and it has been directed mainly at national decisions that do not represent the majority in European terms. This is part of the peculiar nature of European judicial activism [...] (Maduro 1998: 11).

Maduro thus defines EU judicial activism as a "majoritarian activism".

Moreover, the role of the ECJ is to be analysed against the background of *constitutional pluralism* (Maduro 2003; Kumm 1999; Walker 2002). Constitutional pluralism defines a practice in which the use of different sources of law and reference to different legal traditions go along with an increased communication among national and supranational legal institutions. This is indeed a distinctive feature of the European legal system (Maduro 2007). In strictly legal terms, EU political institutions, member states, and their national institutions, are merely either the object or the recipients of ECJ's rulings. However, they are in fact interlocutors involved in a permanent dialogue with the Court. Such a practice frequently transforms the ECJ into an institution situated between the legal and the political sphere (Weiler 2004: 516). Therefore, besides the ECJ's role as law-maker, some authors have also pointed out its function as policy-maker (Rasmussen 1986). The political significance of its rulings stems not only from its creative legal function, but also from its political performative action. Thus, Dehousse (1998) has stressed the influence of the Court of Justice on agenda setting, policy innovation, and as catalyst of EU legislation. The "political review" of judicial activity (Reed 1995) is of key importance in order to gauge the ECJ's ability to step on political ground. The fact that the Council has thus far abstained from using its legislative powers to annihilate the impact of the ECJ's jurisprudence supports the idea that an ex-post legitimacy is bestowed on the latter through the reaction of the "countervailing powers". However, the effectiveness of this legitimacy criterion is still dependent on whether the political consensus necessary for legislative change can be reached. In the light of the constraints to which the institutional environment subjects the ECJ, some authors have nevertheless spoken of a "constrained independence" (Andersen and Glencross 2007: 9).

Against the background of such an institutional interdependence, a transposition of the doctrine of acquiescence to the ECJ is often argued for. Martin Shapiro writes, for example, that

> the member-states acquiesced in the transposition of the treaties from international law into constitutional documents not by debate and vote, but by silent acceptance by their elected governments and case-by-case obedience by their own court (Shapiro 2006: 210).

Similarly, Rasmussen highlights how the legitimacy of judicial policymaking can be assessed on the basis of other players' (such as Council, national courts, legislatives and executives, independent expert opinion, and public opinion) responses to it in the *communitarian game*. In the end, Rasmussen legitimises the ECJ's activity as a counter to *democratic inertia,* inasmuch as difficulties in obtaining the political consensus necessary to pass new legislation shift the onus of furthering integration onto the judicial sphere (Rasmussen 1986: 70–74).[6] The Court should return to self-restrain whenever legislative inertia and impasse would end.[7] Nonetheless, as Weiler points out,

> [t]he question of doctrinal content – the interpretative claim made by the Court – is only part of the picture. It must be followed by an enquiry into the 'persuasion pull' and 'compliance pull' which such doctrinal claims can evoke (Weiler 2004: 516).

Several informal means are available to the member states, Commission and Council to reject the ECJ's jurisprudence. One need only think of the most extreme scenario of the refusal to comply with a ruling or of concerted political measures within the Council. Limitations of the ECJ's activity can also be achieved through *ex ante* measures, as is the case with the second and third pillars, which were summarily subtracted from the jurisdiction of the Court

6 This difficulty has been pointed out by other authors. Miguel Poiares Maduro mentions for instance that "[...] the incapacity to reach decisions in the political forum has left judicial institutions with the responsibility for solving political conflicts" (Maduro 1998: 17).

7 Rasmussen's argument did not go unquestioned. In response, Mauro Cappelletti (1987) pointed out that legal indeterminacy, an inescapable property of law, necessarily involves a margin of interpretative discretion. Weiler (1987) accused Rasmussen's hypothesis of promoting judicial opportunism, leaving the ECJ dependent on the transitory contingencies expressed in the responses of the countervailing powers.

of Justice. However, the extension of the jurisdiction of the ECJ operated by the Lisbon Treaty significantly curtails such pre-emptive constraints on the Court. One must only bear in mind the legally binding nature of the Charter of Fundamental Rights as well as the fact that criminal justice and police co-operation, formerly covered by the third pillar, are now subject to the Court's review.

Despite the several sources of conflict, a general goodwill characterises the relationships between the ECJ and the various national actors, which was only occasionally characterised by controversy. This may come as a surprise, but it may also be understood as an *ex post* legitimisation of legal activity. As Weiler has noted, "[...] the measure of the success of the Court is the almost sacrosanct nature of the venerable *acquis* of the Community vindicated and validated again and again at each IGC" (Weiler 2003: 151). Weiler maintains that the most effective reply to the hermeneutically and normatively powerful arguments raised by Rasmussen's is empirical, and consists in "[t]he remarkable success of the ECJ in persuading the key constituencies in the member states" (Weiler 2006: 22).

The legitimacy of the ECJ's activism: interpretive rationality

According to principle-based and interpretivist theories, the legitimacy of the judicial review stems not only from the necessity to defend the Constitution but also from the *discursive rationality* that underlies constitutional adjudication (Bickel 1962; Rawls 2005: 223–240; Dworkin 2005). The claim is that only the Court possesses the necessary conditions to rule on matters of principle, for only the judicial branch is sufficiently distanced from political pressures to guarantee that its decisions are exclusively *principle-based* (Dworkin 1996).

Alongside theories of discursive rationality, the need to interpret constitutional texts and principles is a further justification of judicial review. Constitutional documents are formulated at an extremely abstract level. This, as well as the fact that constitutional texts and amendments are embedded in a historical context, makes it difficult to pin down any ostensible meaning. The interpretive leeway that results from such indeterminacy poses methodological concerns, regardless of which theory of constitutional interpretation is adopted.

Some authors contend that such a view of constitutional interpretation is actually blueprint for the judiciary's "creative" activity (Bork 2003; Posner 2003). The most sophisticated response to these principle-based theories is given by *originalism*. The originalist thesis proposes that only an interpretation of the Constitution guided by the specific intent of the Framers can avoid illegitimate judicial rulings based on merely personal choices (Scalia 1997).

On the other hand, theories of the *living constitution* reject the relevance of the historical moment of constitutional entrenchment, and argue that it is up for the judiciary to promote an interpretative update of the higher law.[8] Other theories focus on the pivotal role of judicial minimalism or self-restraint (Sunstein 2001; Waldron 2009).

Constitutional interpretation has been the object of an inexhaustible debate which transcends the academic boundaries. In the US, the debate involves also social movements, political officers and members of the judiciary, including some members of the Supreme Court, who advocate particular theories (Scalia 1997; Breyer 2008), which they subsequently call on to justify specific rulings or opinions.

As to the European case, through the mechanism of reference for preliminary ruling the ECJ has checked on the "constitutionality" (i.e. the conformity with the higher law) of both secondary EU law and of national law right from the outset. The parameters of control, in the first case, are the Treaties and, in the second case, both the Treaties and secondary EU law. Although

8 In a recent work Jack Balkin (2011) has argued that originalism and evolutive interpretation are not necessarily antagonistic.

it is possible to identify disparities in the deference shown by the ECJ towards the European legislator and national legislators (Eeckhout 2000; Reich 2012), the interpretive complexity brings about a complex power-play that can ensue between the ECJ, on the one hand, and national and European legislative bodies, on the other.

As is the case with the US Constitution, the EU founding documents also present considerable difficulties on a linguistic level. The context of their ratification offers no relevant contribution towards a consensus as to the scope of their norms.[9] Being the result of a consensus reached at intergovernmental summits, their content clearly represents the political compromise that was possible to reach when they were drafted. Some authors contend, in fact, that it is the very nature of the treaties that stimulates the ECJ's creative activity, for these are essentially policy papers, which define in fairly general and abstract terms the political objectives to be attained without supplying, however, any guidelines or precise definitions as to how these objectives are to be reached in this newly-fashioned institutional framework (Pollicino 2004; Reed 1995: 15). Their rather cryptic language and brevity requires an ingenious and creative interpretative activity, very much alike to the one often employed by the US Supreme Court. The particular nature of the treaties and of the European legislative process, and the multilingual nature of EU law (Derlén 2009; Mancini 2000: 177–178) have been decisive for the choice of the methods of interpretation adopted by the ECJ.[10]

The ECJ's judicial function essentially consists in the supervision of the constitutionality of European directives. The ECJ's mandate in this area is twofold: the interpretative task and the con-

9 For a contrary view see Gerard Conway (2012: 247).

10 The European debate on "constitutional interpretation" does not match the intensity of the American discussion. Instead of focusing on theories of interpretation, it has been directed at the Court's "methods of interpretation". As an exception see Maduro (1998), who attempted the formulation of a normative theory that the Court of Justice had itself been unable or unwilling to formulate.

trol of constitutionality *per se*. The interpretive method adopted by the ECJ is of the utmost importance in appreciating and understanding its jurisprudence. Throughout its existence, the ECJ has understandably employed several interpretative methods. A clear preference for the teleological or "purposive" method and a lesser consideration of the historical element than its US counterpart can nonetheless be identified. The teleological method allows the ECJ to follow the political and normative development of the system, through the Preamble to the Treaty and the general principles of EU law (Bengoetxea 1993; Maduro 2007).

The reasoning behind the decisions is presented according to a formalistic model, with its impersonal style based on an "apparently deductive form of reasoning and a distinctly magisterial tone" (Lasser 2004: 103). The adoption of this formalistic model is consistent with the method of adjudication traditionally followed by the majority of the judicial bodies of the member states, and serves the additional purpose of projecting the appearance of neutrality that the Court of Justice has been keen to maintain. Nonetheless, the publication within the text of the Advocate General's opinion, with its fairly disparate discursive style, allows for the inclusion of an internal element of contention, thus contributing to its legitimization.

The ECJ in context

Both the American and the European debate on judicial activism focus on how creatively each court interprets the fundamental provisions and how legitimately interferes with the choices of the legislative and executive powers. In both cases, several scholars refer to the institutional context of checks and balances in order to justify and even demand the creative action of the judiciary. Such specific checks and balances not only allow for the development of an active judicial agenda, but may also be regarded as a constraint on the courts' own activities.

The difficulties inherent to constitutional change frequently translate political conflicts onto the judicial arena. Political actors can avail themselves of formal and informal mechanisms in order to restore the balance of powers whenever they regard the Court's activity as pernicious. Although the unanimity required in Council at the level of primary law rule represents a considerable element of constraint governmental counter-action,[11] it should be noted that the ECJ has shown a considerable capacity of persuasion, and has often met with the goodwill of national actors. In effect, in contrast to the USSCt, the ECJ lacks the institutional authority inherent to any court integrated within a national legal system.

The differences between the US American and the European debate are also interesting. The originalist or historical element has received much greater emphasis in the American than in the European discourse. The fact that the Treaty of Rome was essentially an international treaty and the secrecy that for a considerable period surrounded the *travaux preparatoires* have made the task of estimating the original intentions of the founders rather onerous. Furthermore, there is a broad consensus in support of the teleological method of interpretation as being the most adequate to the ECJ's functions. The specific European context also seems to undermine the flourishing of dialogue theories that took place among American scholars. Traditionally, such theories are focused on the distinction between law-making and adjudication within a typical state architecture. The ECJ's *constitutional activ-*

---

11 The overruling of judgments at the level of secondary law is not an easy task, either. As de Waele maintains, "[...] secondary law can of course often be adopted by a qualified majority of the Council. Due to the hierarchy of norms, such rules are however of little use when the desire is to counter unwelcome ECJ interpretations of primary law. Moreover, the Commission would have to propose such measures, Parliament would have to approve as well, and the attainment of even a qualified majority can still prove rather difficult. The recent hardships experienced in the attempted adoption of a new Working Time Directive, necessitated by the Court's judgment in Case C-151/02, Landeshauptstadt Kiel v Norbert Jaeger, [2003] ECR I-8389, illustrate the general point" (de Waele 2010: 15, fn 53).

ism is usually directed against a particular member state who does not account alone for the legislative power, which resides either in all member states collectively (on the level of treaties), or on the EU's competent bodies (on the level of secondary law). This rules out any possible formal reaction by single member states on the decisions they may consider illegitimate. Such a reaction could only be attained if a broad consensus is reached among the member states. Informal mechanisms are scarcely available to individual member states. Besides the drastic scenario of disobedience, only political pressure inside EU institutions is viable. This may account for the fact that dialogue metaphors have emerged in European literature only with respect to relationships between courts.

Unlike in the US, members of the ECJ do not tend to participate in the debate regarding the Court's methods of interpretation, nor do they publicly discuss the functions that this institution should exercise within the European institutional framework. The secret nature of the ECJ's deliberation process, the requirement that in case of majority vote any minority remain officially silent, the fact that no dissenting opinions are ever issued, and the explicit obligation not to reveal the content of the discussions leading to the deliberation, all this makes sure that important elements of judgement are subtracted from the scrutiny of the European public, unlike in the US.[12] As a consequence, legal and political communities are often left to speculate on the real motivations behind ECJ's decisions.

Nevertheless, the ECJ retains the responsibility of operating in a context of constitutional pluralism in which the risk of clashes with national, and in particular constitutional, courts permanently threatens the balance of the European legal order. The ECJ has therefore every interest in strengthening its persuasive capacity. If the traditional formalistic style has previously proven adequate to the integration process, it is nonetheless the case that the frequently cited democratic deficit (to which the ECJ also ultimately

12 These features also impair studies on judicial behaviour which are frequent in the American focus on the Supreme Court. See Shapiro (2006: 200).

falls prey)[13] may require new approaches to legal decision-making. On the style of ECJ judgments, Weiler wrote:

> I think the Court should abandon the cryptic, Cartesian style which still characterizes many of its decisions and move to the more discursive, analytic and conversational style associated more with the common law world – though practiced by others as well, notably the German Constitutional court. [...] Especially in its Constitutional jurisprudence, it is crucial that the Court displays in its judgments that national sensibilities were fully considered and taken into account. And it must amply explain and reason its decisions if they are to be not only authoritarian but also authoritative. The Cartesian style with its pretence of logical legal reasoning and inevitability of results is not conducive to a good conversation with national courts. In the same vein, I would argue for the introduction of separate and dissenting opinions. One of the virtues of separate and dissenting opinions is that they force the majority opinion to be reasoned in an altogether more profound and communicative fashion. The dissent often produces the paradoxical effect of legitimating the majority because it becomes evident that alternative views were considered even if ultimately rejected (Weiler 2001: 225).

Such a change of style may not be limited to the rulings themselves, but also to the manner in which these are received by the legal community in general. A growing interest for a normative approach that is critical of the ECJ's jurisprudence (Conway 2012; de Waele 2010; Weiler 1994) may demand a different approach to the "persuasion pull" (Weiler 1994: 516) of the Court's decisions. If this is the case, perhaps the premises behind the ECJ's current mode of reasoning will find themselves being decidedly questioned in the future.

---

13 Weiler contends that the ECJ is not only a victim of the democratic deficit but also the cause of this same problem: "[w]hatever the hermeneutic legitimacy of reaching supremacy and direct effect, the interaction of these principles with the non-democratic decision making process is, to put it mildly, highly problematic [...]. The paradox is thus that the legitimacy challenge to the Court's constitutional jurisprudence does not rest as often has been assumed in its hermeneutics – a good outcome based on a questionable interpretation. But quite the opposite: An unassailable interpretation but an outcome which underpins, supports and legitimates a highly problematic decisional process" (Weiler 2006: 125).

References

ALTER, Karen (2008), Agents or Trustees? International Courts in their Political Context. *European Journal of International Relations*, Vol. 14, N. 1, pp. 33–63.

ANDERSEN, Stine, and Andrew GLENCROSS (2007), Pre-Empting the Court: member state Expectations, Political Oversight and the Nexus of Law and Politics in the EU. Paper Presented at the EUSA Biennial Conference, Montreal, 17–19 May, 2007, available at: http://www.unc.edu/euce/eusa2007/papers/glencross-a-01c.pdf (last accessed October 11, 2012).

BALKIN, Jack (2011), *Living Originalism*. Cambridge: Harvard University Press.

BARAK, Aharon (2006), *The Judge in a Democracy*. Princeton: Princeton University Press.

BENGOETXEA, Joxerramon (1993), *The Legal Reasoning of the European Court of Justice – Towards a European Jurisprudence*. Oxford: Clarendon Press.

BICKEL, Alexander M. (1986), *The Least Dangerous Branch – The Supreme Court at the Bar of Politics*. New Haven: Yale University Press.

BORK, Robert (2003), *Coercing Virtue. The Worldwide Rule of Judges*, Washington: The AEI Press.

BREDIMAS, Anna (1978), *Methods of Interpretation and Community Law*, Oxford: North-Holland Pub.

BREYER, Stephen (2008), *Active Liberty: Interpreting a Democratic Constitution*, Oxford: Oxford Univ. Press.

CAPPELLETTI, Mauro (1987), Is the European Court of Justice Running Wild?. *European Law Review*, N. 12, pp. 3–17.

COLIN, Jean-Pierre (1966), *Le gouvernement des juges dans les Communautées Éuropéenes*. Paris: Librarie génerale de droit et de jurisprudence.

CONWAY, Gerard (2012), *The Limits of Legal Reasoning and the European Court of Justice*. Cambridge: Cambridge University Press.

DAHL, Robert (1957), Decision-Making in a Democracy: The Supreme Court as a National Policy-Maker. *Journal of Public Law*, N. 6, pp. 279–295.

DEHOUSSE, Renaud (1998), *The European Court of Justice. The Politics of Judicial Integration*. London: Macmillan Press.

DERLÉN, Matias (2009), *Multilingual Interpretation of European Union Law*. Alphen aan den Rijn: Kluwer Law.

DWORKIN, Ronald (2005), *Taking Rights Seriously*. London: Duckworth.

— (1996), *A Matter of Principle*. Oxford: Clarendon Press.

EECKHOUT, Piet (2000), The European Court of Justice and the legislature. *Yearbook of European Law*, N. 18, pp. 1–18.

FISCHER, Louis (1988), *Constitutional Dialogues. Interpretation as Political Process*. Princeton: Princeton University Press.

HAMILTON, Alexander, James MADISON and John JAY (2009), *The Federalist.* Cambridge: The Belknap Press.
HIRSCHL, Ran (2004), *Towards Juristocracy – The Origins and Consequences of the New Constitutionalism.* Cambridge: Harvard University Press.
KOMESAR, Neil (1994), *Imperfect Alternatives. Choosing Institutions in Law, Economics and Public Policy.* Chicago: The University of Chicago Press.
KUMM, Mathias (1999), Who is the Final Arbiter of Constitutionality in Europe?. *Common Market Law Review,* Vol. 36, N. 2, pp. 351–386.
LASSER, Mitchel (2004), *Judicial deliberations: A Comparative Analysis of Judicial Transparency and Legitimacy.* Oxford: Oxford University Press.
MANCINI, G. Federico (2000), *Democracy and Constitutionalism in the EU.* Oxford: Hart.
NEILL, Patrick (1995), *The European Court of Justice: A Case Study in Judicial Activism.* London: European Policy Forum.
MADURO, Miguel Poiares (1998), *We, The Court. The European Court of Justice & the European Economic Constitution – A Critical Reading of Article 30 of the EC Treaty.* Oxford: Hart Publishing.
— (2003), Contrapunctual Law: Europe's Constitutional Pluralism in Action. In Neil Walker (ed.), *Sovereignty in Transition.* Oxford: Hart, pp. 501–537.
— (2007), Interpreting European Law: Judicial Adjudication in a Context of Constitutional Pluralism. *European Journal of Legal Studies,* Vol. 1, N. 2, pp. 1–21.
MONTESQUIEU, Charles de (1995 [1748]), *The Spirit of the Laws* (transl. Anne M. Cohler, Basia Carolyn Miller, Harold Samuel Stone). Cambridge: Cambridge University Press.
POLLICINO, Oreste (2004), Legal reasoning of the Court of Justice in the context of the principle of equality between judicial activism and self-restraint. *German Law Journal,* N. 3, pp. 283–317.
POSNER, Richard (2003), *The Problems of Jurisprudence.* Cambridge: Harvard University Press.
RASMUSSEN, Hjalte (1986), *On Law and Policy in the European Court of Justice: A Comparative Study in Judicial Policymaking.* Dorderecht: Martinus Nijhoff Publishers.
RAWLS, John (2005), *Political Liberalism.* New York: Columbia University Press.
REED, J.W.R. (1995), Political Review of the European Court of Justice and its Jurisprudence. *Jean Monnet Working Papers,* N. 1, available at: http://centers.law.nyu.edu/jeanmonnet/archive/papers/95/9513ind.html (last accessed October 11, 2012).
REICH, Norbert (2012), How Proportionate is the Proportionality Principle? Some critical remarks on the use and methodology of the proportionality principle in the internal market case law of the ECJ. In Micklitz, Hans-Wolfgang, Bruno de Witte (eds.), *The European Court of Justice and the Autonomy of the member states.* Cambridge: Intersentia, pp. 83–111.

SCALIA, Antonin (1997), *A Matter of Interpretation*. Princeton: Princeton University Press.

SHAPIRO, Martin (2005), Rights in the European Union: Convergent with the USA? In Nicolas, Jabko, Craig Parsons (eds.), *The State of the European Union: With US or Against US? European Trends in American Perspective*, Volume 7. Oxford: Oxford University Press, pp. 371–390.

— (2006), The US Supreme Court and the European Court of Justice Compared. In Anan Menon & Martin A. Schain (eds.), *Comparative Federalism: The European Union and the United States in Comparative Perspective*. Oxford: Oxford University Press, pp. 195–220.

STEIN, Eric (1981), Lawyers, Judges and the making of a Transnational Constitution. *The American Journal of International Law*, Vol. 7, N. 1, pp. 1–27.

SUNSTEIN, Cass (2001), *One Case at a Time: Judicial Minimalism in the Supreme Court*. Cambridge: Harvard Univ. Press.

TOCQUEVILLE, Alexis de (2004 [1840]), *Democracy in America*, New York: Library of America.

TUSHNET, Mark (2009), *The Constitution of the United States of America – A Contextual Analysis*. Oxford: Hart Publishing.

DE WAELE, Henri (2010), The Role of the European Court of Justice in the Integration Process: A Contemporary and Normative Assessment. *Hanse Law Review*, 6(1), pp. 3–26.

WALKER, Neil (2002), The Idea of Constitutional Pluralism. *Modern Law Review*, Vol. 65, N. 3, pp. 317–359.

WEILER, Joseph H.H. (1987), The Court of Justice on Trial. *Common Market Law Review*, N. 24, pp. 555–589.

— (1993), Journey to an Unknown Destination: A Retrospective and Prospective of the European Court of Justice in the Arena of Political Integration. *Journal of Common Market Studies*, Vol. 31, N. 4, pp. 417–446.

— (1999), *The Constitution of Europe: "Do the New Clothes Have an Emperor?" and other essays on European integration*. Cambridge: Cambridge University Press.

— (2003), Rewriting Van Gend en Loos: Towards a Normative Theory of ECJ Hermeneutics. In O. Wiklund (ed.), *Judicial Discretion in European Perspective*. Dordrecht: Kluwer, pp. 150–163.

— (1994), A Quiet Revolution: The European Court of Justice and its Interlocutors. *Comparative Political Studies*, Vol. 26, N. 4, pp. 510–534.

— (2006), The Essential (and Would-Be Essential) Jurisprudence of the European Court of Justice: Lights and Shadows Too. In Ingolf Pernice, Juliane Kokott, Cheryl Saunders (eds.): *The Future of the European Judicial System in a Comparative Perspective*. Baden-Baden: Nomos Verlag, pp. 117–127.

— (2001), The Judicial Après Nice. In J.H.H. Weiler, Gráinne de Búrca, *The European Court of Justice*. New York: Oxford University Press, pp. 215–226.

Section IV
Expectations and Reality

The Charter of Fundamental Rights After Its First Decade: Legal Impact and Political Consequences

A Conversation with MIGUEL POIARES MADURO[1]

Prof. Maduro, over the past ten years you have repeatedly dealt with the Charter of Fundamental Rights of the European Union (CFR) both in your scholarly work and as Advocate General at the European Court of Justice (ECJ). Your initial view was that the Charter was shred in a peculiar ambiguity: it could be seen either as an instrument to guarantee that the powers of the Union conform to the fundamental rights of member states, or it could be seen as a first and decisive step towards a genuine component of a true constitutional project. In the first case, the Charter would impose a limitation on the legislative acts of European institutions, whereas in the latter it would mainly work as an instrument of further political integration of a federalist type. The one does not rule out the other, but from a political point of view the two options reflect the well-documented, contradictory intentions and political wills that stood behind the adoption of the Charter. How do you assess this alternative ten years after its drafting?

In my view we have not witnessed a resolution of that ambiguity. If anything, such an ambiguity has grown. The Charter has nei-

1 Miguel Poiares Maduro is Professor at the Department of European Law and Director of the Global Governance Programme of the Robert Schuman Centre for Advanced Studies, European University Institute, Florence. He served as Advocate General at the European Court of Justice in Luxembourg from 2003 to 2009 and is Founding Editor in Chief of the Journal *Global Constitutionalism* (Cambridge University Press). The interview was conducted by Gabriele De Angelis with the contribution of Paulo Barcelos and Giovanni Damele.

ther predominantly become a tool for further political integration, nor has it put a limit to it. Instead, the ambiguity has grown in both senses. In part, it is even a product of the Charter and of the use that has been made of it, and it's even more the result of the political evolution of the European Union. This evolution has only made that tension more acute, more real, and also clearer. When the French government took certain steps that were considered a limitation to the rights of Roma people in France,[2] the reactions have been indicative in this respect. People used the rhetoric of the Charter, they mentioned the Charter to argue that the European Union should intervene either to sanction France or to restrain the action of the French government. And yet, on the basis of a strictly legal interpretation it is not at all clear whether the Charter is intended to endow the Union with the competence to intervene in member states' internal matters concerning fundamental rights.

Something similar is happening in Hungary.[3] Also in this case we can develop legal arguments to support the thesis that the UE does have a competence and a jurisdiction to intervene even in the internal matters of that state, if fundamental rights are affected. In the light of what has been the case law of the European Court of Justice, there are nevertheless other cases in which it is more difficult to make that argument. In spite of all this, we witness ever more insisting claims that the European Union must do something to grant the respect of fundamental rights even inside

2 In 2010 the French government deported around ten thousand Romanians and Bulgarians of Roma ethnicity, also destroying a great number of illegal camps. Following those events, in September 2010 the European Commission, through the voice of Commissioner Viviane Reding, warned France that it could face an infringement procedure for breaching the principle of freedom of movement. The case was not initiated.

3 In the aftermath of the 2010 parliamentary election, the coalition between the Fidesz Party of Prime Minister Viktor Orban and the Christian Democratic People's Party made pass a new electoral law, new procedures for appointing officials of the judiciary, alterations in the Electoral Commission and the central bank, as well as a new regulation of the media. These measures were seen as authoritarian and raised therefore consistent worries in numerous EU member states.

member states, and this happens with direct reference to the Charter and to the idea that the protection of fundamental rights is of paramount importance for European identity.

At the same time, we become aware of growing concerns from within member states regarding the scope of EU competences, and the Euro crisis may have well made such concerns even more acute. It is therefore no wonder that the Charter is sometimes also used as an argument to protect the diversity and identity of member states. In this respect, in political discourse the Charter is referred to in order to restrain EU powers. Such a consequence of the Charter's adoption is all the more remarkable inasmuch as the Court itself has enhanced its degree of judicial scrutiny of EU legal acts regarding fundamental rights violations. Kadi[4] is a case, but we have others. In virtue of the Charter, the Court feels possibly more empowered in this respect.

So, I still see the Charter as furthering European integration and giving enhanced powers to the European Union to intervene in the member states' domestic affairs whenever fundamental rights may be affected. On the other hand, the Charter is being used in order to restrain the power of the European Union. I think both uses have been made, and the importance of both of them

---

4 *Yassin Abdullah Kadi and Al Barakaat International Foundation v Council and Commission* (JOINED CASES C-402/05 P AND C-415/05 P, September 2008). The Kadi case witnessed a clash between two legal systems: Community law and international law, in particular a United Nations Security Council Resolution (1267, 1999) requiring that the assets of suspects of terrorist activities be frozen. The ECJ declared that such a measure would have breached fundamental rights as protected in the European legal space, and therefore could not be applied. The ECJ based its ruling on the separateness and autonomy of the Community's legal system, stating that "an international agreement cannot affect the allocation of powers fixed by the Treaties" (para 282). Miguel Poiares Maduro was the appointed ECJ's Advocate General for this case. He stated, in the same vein that the "relationship between international law and the Community's legal order is governed by the Community legal order itself, and international law can permeate that legal order only under the conditions set by the constitutional principles of the Community" (*Opinion of Advocate General Poiares Maduro, Case C-415/05 P*, delivered on 23 January 2008).

has grown. We still have to deal with a tension between those two consequences of the Charter, and we still have to answer the question as to the reason why we want fundamental rights protection at EU level. Do we want them to restrain EU powers, or do we also want them as a further competence that we assign to EU institutions in order to limit member states powers whenever they happen to violate fundamental rights? That tension is now even more present than it was when the Charter was adopted.

Allow me an additional question: the ambiguity that you pointed out seems to stem from a "dissonance" between a strictly legal implementation of the Charter as regards the review of EU legislation, and the Charter's "political" implementation as regards what happens inside the member states in terms of fundamental rights protection. In this latter case a kind of "moral suasion" or forms of political pressure seem to take place, and not legal action properly.

Well, let's put it like this. The Court of Justice has developed the idea that fundamental rights are part of the general principles of EU law, and it has done so to review acts of EU institutions, not of member states. This is well known. So, the EU had no competence with respect to fundamental rights as far as member states are concerned. This is, instead, the domain of the Council of Europe, the Convention for the Protection of Human Rights and Fundamental Freedoms. Now, it's well known that even in the ECJ case law, the Court slowly expanded fundamental rights review also to cover national acts, but did so in a limited fashion. The Charter does not seem to increase the scope of these interventions. If anything, the opposite is true, for the Charter is very clear in this respect, and states explicitly that it applies to European Union institutions and to Member-States while they implement EU law.[5] Therefore, it does not extend to member states actions as long as they are not applying EU law. Such is the legal level of EU-wide protection that the Charter basically makes possible. That seems, by the way, to narrow down the scope of inter-

5 CFRUE, Art. 51.

vention in comparison to the traditional case laws of the ECJ. Fundamental rights "exist" mostly by means of its legal provisions on their scope of application in the European communities. The RCJ seems to endorse the position according to which that the Charter is aimed at guaranteeing that the actions of European institutions do not violate fundamental rights, and does not primarily address member states.

That said, the political project behind the Charter was much more ambitious. It aimed to establish values that would reflect European identity, and European identity had to rest primarily, or at least to a considerable extent, on the protection of fundamental rights. The tension that we detect between the extensive and the restrictive implementation of the Charter with regard to the integration process stems from the fact that the "original" project represents sort of an appeal for an EU-wide fundamental rights protection beyond its traditionally limited scope of application. So, the political project of the Charter, thus considered, is somehow at odds with the intended legal scope of the latter. Surely, that doesn't mean that these two aspects are fully independent of one another. I don't see them as strictly separated. In the US, the Bill of Rights was initially adopted to be applied only to the federal government. It was the Supreme Court that incorporated it into the due process clause that was applied also to the states. Therefore it now applies most of the Bill of Rights also to the states. Analogously, it is possible to consider domestic violations of fundamental rights as violations of other EU provisions. For example, we can say that in a state with no freedom of expression the free movement of persons is not guaranteed either. As a matter of fact, who wants to go and live in a state where you cannot enjoy your freedom of expression?

Thus, it is possible to make legal arguments to expand the scope of application of EU fundamental rights protection. As far as I can see, the Charter prompts political claims that conversely promote the extension of the Charter's application into the internal sphere of the states. A dynamic arises that leads to the adoption and endorsement of legal interpretations of existent provisions that expand their scope of application in this sense. So, although the Charter's legal scope was originally much narrower than the political ambitions would have wished, this does not mean that the political dimension of the Charter will not end up affecting the interpretation of EU rules with regard to member states' actions in such a way as to extend its legal scope.

Nevertheless, this tension is still there. This may either create a risk of a gap, in the sense that the Charter generates public expectations and political claims that are not legally viable, or its legal scope may indeed broaden. If the latter occurs, this will not be without risks, contestations, and conflict, either.

Despite the ambiguous nature of the Charter and the double reading that could be given of it you have repeatedly stated that we should not expect any dramatic change in the standard of fundamental rights protection in Europe. Is this still your opinion or do you see any innovation that the Charter may have brought along in this respect?

That depends of what you mean by standard of fundamental rights. In a narrow sense, by this we may intend the degree of judicial scrutiny that is exercised in reviewing measures restrictive of a certain fundamental right. This would be the "highest" standard of protection in judicial terms. And yet, a different, but relevant aspect of your question concerns the scope of application of fundamental rights protection, that is, the set of circumstances to which it is applicable. From this point of view, I certainly think that the pressure is on the Court to expand the scope of application of the Charter. The examples I gave you regarding France and Hungary (there are many others, though) speak to the point. Noteworthy are also cases in which matters of citizenship are seen in immediate conjunction with fundamental rights, such as Zambrano, McCarthy and the like,[6] in which the Court is being

6 Both the Zambrano (Zambrano vs. Office national de l'Emploi, C-34/09) and the McCarthy (McCarthy vs. SSHD, C-434/09) cases concern the free movement of EU citizens for assisting family members who are third country nationals. In the Zambrano case the Court asserted that national measures limiting the free movement of persons so as to deprive EU nationals of the

pushed towards applying fundamental rights to a much broader set of circumstances, including domestic ones that would have traditionally been outside the jurisdiction of the European Union institutions. So, there has been some extension to the scope of application of fundamental rights protection in Europe, but to a limited extent.

The reason why it is, and I believe will remain, limited, is workload. This is the most significant constrain to EU institutions' having as clear a saying in matters of fundamental rights as have national institutions. If the Court would someday say "yes, we will also review issues of fundamental rights in the domestic sphere of the member states with respect to the Charter", if the Court would say that, it would be overloaded with cases. It would be unworkable for the judicial system as it is today. So, if we want the Court to play a larger role in the protection of fundamental rights also inside the member states, we need to rethink the judicial system, because otherwise it will not work, it will not come to terms with the challenge for practical reasons.

The same can be said of the standard of protection. Again, the Court is applying a higher level of scrutiny, and I believe this is not only a consequence of the Charter, although due to the Charter the Court is not simply enforcing fundamental rights that the Court itself has developed as part of the general principles and the common constitutional tradition of member states, which, in terms of legitimacy, will always be more subject to contestation. Now the Court says "We are enforcing the Charter, we are applying the Charter". As a consequence, the Court is additionally empowered in that respect, and can exercise an additional degree of judicial scrutiny.

"genuine enjoyment of the substance of the rights attaching to the status of European Union citizen" were disallowed. The case dealt in particular with two children of Belgian nationality, whose parents (two Colombian asylum seekers) had been ordered by Belgian authorities to leave the country. In the McCarthy case the Court further specified the first ruling, limiting its application to cases in which national measures impact on rights anchored in EU law.

But there are two other circumstances, in my view, to explain the stronger degree of judicial scrutiny and therefore the higher standard of fundamental rights protection that the Court can now afford. One is the fact that the European Union is increasingly intervening in areas in which questions of fundamental rights do require a higher degree of judicial scrutiny, such as immigration, criminal or quasi-criminal sanctions, and individual freedoms. As long as the EU areas of competence were mostly limited to the internal market and economic regulation, the courts, including national constitutional courts, often allowed in those areas a much larger margin of discretion to the political process. Given the new competences of the EU in areas such as internal justice, freedom, and security, the ECJ is more expected to exercise a stronger degree of judicial intervention when fundamental rights are at stake.

There is a further important source of evolution of the ECJ that we need to take into account. As the EU moves from a unanimity-based towards a majority-based system, that is, as decision making takes more and more the form of majority decision, the Court is likely to play an increased counter-majority role. We could say that while the EU political process has been operating in a logic of unanimity, its internal constrains in terms of decision making were very high. There were therefore several mechanisms of control that were built into the political process itself. As the system becomes more and more majoritarian, the court may need to protect minorities in terms of fundamental rights respect.

You repeatedly said that you expected an increased level of litigation at EU level due to the entrenchment of fundamental rights by means of the Charter. Do you see any substantial sign of this in recent legal practice?

I haven't made any empirical study in this respect. It would be interesting if someone worked out how many times fundamental rights have been claimed before the court in the course of the years. The anecdotal evidence I have is that they have indeed increased. The use of legal arguments based on fundamental rights as a reason for challenging either a national or a EU decision before the ECJ has increased after the Charter came into effect. That's my perception, at least.

On the basis of what I said before, The Charter was likely to create this kind of dynamic because of the political claims that went along with the entrenchment of fundamental rights. So, I'm not surprised. This puts the Court under the pressure that I have mentioned before [to extend the scope of judicial review]. But the Court is very careful, sometimes it seems that it's ready to expand the scope of application of fundamental rights, sometimes it narrows it down. This has to do with the institutional restriction I've mentioned earlier on: workload. The court could not work if it had a general jurisdiction on fundamental rights. It would be overloaded and blocked.

European institutions as well as actors from civil society see in the progressive acquisition of ever new competences by European institutions a chance to broaden their own overall sphere of influence. For instance, once the Commission includes gender equality among its competences, the temptation to do the same for other fundamental rights almost naturally arises. This has been observed several times in the course of EU studies. Indeed, the method used to draft the Charter, the emphasis that the drafting Convention put on including actors from civil society, shows exactly this mechanism. This may perhaps account for the fact that many actors involved in the process of drafting the Charter as well as many of those who then pushed for its formal adoption and inclusion in the Treaties seemed to consider it more as a political than a legal document. Do you think this piecemeal nature of the Charter made any difference in its effectiveness or coherence in the light of its subsequent legal implementation?

I would say that the piecemeal nature is not so much a characteristic of the Charter, actually, but of the role of fundamental rights in general in the EU. Let's ask a simple question: why does the EU have general competence in areas of fundamental rights such as non-discrimination on the bases of race, religion, sexual orientation, gender, etc., and not in other areas? Why should the EU have a general competence with respect to one particular right, such as non-discrimination, i.e. a competence to adopt a legislation that applies even to private relations within the member states? And why doesn't this happen for other fundamental rights? Well, this is an example of the piecemeal nature of the fundamental rights architecture in the EU. Sometime a right was introduced with a given purpose, for example economic integration, then it became a right of its own. Why? Because social actors mobilise around that right, spur the EU to action, and demand a fully-fledged EU policy in that area. That happened with non-discrimination, but not in other areas.

Now, this teaches us two things. The first is that one might expect the same process to occur with respect to many of the provisions of the Charter. As the Charter generates political claims even with its currently limited legal scope, those claims will sooner or later bring about a stronger legal intervention. If they don't, the political tension it creates will become very difficult to withstand. This is exactly what the Commission is experiencing, because it is constantly been criticized for not implementing some things that people derive from the Charter. And yet, the legal means in the hand of the Commission are rather limited. And this is again a result of the piecemeal nature of fundamental rights protection and inclusion at EU level.

Fundamental rights are often the argumentative instrument that people use to try to raise first new political, then new legal claims. The last resource of any party who somehow feels that the right she believes her own is not protected, is to try to derive an argument from fundamental rights. And this also means that fundamental rights often acquire a piecemeal nature. This is the second thing we learn. Let's consider, for instance, the argument from human dignity. It may happen to shield some claims, but not others. This may be because no one has yet developed adequate legal claims in conjunction with this argument, or because a court was open to consider certain kinds of claim as supported by the argument from human dignity, but not others. This may be a consequence of the plausibility of the claim itself, but it may also be due to other circumstances, for instance to institutional limits, as I mentioned before. The court might suddenly perceive that if it continued down the path opened up by a certain interpretation of human dignity, it may open the gate to a flood of other cases, and narrow it on this consideration. So, fundamental rights are an area in which a lot of variation occurs in the courts' case law. It is only with time that it starts to stabilise itself. This is indeed an area in which legal claims tend to multiply themselves, in which innovative legal claims are often developed by recourse to the rhetoric and the narratives of fundamental rights, and in which the consequences of judicial action are most uncertain.

What you say is indeed very interesting, and yet weird, in a way, if we consider that what many people expected from the Charter of Fundamental Rights was to help establish a Europe-wide legal culture with regard to fundamental rights. This should have implied more coherence and less piecemeal work.

Lawyers like to think this way. They like to think that, because they have a Charter with all these beautiful rights, all will be very coherent. Consider, though, the principle of non-discrimination. What does non-discrimination mean? Does it mean that gay people should have the right to marry? Some people would say Yes, some people would say No. What does the right to life mean? Does it mean that an unborn has a right to life? And how is this to be balanced with other fundamental rights? In theory, the provisions of the Charter look all very well-balanced as a series of universal rights that we all agree upon, but which claims can actually be derived from it is often highly controversial. This is due not least to the fact that fundamental rights are actually what excluded groups, groups that feel put to a disadvantage or attempt to get more of a hearing, base their arguments upon for the protection of their interests or of what they consider to be their rights. This makes fundamental rights much more contestable than other areas of law. So, in the books human rights receive the aesthetically most beautiful, well-grounded, and systematic exposition, but in the practice they often are the messiest, most difficult and sometimes even inconsistent area of law.

Your remarks are highly interested, but also somehow disconcerting. After all, several observers expect legal practice to bring about more clarity to the provisions of the Charter and their application. Would you say that this actually happened?

Yes and no. The practice of interpreting fundamental rights will clarify some issues, create path dependencies, and provide legal certainty. At the same time, fundamental rights are often the legal basis from which people mostly derive new rights, so that a fundamental right can in fact be multiplied in diverse new rights. Even though there is sometimes a period of increased stability when courts consolidate the interpretation of a given fundamental right, suddenly someone may come up and develop an argument that no one has ever thought about with respect to that same fundamental right. Non-discrimination as including discrimination on the basis of age is a case in point. For many years no one ever considered that. Then suddenly someone brought that up. All of a sudden new expectations, new elements of uncertainty turn up. Some people see as a violation, as a form of discrimination, what others see otherwise. The courts have then to debate to which extent discrimination on the basis of age must be prohibited. It will come to a point in which the case law becomes stabilised around an interpretive practice, until a different factor of discrimination is fed into the debate: level of education, for instance. Consequently, we will have an "exploitation" (in a neutral sense, I mean) of that fundamental right, because that is what fundamental rights are about: they provide an opportunity for groups to develop a discursive process about their interests, the degree of their exclusion or inclusion in the political process, etc. When a group attempts to further its members' rights and interests in the political process, arguing on the basis of a fundamental right is a good strategy. Sometimes are groups successful, so that something that we have never thought of as a possible violation of a fundamental rights becomes indeed a violation.

This is highly interesting. Let's turn, however, to another lively debated question: legal argumentation and pluralism. Both the ECJ and the European Court of Human Rights (ECHR) have continuously worked on a "comparative" basis. In other words, they have to take into account a plurality of legal sources and traditions: international regulations, national legislations, and constitutional traditions. At times, they have more or less explicitly referred to the "comparative method", as you have also highlighted in some of your articles. A typical objection against this method is levelled against its excessive "openness" and ad hoc character, which would make room for shaping judicial review on "political" considerations of opportunity, instead of relying on "pure" principles of legality and justice. In short, legal certainty and coherence would be in danger. How do you assess the role of the ECJ as a custodian of Community law against the background of these criticisms?

This is a difficult question, because it all depends on what is meant by "political considerations of opportunity", and on what we understand to be the principles of justice. For someone, the latter may help fill a gap, an indeterminacy, or remedy a lacuna in the law, whereas for others it may the latter the court may be simply adjusting its rulings on the basis of "political considerations". It is very difficult for me to answer without clarifying what we mean by these labels. Law is by its nature open, which implies a gap between legal texts and reality. The courts fill this gap by means of what I call the "legal software of judges": the methods of interpretation that are acceptable in their community of reference. Courts make use of what is recognised within the dominant constitutional culture of the political community that constitutes their environment. Their rulings result from political culture as well as from the practices of political and legal interpretation of that specific fundamental right or that specific norm. Rulings also result from what I often define as the "normative systemic preferences" that judges employ when deliberating upon a case. Such preferences often determine how to strike a balance between different possible methods of reasoning and possible interpretations. In my view, these systemic normative preferences come not only from the interpretation of specific norms, but from an understanding of what are the underlying balances of our legal and political order. What is it that the judges attempt to achieve with their rulings? What kind of balance do they try to preserve in society? These options, these choices represent their normative preferences. Courts use them whenever they interpret a rule against the background of a given social and economic reality. Courts have to mediate between the rule as a text and the rule as a reality. Legal rules only make sense as long as they are considered in relation with their economic, political, and social consequences. If we don't consider the rules as embedded in such a reality, how can we know that the rules achieve the purpose they are intended to achieve?

Now, considerations of political opportunity do not intervene in the sense that the judges ask what is best for them as judges or for the court as an institution. They intervene, instead, to the extend to which rules aim to be normative, really normative, in the sense of shaping reality. Judges must then take into account what will happen in reality as a consequence of a certain interpretation of the rules. Accordingly, judges must consider the "systemic identity" of the legal political order in which they operate. They have to preserve the key balances in that legal and political order.

I take it that what scholars and practitioners aim to highlight when criticising the comparative method is that it allows the judges to pick the legal material, the norms and traditions they think fit for their rulings to be acceptable to the institutions they address. This would in a way impinge on the very sense of judicial review.

Exactly because of that I think it so important that the judges articulate their leading normative principles and clearly state their understanding of the legal system as a whole. They ought to specify what is guiding them in the application of a specific legal rule in the cases at hand. This is what guarantees that they are coherent in the interpretation of the law in the long-term; this is what guarantees that they are using the comparative method not instrumentally, but in the light of a given normative understanding of the overall legal order. This would strengthen the need and the request of justification in any case in which that normative understanding is used to support fully unexpected rulings, or when judges seem to stray away from their own interpretive pattern. Coherence: this is one of the mechanisms of courts' accountability.

However, coherence means not simply to decide the same legal question always in the same way. To be coherent is to decide the same legal question in a way that is coherent with how we decide a number of different legal questions in the light of the overall systemic understanding of the legal order in which we operate. That is the real coherence that we should require from judges. And if we require that kind of coherence in the application of comparative law, then comparative law does not become fully instrumental in the sense that a judge decides one day this way, the other day, another, just picking the answer that is best for what you want to achieve on a case by case basis.

That leads me to a follow-up question. The idea to constitutionalise the UE was meant exactly as you say. The entrenchment of fundamental rights was meant to encourage the kind of coherence you are talking about. In the long run, this should have brought in order the rulings of the ECJ. Do you think this is happening?

Well, I think fundamental rights are not enough to do that for the reasons I have mentioned. I think that we need to articulate, to make explicit our conception, our interpretation of fundamental rights. We need to make clear the purpose we ascribe to particular fundamental right in the context of the legal and political order of the EU. That's what I mean by coherence. By themselves, fundamental rights can be subject to radically different interpretation. We do not simply need a Charter of Fundamental Rights, we need a theory of fundamental rights. That is what we are still missing.

The Charter may be useful in this respect inasmuch as it creates incentives for the Court to articulate a theory of fundamental rights. I don't mean to say that the Court needs to write a legal textbook on fundamental rights. Instead, the court needs, for example, to slowly make clear why it is exercising a certain degree of judicial scrutiny in a given set of cases and a weaker or stronger degree of scrutiny in another set of cases. Whether we agree with it or not, an example of a theory of fundamental rights or a part of a theory of fundamental rights is the famous Carolene Products Footnote of the US Supreme Court (USSC).[7] In this ruling the USSC stated that whenever legislation would affect, discriminate, or differently treat discrete and insular minorities (racial ones, for instance), the Court would exert an additional degree of judicial scrutiny and therefore require additional justification from the political decision-maker in comparison to legislation that would not have the same impact on minorities. In this case, the USSC provided legal justification as to why a given rule, such as non-discrimination, would lead to a different degree of judicial scrutiny in different categories of cases and different sets of circumstances. This is an example of how the application of a given fundamental right triggers a theory of fundamental rights. Something of this sort is what we need to develop.

My last question concerns the current sovereign debt and Euro-crisis. When we discuss the role of constitutional jurisprudence in European integration we often address the relationship between national Constitutional Courts and the European Court of Justice. This seems to be needed again due to the development we currently witness regard-

7 Footnote 4 of the USSC's ruling in *United States vs. Carolene Products Co.* has had a longstanding influence on the US legal system, for in it the Court enunciates its conception and practice of judicial scrutiny of legislation. Firstly, the Court rejects competence on regulatory and social welfare legislation. The assessment of constitutionality should be solely directed to the devices and proceedings that might hinder the political process to run in a democratic way, but not to the content of the laws arrived at in a legitimate way. Judicial scrutiny should, in this way, be directed to protecting "those political processes which can ordinarily be expected to bring about repeal of undesirable legislation" (paragraph 2). Furthermore, as an example of what is to be understood as a hindrance to the democratic political process the Court refers to the judicial protection of those minorities which, inasmuch as they constitute "discrete and insular" social groups, are excluded from participation in the political process by discriminatory measures. Being the African American community a clear example of this kind of oppressed groups, this statement paved the way for the attack on the American system of racial segregation.

ing constitutional matters in the Eurozone. In deference to German worries, the Euro countries have recently concerted to introduce a constitutional amendment in their own national constitutions in order to entrench a limit to state budget deficit and public debt. The Euro countries have, however, different mechanisms of judicial review. Their constitutional courts operate in different ways and play different roles in their respective legal systems. Therefore, it stands to reason to assume that the constitutional amendment in question will not yield the same results in all countries, for the limitation it imposes on governments will work differently. Do you share this mixed expectation with regard to this specific arrangement, or do you think this is indeed a factual step forward in European legal integration?

I would probably need more time to answer this. This is not a question about the merits and demerits of constitutionalisation of debt breaks or limits to budgetary deficits. I think there are constitutional and democratic reasons for welcoming such rules, reasons that have to do with the externalities that a country's financial behaviour causes in other states as well as with the intergenerational consequences of deficit spending. There are, however, further reasons to be sceptical of such constitutional breaks. In the case of the European Union I would defend very different mechanisms, but let's not get into this now.

The issue at stake is whether these constitutional mechanisms do make a difference, especially once we consider that a similar provision is to be constitutionally entrenched in states with different constitutional cultures. Yes, they do make a difference.

However, we first have to take notice of the fact that this treaty does not require such an entrenchment.[8] It states, instead, that

8 In December 2011, 25 of the 27 EU member states (the United Kingdom and the Czech Republic opted out) signed an intergovernmental agreement that specified procedures for a more harmonized budgetary co-ordination. The *Treaty on Stability, Coordination and Governance in the Economic and Monetary Union* includes a "balanced budget rule" to be given constitutional or equivalent status in the signatory states' legal systems. These rules are meant to be enforced by means of automatic measures of budgetary restriction that apply in case of non-compliance.

such an entrenchment is preferable, but not mandatory. In fact, there is in some states no tradition of constitutional and judicial review at all. Some other states have a tradition in this sense, but make little use of such a instrument. Actually, I don't think the Treaty really aims to guarantee a uniform level of protection from budgetary deficits in all member states through constitutional instruments. I do not think this would be a sensible goal, precisely because constitutional and political cultures are so different. In some member states you do not even need anything of the kind, because the political culture is such that the government is aware that it would pay a high political price, if the deficit would grow too much. This is because the public opinion has constructed a narrative according to which deficits are bad. In some countries you may not need a constitutional debt break at all.

In other states it is exactly the other way around. In some countries you might need such a break, because the risk that political decisions make the deficit grow is higher. Besides, in these countries the courts may also be less effective in exercising their control.

All in all, I do not expect the power of this provision to reside in automatic and effective judicial control. I expect this provision to play a twofold function. One is to be an additional instrument for empowering the European Commission to enforce the Growth and Stability Pact. It is a political empowerment in that the Commission may confront member states with their commitment, to which the constitutional form may lend more credibility and more loss of face in case of non-compliance. Alongside the new powers that the Treaty bestows on it, the Commission will have an additional and important role to play in this respect.

The other function that I would expect entrenchment to fulfil is to provide some governments with more political backing. I mean the governments of those states whose public opinions are very resistant to help other Euro partners, and I am talking mostly of Germany. This may actually be the key function of the stability treaty. It may lend additional support to governments inasmuch as they can now point out how much they did to guarantee fiscal discipline on the side of formerly so undisciplined countries. These governments have now additional arguments to reassure their public opinions that the money they will be going to pump into the system will be used appropriately. This is the purpose I see in the stability treaty. I don't know whether this answers your question, but I think this is as much as I can say now.

LISBON PHILOSOPHICAL STUDIES

uses of language in interdisciplinary fields

A Publication from the Institute of Philosophy of Language at the New University of Lisbon

Lisbon Philosophical Studies – Uses of Language in Interdisciplinary Fields is the book series of the Institute of Philosophy of Language at the New University of Lisbon. Its aim is the publication of high-quality monographs, edited collections and conference proceedings in areas related to the philosophy of language, such as aesthetics, argumentation theory, epistemology, ethics, logic, philosophy of mind and political philosophy. The purpose of the series is to reflect the activities of the Institute as well as contemporary research in these areas, encouraging the interchange of arguments and ideas between philosophy and other disciplines.

Address for Correspondence:

Instituto de Filosofia da Linguagem
Faculdade de Ciências Sociais e Humanas
Universidade Nova de Lisboa
Av. de Berna, 26-C
1069-061 Lisboa
Portugal

www.ifl.pt

Vol. 1 António Marques & Nuno Venturinha (eds)
Wittgenstein on Forms of Life and the Nature of Experience.
2010. ISBN 978-3-0343-0491-7.

Vol. 2 Luca Baptista & Erich Rast (eds)
Meaning and Context.
2010. ISBN 978-3-0343-0574-7.

Vol. 3 Maria Filomena Molder, Diana Soeiro and Nuno Fonseca (eds)
Morphology. Questions on Method and Language.
2013. ISBN 978-3-0343-1376-6.

Vol. 4 Paulo Barcelos & Gabriele De Angelis (eds)
The Long Quest for Identity.
Political Identity and Fundamental Rights Protection in the European Union.
2013. ISBN 978-3-0343-1083-3.

www.ingramcontent.com/pod-product-compliance
Ingram Content Group UK Ltd.
Pitfield, Milton Keynes, MK11 3LW, UK
UKHW021012120926
8556IPUK00039B/1047

9 783034 310833